THEOLOGY OF THE HEBREW BIBLE, VOLUME 1: METHODOLOGICAL STUDIES

RESOURCES FOR BIBLICAL STUDY

Editor
Hyun Chul Paul Kim, Old Testament/Hebrew Bible

Number 92

SBL PRESS

THEOLOGY OF THE HEBREW BIBLE, VOLUME 1: METHODOLOGICAL STUDIES

Edited by

Marvin A. Sweeney

SBL PRESS

Atlanta

Copyright © 2019 by Society of Biblical Literature

Library of Congress Cataloging-in-Publication Data

Names: Sweeney, Marvin A. (Marvin Alan), 1953– editor.
Title: Theology of the Hebrew Bible / edited by Marvin A. Sweeney.
Description: Atlanta : SBL Press, 2018– | Series: Resources for biblical study ; Number 92 | Includes bibliographical references and index.
Identifiers: LCCN 2018033061 (print) | LCCN 2018037140 (ebook) | ISBN 9780884143024 (ebk.) | ISBN 9781628372144 (v. 1 : pbk. : alk. paper) | ISBN 9780884143017 (v. 1 : hbk. : alk. paper)
Subjects: LCSH: Bible. Old Testament—Theology. | Bible. Old Testament—Hermeneutics.
Classification: LCC BS1192.5.A1 (ebook) | LCC BS1192.5.A1 T44 2018 (print) | DDC 230/.0411—dc23
LC record available at https://lccn.loc.gov/2018033061

Printed on acid-free paper.

Contents

Abbreviations

AB	Anchor Bible
ABD	Freedman, D. N., ed. *Anchor Bible Dictionary*. 6 vols. Garden City, NY: Doubleday, 1992.
AFLR	*Aersbok för föreningen lärare i religionskunskap*
AnBib	Analecta Biblica
ANEP	Pritchard, J. B., ed. *The Ancient Near East in Pictures*. 3rd ed. Princeton: Princeton University Press, 1969.
ANET	Pritchard, J. B., ed. *Ancient Near Eastern Texts Relating to the Old Testament*. 3rd ed. Princeton: Princeton University, 1969.
ATANT	Abhandlungen zur Theologie des Alten und Neuen Testaments
ATD	Das Alte Testament Deutsch
AYB	Anchor Yale Bible
b.	Babylonian Talmud
B. Bat.	Bava Batra
Bar	Baruch
BBRSup	Bulletin for Biblical Research, Supplements
BEATAJ	Beiträge zur Erforschung des Alten Testaments und Antiken Judentum
Ber.	Berakhot
BETL	Bibliotheca Ephemeridum Theologicarum Lovansiensium
Bib	*Biblica*
BibInt	*Biblical Interpretation*
BSac	*Bibliotheca Sacra*
BThSt	Biblisch-Theologischer Studien
BWANT	Beiträge zur Wissenschaft vom Alten und Neuen Testament

BZAW	Beihefte zur Zeitschrift für die alttestamentliche Wissenschaft
CBQ	*The Catholic Biblical Quarterly*
CCAR	*Central Conference of American Rabbis*
ContC	Continental Commentaries
CSHJ	Chicago Studies in the History of Judaism
CTS	Contextual Theology Series
Doctr. chr.	*De doctrina christiana*
EBR	Klauck, H.-J., et al., eds. *The Encyclopedia of the Bible and Its Reception.* Berlin: de Gruyter, 2009–.
EncJud	Roth, Cecil, ed. *Encyclopedia Judaica.* Jerusalem: Keter and MacMillan, 1971–1972.
1 Esd	1 Esdras
FAT	Forschungen zum Alten Testament
FOTL	Forms of the Old Testament Literature
GAT	Grundrisse zum Alten Testament
HBT	*Horizons in Biblical Theology*
HS	*Hebrew Studies*
HSM	Harvard Semitic Monographs
HTR	*Harvard Theological Review*
HUCA	*Hebrew Union College Annual*
IBC	Interpretation: A Bible Commentary for Teaching and Preaching
ICC	International Critical Commentary
Int	*Interpretation*
JBL	*Journal of Biblical Literature*
JCSHS	Jewish and Christian Heritage Series
JPS	Jewish Publication Society
JPSBC	JPS Bible Commentary
JR	*Journal of Religion*
JSNT	*Journal for the Study of the New Testament*
JSNTSup	Journal for the Study of the New Testament Supplement Series
JSOT	*Journal for the Study of the Old Testament*
JSOTSup	Journal for the Study of the Old Testament Supplement Series
JSQ	*Jewish Studies Quarterly*
JTI	*Journal of Theological Interpretation*
KST	Kohlhammer Studienbücher Theologie

LBT	Library of Biblical Theology
LHBOTS	Library of Hebrew Bible/Old Testament Studies
LXX	Septuagint
m.	Mishnah
Meg.	Megillah
MJ	*Modern Judaism*
MT	Masoretic Text
NAC	New American Commentary
NCBC	New Cambridge Bible Commentary
NICOT	New International Commentary on the Old Testament
NN	*Nations and Nationalism*
NSKAT	Neuer Stuttgarter Kommentar, Altes Testament
OBT	Overtures to Biblical Theology
OLR	*Oxford Literary Review*
OOTT	Overtures to an Old Testament Theology
OTL	Old Testament Library
OtSt	Oudtestamentische Studiën
Pes.	Pesaḥ
Presb	*Presbyterion*
Proof	*Prooftexts: A Journal of Jewish Literary History*
PRSt	*Perspectives in Religious Studies*
PTMS	Pittsburgh Theological Monograph Series
Qidd.	Qiddušin
QTS	Queering Theology Series
RBL	*Review of Biblical Literature*
RD	Religions and Discourse
Šabb.	Šabbat
SAC	Studies in Antiquity and Christianity
San.	Sanhedrin
SBLDS	Society of Biblical Literature Dissertation Series
SBLSymS	Society of Biblical Literature Symposium Series
SEÅ	*Svensk exegetic Årsbok*
Sipre Deut.	Sipre Deuteronomy
SJOT	*Scandinavian Journal of the Old Testament*
SJT	*Scottish Journal of Theology*
SRA	*Svensk religionsgustoris aersskkrift*
StBibLit	Studies in Biblical Literature (Lang)
StThT	Studia Theologica—Teresianum
t.	Tosefta

Ta'an.	Ta'anit
TDOT	Botterweck, G. Johannes, Helmer Ringgren, and Heinz-Josef Fabry, eds. *Theological Dictionary of the Old Testament*. Translated by John T. Willis et al. 15 vols. Grand Rapids: Eerdmans, 1974–2006.
TE	*Topics in Education*
ThSt	Theologische Studiën
TLZ	*Theologische Literaturzeitung*
Tob	Tobit
TSAJ	Texte und Studien zum Antiken Judentum
UBL	Ugaritische-biblische Literatur
VT	*Vetus Testamentum*
VTSup	Supplements to Vetus Testamentum
WBC	Word Biblical Commentary
WMANT	Wissenschaftliche Monographien zum Alten und Neuen Testament
y.	Jerusalem Talmud
Yad.	Yadayim
ZABR	*Zeitschrfit für altorientalische und biblische Rechtsge-schichte*
ZAW	*Zeitschrift für die altestamenltiche Wissenschaft*

Introduction

Marvin A. Sweeney

The Society of Biblical Literature Section on Theology of the Hebrew Scriptures was established to foster scholarly discussion by Jews and Christians concerning the theological interpretation of the Hebrew Bible, known as the Tanak in Judaism and the Old Testament in Christianity. The need for such discussion was evident in the early years following World War II. Prior to the war, biblical theology was almost exclusively a Christian theological enterprise that was intended to relate biblical interpretation to the concerns of dogmatic and later systematic theology. Jews were not well represented in modern critical scholarship prior to the war, and the overarching viewpoint among Christian scholars during the eighteenth through the early twentieth century was that Jews, who were largely responsible for the redaction of biblical texts, had fundamentally misunderstood the theological insights of early "Israelite" literature, such as the J source of the Pentateuch or the original oracles of the Prophets, and had corrupted the meaning of the text by attempting to introduce alleged Jewish concerns for legalism, ritual, and parochial national identity into a text that originally was intended to address the entire world with its notions of universal salvation, moral order, and conceptualization of G-d.

But the experience of World Wars I and II raised fundamental questions concerning the notions of universal salvation, ethics, and spirituality associated with G-d during the period of the Enlightenment as theologians began to recognize that supposedly rational human societies had failed miserably as ideals such as National Socialism, fascism, communism, and Japanese imperialism played key roles in bringing about worldwide war that saw the deaths of some seventeen million people in World War I and sixty million people in World War II, including the deliberate genocidal murder of some six million Jews as well as millions of Gypsies, gays and lesbians, Slavic groups, and persons deemed mentally or physically deficient. Despite noteworthy efforts by Christian theologians such as Paul Tillich, Dietrich Bonhoeffer, and Karl Barth, the Christian churches were largely silent during the Shoah, in part for fear of retaliation by the Nazi-controlled or influenced governments of Germany and its allies, and in part due to the belief that Jews had sinned in rejecting Jesus and participating in his crucifixion and therefore deserved punishment.

Walther Eichrodt's Old Testament theology, originally published in 1933–1939, offered an understanding of the covenant between G-d and human beings that asserted Judaism as a "torso-like" appearance in the covenantal history; Gerhard von Rad's 1955–1958 theology of the Old Testament completely ignored Judaism in asserting that the Old Testament proclaimed salvation history for humankind as the theological core of the Old Testament. Neither scholar treated the book of Esther, which takes seriously the question of what happens when a government deliberately attempts to murder its Jewish population, and instead denied the theological character of the book, insofar as G-d is never mentioned in it, or decried Jewish violence against gentiles at the end of the book. When the modern state of Israel was created in the aftermath of the Shoah, in part to ensure that Jews would never find themselves without a homeland again, many scholars rejected the Jewish state as antithetical to divine and biblical intentions.

But as Jewish scholars such as Richard Rubenstein, Emil Fackenheim, Eliezer Berkovitz, Abraham Joshua Heschel, and Elie Wiesel began to write about the theological and moral problems posed by the experience of the Shoah, Christian scholars such as Paul Tillich, Clark Williamson, and even Pope John XXIII began to recognize the need to rethink Christianity and its relationship with Judaism in the aftermath of the Shoah. As historical scholars engaged in textual analysis and archaeology as means to understand the historical character of ancient Israel and Judah, theological scholars began to reexamine the theological viewpoints of biblical literature on Israel's formation, history, and destruction in efforts to understand better the nature of G-d's covenant with Israel and the recognition that it might point to the ongoing life of Israel, the Jewish people, and Judaism beyond the time of Jesus and the New Testament. Although Christianity did not bring about the Shoah, its anti-Jewish statements, particularly the charge that Jews were responsible for the crucifixion of Jesus, had actually constituted a major basis for Nazi views of Jews and their efforts to exterminate them.

The result was a rapprochement between Judaism and Christianity, particularly in the field of biblical theology, as Jewish and Christian

scholars began to examine the interrelationships between the two traditions and their reading of biblical texts. Jewish scholars such as Jon D.
Levenson, Michael Fishbane, Tikva Frymer-Kensky, Isaac Kalimi, Benjamin Sommer, Tamar Kamionkowski, the present writer, and many others
began to enter the field of biblical theology—even when they had reservations about its Christian character. Christian scholars such as Rolf
Rendtorff, John J. Collins, Katherine Pfisterer Darr, Kathleen O'Connor,
Walter Brueggemann, Leo Perdue, Wonil Kim, and many others began to
engage in dialogue with Jewish biblical scholars in their efforts to understand better the theological perspectives of the Bible.

One outcome of the intensive efforts to study the historical and theological dimensions of the Hebrew Bible throughout the latter twentieth
and the early twenty-first century was the recognition that the earlier
assertions of objective historical research and critical theological analysis
could not be sustained. Biblical historical works such as the Pentateuch,
the Deuteronomistic History, and the Chronicler's History each has its
own set of theological and historiographical principles that underlie and
define its literary presentations of ancient Israelite and Judean history and
thought. Furthermore, historical and theological study of the Hebrew Bible
is heavily dependent upon the preexisting perspectives of the scholars
undertaking the research. As historical research began to decline, ideolog-
ically and theologically based perspectives such as feminist and gendered
interpretation of the Bible, African and African American interpretation
of the Bible, Latino/a readings of the Bible, Asian and Asian American
perspectives, and others began to emerge in the field together with strong
reactions against the Bible for its relationships to modern Zionism, that
is, the movement to establish a Jewish homeland in the land of Israel, its
propensity for blaming the victims of oppression for sins that would then
explain their victimization, and a parochial perspective that upholds Israelite and Judean interests over those of other nations.

The result has been an influx of studies in the field that have raised
questions about contemporary biblical theology. Does the Hebrew Bible
belong exclusively to the Jewish people and to Judaism, or does it also
address other nations, ethnic groups, and religious traditions? Is the same
Bible read in Christianity and in Judaism, or does it appear in a multiplicity of forms that must be considered in the larger context of biblical
theological interpretation? Do Jews and Christians read the Bible the same
way, or are there distinctively Jewish and Christian perspectives that must
be considered in the theological reading of the Bible? Questions such as

these underlie the work of the Society of Biblical Literature Theology of the Hebrew Scriptures Section and the papers that appear in this volume.

Many of the papers published here were presented in the various panels and sessions of the Theology of the Hebrew Scriptures Section during the course of the 2013, 2014, 2015, and 2016 Society of Biblical Literature Annual Meetings in Baltimore, San Diego, Atlanta, and San Antonio. Others were submitted or solicited from scholars who have had past relationships with the Theology of the Hebrew Scriptures Section or who have an ongoing interest in the work of the section.

"Disputed Issues of Biblical Theology," by Georg Fischer, SJ, was originally presented as part of the Theology of the Hebrew Scriptures panel discussion on "What Is Biblical Theology?" at the 2013 Annual Society of Biblical Literature Meeting in Baltimore. Fischer notes the recent renaissance in biblical theology and turns first to the question of the necessity of biblical theology. He understands the term to refer to speaking about G-d but well recognizes the issue of canonical differentiation in the various traditions that employ the Bible as sacred Scripture. A full picture of G-d accounts for both divine love and divine violence. He discusses seven disputed issues, such as the question of where to begin, what to search for, how to approach it, how far the study should extend, the role of faith, whether biblical theology is descriptive or also critical, and whether there is a core to biblical theologies. He offers a rich discussion that maintains throughout the centrality of YHWH in biblical theology.

My own paper, "What Is Biblical Theology? With an Example on Divine Absence and the Song of Songs," was originally presented as two separate papers in the 2013 Theology of the Hebrew Scriptures panel discussion on "What Is Biblical Theology?" in Baltimore and in the 2015 Theology of the Hebrew Scriptures panel discussion on "Divine Hiddenness in the Hebrew Bible" in Atlanta. I played a major role in developing these panels as current cochair (2013–2018) of the Theology of the Hebrew Scriptures Section. The first part of the paper notes the changes that have taken place in the field since World War II and argues for the need to consider canonical context in defining what Bible is read in the various traditions of Judaism and Christianity. It studies the differences in the formal structures of the Jewish Tanak and the Christian Old Testament. It argues that the Tanak is based in a cycle that articulates the ideals of Jewish life and relationship with G-d in the Torah, the disruption of that ideal in the Prophets, and the attempts to reconstitute that ideal in the Writings; the Old Testament, on the other hand, displays a linear presentation that ultimately points to the New Testament and begins with treatment of the early history of the world and Israel in the Pentateuch, the later history of Israel in the historical books, theological and philosophical issues in the poetic and wisdom books, and a view of the future in the prophetic books. A similar structure appears in the New Testament, which points to the second coming of Christ. It also discusses the dialogical dimensions of the Bible to argue that there is no center to the Bible and that its constituent books are often in disagreement, in some cases positing that G-d is sometimes absent, impotent, or unjust. The second part of this paper examines the issue of divine absence in the Song of Songs, arguing that human beings must also be recognized as partners with G-d in bringing about creation and sanctification in the world.

"Biblical Theology in Context(s): Jewish, Christian, and Critical Approaches to the Theology of the Hebrew Bible," by Julia M. O'Brien, was originally presented as part of the 2014 Theology of the Hebrew Scriptures panel discussion in San Diego. O'Brien, the former cochair of Theology of the Hebrew Scriptures (2011–2016), admits that the title for the sessions leaves her unsettled, despite her role in formulating the title, as none of the three labels offered—Jewish, Christian, and critical—accurately describes her own understanding of biblical theology. She maintains that theological exegesis in Christianity is flawed because it presumes commonality among Christian theologians that does not exist and in practice privileges only a few voices in the discussion. Such practice leaves her unsatisfied calling biblical theology Christian. She is also uncomfortable with the description of biblical theology as critical, insofar as such a term presumes an objectivity in method and viewpoint that does not exist in the field. She rightly notes that the label Jewish is not hers to choose, as she is not a Jewish biblical theologian, despite having been trained in part by Jewish scholars and engaging the work of Jewish scholars in her publications and in dialogue. Despite the problems she observes, she endorses the task of doing biblical theology in context, as it leads to better understanding of the issues of justice and fairness, trauma, and identity in the world.

"Hebrew Bible Theology: A Jewish Descriptive Approach," by Dalit Rom-Shiloni, a former Theology of the Hebrew Scriptures steering committee member (2011–2016), was presented at the 2014 Theology of the Hebrew Scriptures panel discussion on "Biblical Theology in Context: Jewish, Christian, and Critical Approaches to the Theology of the Hebrew Bible" in San Diego. Her paper was published under the same title in the *Journal of Religion* 96 (2016): 165–84, and it is republished here with permission. Rom-Shiloni represents the voice of a Jewish, Israeli, nonreligious scholar in reading the Hebrew Bible. She first discusses the proper borders of the literary corpus that constitutes the Hebrew Bible and the question of dialogical method for reading that literature. She raises questions as to whether the Hebrew Bible should be read as a self-contained literary and theological work and whether or not from a Jewish standpoint the Bible should be put into dialogue with later postbiblical Jewish literature. In the end, she recognizes the diachronic distinctions between the Bible and later Jewish literature while calling for dialogue between them. She then turns to the question of non-Christian terminology for the field of biblical theology, particularly in relation to the problems posed by Christian supersessionism. She examines problematic terminology, such as anthropomorphism, which often overlooks the metaphorical character of the portrayal of G-d for many Christian scholars. In the end, she calls for a descriptive theological approach—that is, what the text meant for the Israelite and Judean writers—that must be examined and put into dialogue with the constructive theological approaches advocated by so many Jewish and Christian scholars.

"Beyond Dialogue: Toward a Dialectical Model of Theology of the Hebrew Scripture/Old Testament," by Wonil Kim, former cochair of Theology of the Hebrew Scriptures, examines the ethnocentric, xenophobic, and militaristic character of the biblical narratives of Israelite origins in an effort to develop a clear and responsible method for biblical theology. He further notes the problems posed by the plurality of theologies that appear within the Hebrew Bible. Kim proposes a dialogical model for biblical theology in an effort to put this plurality of theologies into dialogue with each other and avoid the problems posed by a purely descriptive biblical theology that would pass over the problems acknowledged above. Kim's dialogical and dialectical model presupposes the role of the reader who enters into a dialogue with the text as well and raises questions concerning the assertions of the biblical narratives, that is, to what extent the reader says no to the models presented in Scripture as a basis for learning from the problems prompted by the perspectives of the biblical literature itself. Such a model entails that we modern readers are active participants in the act of reading and that we have the capacity both to say no to the Bible and to offer an alternative model based on what we have learned from reading the biblical texts. Although Kim's model does not self-consciously engage in questions of Jewish or Christian readings of the Bible, it does raise questions for contemporary readers of all—or no—traditions.

Andrea L. Weiss's "Making a Place for Metaphor in Biblical Theology" was one of the presentations for the 2013 Theology of the Hebrew Scriptures panel on "What Is Biblical Theology?" at the Society of Biblical Literature Annual Meeting in Baltimore. Weiss provides a brief review of the emergence of biblical theology among Jewish scholars by first noting the initial resistance to the field and then surveying a number of key publications by Jewish scholars engaged in the field. She follows Collins, who argues that biblical theology should involve the critical evaluation of biblical speech about G-d, and turns to the study of metaphor about G-d as a central element in the field. In the past, scholars such as Brueggemann have employed rhetoric to conceive metaphors concerning G-d in nominal form, but Weiss argues that interpreters must pay closer attention to linguistic and metaphor theory to provide the necessary full range of metaphor that biblical speech concerning G-d requires. Her study of texts from Deuteronomy, Jeremiah, and Hosea demonstrates that no single metaphor properly encapsulates the character of G-d, but each text includes multiple metaphors or metaphor clusters that provide a wide range of metaphorical portrayals of G-d that can begin to demonstrate the wide range necessary to prevent the portrayal of G-d to become just another form of idolatry.

"A Theology of Creation—Critical and Christian," by Jacqueline E. Lapsley, originally appeared as part of the 2014 Theology of the Hebrew Scriptures panel on "Biblical Theology in Context: Jewish, Christian, and Critical Approaches to the Theology of the Hebrew Bible" at the Society of Biblical Literature Annual Meeting in San Diego. Lapsley rejects a common understanding that biblical theology is a Christian theological field that attempts to trace the progressive history of G-d's self-revelation to humanity culminating in Jesus Christ as unrecognizable to her and many contemporary colleagues. Recognizing that all approaches, including critical approaches, are confessional to some degree, she asks whether biblical theology should be descriptive or constructive and recognizes that biblical theology must be able to account for the diversity of the texts in the Bible rather than attempting to reduce discussion to a single or a few sets of themes. She proposes a creational theology that is fundamentally concerned with the question of human dignity as one example of the multifaceted approaches that biblical theology requires. The key aspect of her proposal is the focus on the responsibility that human beings have for the world of creation that human capabilities and partnership with G-d entails. Ironically for a Christian scholar, Lapsley's proposal is consistent with Jewish views on the task of the human being within creation.

David Frankel's "Toward a Constructive Jewish Biblical Theology of the Land" first appeared as a panel presentation for the 2014 Theology of the Hebrew Scriptures panel in San Diego on "Biblical Theology in Context: Jewish, Christian, and Critical Approaches to the Theology of the Hebrew Bible." Frankel points to the foundational work of Martin Buber, who in his concern to demonstrate the relevance of the Bible for modern human beings as well as for Israel as a nation, viewed the Bible as a fundamentally unified work that expressed a form of religious humanism as a basis for Buber's theopolitical version of Zionism and his teachings about G-d, humanity, Israel, and human society more generally. Most contemporary Israeli scholars would reject Buber's approach, arguing instead that the Bible presents a wide variety of positions on a multitude of topics, making it difficult to establish a biblical basis for any major issue in modern Israeli society. In proposing a new basis for Jewish biblical theology in Israel, Frankel points to the fundamentally exegetical character of Jewish thought, insofar as all of Jewish tradition traces its roots back to the interpretation of biblical texts. He cites Deut 29:14 to assert that biblical texts are addressed both to those of the past who are no longer with us and to those of the present who are with us today. He employs his approach to address the issue of the ultranationalist religious right in Israel, who assert that Jewish sovereignty over the entire land is a cardinal element of Jewish faith in what is perceived to be a messianic era. Insofar as he finds such a position morally disturbing and politically dangerous, Frankel calls for a return to Buber's religious humanism to construct a new Jewish biblical theology of the land that takes into consideration pragmatic and dispassionate thinking, G-d's absolute freedom, Maimonides's demotion of messianism, the importance of prioritizing religious values, the claim that there is no need for territorial completeness, and the recognition that the land is not innately holy. In Frankel's view, such a nonmessianic Jewish biblical theology of the land will do much to promote accommodation and justice in the land of Israel.

"Characterizing Chiastic Contradiction: Literary Structure, Divine Repentance, and Dialogical Biblical Theology in 1 Samuel 15:10–35," by Benjamin J. M. Johnson, was first presented in the 2016 Theology of the Hebrew Scriptures San Antonio session of open papers devoted to "Theological Interpretation of Selected Biblical Texts." Johnson's paper draws on the dialogical reading strategies of Mikhail Bakhtin and others in an effort to demonstrate their importance for reading a text such as 1 Sam 15:10–35, which portrays YHWH's repentant and unrepentant nature in relation to the rejection of Saul as king of Israel. Whereas the literary frame of the passage asserts YHWH's repentance over Saul, Samuel's statements in the core of the passage maintain that the divine YHWH should not repent. Johnson surveys past attempts to address the issue through harmonizing readings, source-critical readings, narrative-critical approaches, and paradoxical approaches. Johnson's own approach to the paradox employs a chiastic reading of 1 Sam 15:10–35 to demonstrate a dialogical reading of the text. Although the outer limits of the text assert YHWH's repentance at choosing Saul, Samuel's denial of YHWH's need to repent serves as the turning point within the chiastic structure of this text. The text thereby creates deliberate tension concerning YHWH's character that prompts readers to engage the question of the nature of YHWH as a deity who remains unpredictable and yet faithful and trustworthy.

"Ashamed before the Presence of God," by Soo J. Kim, current cochair of the Theology of the Hebrew Scriptures Section (2017–2022), was originally presented as part of the 2013 Baltimore Theological Perspectives on the Book of Ezekiel session on Ezekiel 40–48 and Its Relationship to Pentateuchal Legal Texts and Conceptions. Kim challenges prior assertions by Baruch Schwartz that the restoration of Israel in Ezek 40–48 entailed a damaged reputation for YHWH and no repentance from Israel. She poses a number of crucial questions: Is this pessimistic view really the end of the exilic community story and the goal of the writing? What would be the first step in bringing the exiles home if they are victims who refuse to confess their guilt? Which party should initiate reconciliation if the guilty party refuses to do so? What role does shame play in the restoration? Finally, what is Ezekiel's conceptualization of exile? She carefully defines the literary audience and implied audience of Ezek 43:10–11, which urges its audience to be humiliated and ashamed before G-d. Her detailed analysis of each passage points to its key concerns: Ezek 43:10–11 calls for the people to feel shame for their past so they might acquire the knowledge necessary for a more advanced relationship with G-d in the course of the restoration envisioned in Ezek 40–48. By reaching such a deep knowledge of G-d and of self, the people lay the foundations to maintain the relationship forever.

Altogether these essays address various aspects of the question: What is biblical theology?

Disputed Issues of Biblical Theology

Georg Fischer, SJ

1. Introduction

In recent years there has been a kind of renaissance of biblical theology. A large number of monographs have appeared since 1990, notably by Horst Dietrich Preuß, Brevard S. Childs, Walter Brueggemann, Paul R. House, Erhard S. Gerstenberger, R. W. L. Moberly, John Kessler, among many others.[1] Two of the newer books are *Tanak: A Theological and Critical Introduction to the Jewish Bible*, by Marvin A. Sweeney, which has an interesting first part dealing with the differences between Jewish biblical theology and Christian Old Testament theology, and *Ein Gott, der straft und tötet?*, by Bernd Janowski, treating the problem of a violent God who punishes and kills.[2]

I thank Felicity Stephens for the correction of the English in this article.

1. Horst Dietrich Preuß, *Theologie des Alten Testaments*, 2 vols. (Stuttgart: Kohlhammer, 1991–1992); Brevard S. Childs, *Biblical Theology of the Old and New Testaments: Theological Reflection on the Christian Bible* (Minneapolis: Fortress, 1993); Walter Brueggemann, *Theology of the Old Testament: Testimony, Dispute, Advocacy* (Minneapolis: Fortress, 1997); Paul R. House, *Old Testament Theology* (Downers Grove, IL: InterVarsity, 1998); Erhard S. Gerstenberger, *Theologien im Alten Testament: Pluralität und Synkretismus alttestamentlichen Gottesglaubens* (Stuttgart: Kohlhammer, 2001); R. W. L. Moberly, *Old Testament Theology: Reading the Hebrew Bible as Christian Scripture* (Grand Rapids: Baker Academic, 2013); John Kessler, *Old Testament Theology: Divine Call and Human Response* (Waco, TX: Baylor University Press, 2013).

2. Marvin A. Sweeney, *Tanak: A Theological and Critical Introduction to the Jewish Bible* (Minneapolis: Fortress, 2012); Bernd Janowski, *Ein Gott, der straft und tötet? Zwölf Fragen zum Gottesbild des Alten Testaments* (Neukirchen-Vluyn: Neukirchener Verlag, 2013). "Newer" refers to the date when this paper was read in 2013.

These are just a few of the authors and titles that have emerged from a flourishing field of research and publications in several languages. Among recent articles, Manfred Oeming's "Viele Wege zu dem Einen" and Friedhelm Hartenstein's "Jhwhs Wesen im Wandel" are stimulating and reflect on critical problems.[3] On another level, Konrad Schmid's *Gibt es Theologie im Alten Testament* is valuable for providing historical background to our topic and for presenting various inspiring positions.[4]

Personally, biblical theology has held my interest since I encountered it in my early studies in the 1970s. Arnold Gamper, who had worked extensively on "Gott als Richter," was my teacher, and to him biblical theology was always the climax in dealing with the Bible. He regularly gave lectures on themes such as *Bund*, *Messias*, and *Erlösung*, covering main concepts of the Bible and their development throughout its various books.[5]

Following in his footsteps, I have continued to offer courses in biblical theology. Main themes in the first years were *Berufung*, *Sühne und Versöhnung*, *Gebet*, and *Heil und Heilung*.[6] However, my focus shifted slowly in the course of the following years. I started to concentrate more on the way in which God himself is portrayed in the biblical books and became ever more fascinated by the variety of presentations. This led to the desire to show to others the Bible's richness in talking about God and, in consequence, to the project of writing books on the subject, the first volume of which is *Theologien des Alten Testaments*.[7]

---

3. Manfred Oeming, "Viele Wege zu dem Einen: Die 'transzendente Mitte' einer Theologie des Alten Testaments im Spannungsfeld von Vielheit und Einheit," in *Viele Wege zu dem Einen: Historische Bibelkritik—die Vitalität der Glaubensüberlieferung in der Moderne*, ed. Stefan Beyerle et al., BThSt 121 (Neukirchen-Vluyn: Neukirchener Verlag, 2012), 83–108; Friedhelm Hartenstein, "Jhwhs Wesen im Wandel," *TLZ* 137 (2012): 3–20.

4. Konrad Schmid, *Gibt es Theologie im Alten Testament: Zum Theologiebegriff in der alttestamentlichen Wissenschaft*, ThSt 7 (Zürich: TVZ, 2013).

5. Arnold Gamper's thesis and his "Habilitationsschrift" appeared together as *Gott als Richter in Mesopotamien und im Alten Testament: Zum Verständnis einer Gebetsbitte* (Innsbruck: Wagner, 1966). He was my predecessor in the chair of Old Testament Biblical Sciences and Oriental Languages at the Theological Faculty of the University of Innsbruck. The English equivalents of *Bund*, *Messias*, and *Erlösung* are, respectively, covenant, Messiah, and redemption.

6. In English, call/vocation narratives, atonement and reconciliation, prayer, salvation, and healing, respectively.

7. Georg Fischer, *Theologien des Alten Testaments*, NSKAT 31 (Stuttgart: Katholisches Bibelwerk Stuttgart, 2012).

Before starting to expose some of the major concerns in dealing with biblical theology today, I would like to confess my indebtedness to Jewish interpreters and exegesis. I have profited a great deal from medieval commentators such as Rashi and Ibn Ezra and, from the last century, Benno Jacob, Moshe Weinfeld, Moshe Greenberg, Jacob Milgrom, and others, besides many still living. I admire their thorough knowledge of the Bible, their acute observations, and their extraordinary sensitivity to even the smallest details. They have had a great influence on my thinking and interpretation.

What follows here is based on the fruits of recent discussions, together with the relevant literature, part of which is mentioned above, and also on experiences gleaned over more than thirty years of teaching and writing. After a short reflection on the need to engage with biblical theology (§2), I will concentrate on the decisions and the steps to be taken to achieve this goal (§3) and finally, in conclusion, indicate some results (§4).

2. The Necessity for Biblical Theology

Before addressing this issue, a short clarification of the term *biblical theology*, already used several times above, might be appropriate. In my view, the Greek origin of "theology," θεός and λόγος, in its specific sense as "word/speaking (about) God," directs us to keep the focus on God (see also below, §3.2) rather than on other issues.[8] The other word, *biblical*, is fluid in its meaning, according to the various denominations; this will be discussed under the topic *canon* (below, §3.4.2) and for the moment can remain open. As a "working agreement," we may understand biblical theology as those studies dealing with statements about God present in the Holy Scriptures whose extent varies according to the different faith groups.

After this clarification, there arises the question of whether biblical exegesis is necessary at all. Why isn't it sufficient simply to read individual biblical texts and interpret them, that is, do the *exegesis* of distinct passages, without caring about their theological intentions and their connections? I can offer three main arguments against that approach:

---

8. This is also one outcome of my recent article on various biblical theologies: Georg Fischer, "Biblical Theology in Transition—an Overview of Recent Works, and a Look Ahead at How to Proceed," in *Biblical Theology: Past, Present, and Future*, ed. Carey Walsh and M. W. Elliott (Eugene, OR: Wipf & Stock, 2016), 79–90, esp. 87.

(1) One cannot understand single theological statements correctly without taking into account related texts and the broader background. The following two examples demonstrate this.

First, in Ezek 9:3–11:23, YHWH's glory is depicted as leaving his temple in three steps.[9] Unless one also considers Ezek 43:1–5, any interpretation of Ezek 8–11 will remain limited and not do full justice to the motif of God's glory, namely, that these chapters only describe a *temporary* absence.

Second, Jer 12:8 says that God hates his inheritance.[10] To conclude from this passage that the biblical God is misanthropic fails to take into account passages such as Jer 31:3: "I have loved you with eternal love." Interpreting Jer 12:8 without bringing in other texts would result in a one-sided, incorrect picture of God.[11]

Thus it seems necessary to interpret single passages within a larger context. In the cases mentioned here, this is, in the first instance, the respective book. Statements about God, especially when they do not seem to fit into "normal" concepts of him, need to be considered within a broader framework.

(2) The actual discussions about divine violence are urgent, and one must address them.[12] As the last example, Jer 12:8, shows, one cannot do this by referring to single texts. One needs systematic, critical reflection, such as Janowski has provided paradigmatically in his recent book.[13] This is all the more important as recent worldwide developments raise the issue

---

9. For its importance, see Moshe Greenberg, *Ezekiel 1–20*, AB 22 (New York: Doubleday, 1983), 176, 191, 195.

10. The passage coming closest to it is Hos 9:15. There, too, God's hatred is directed against humans, and he dispels them from "my house"; the latter occurs in Jeremiah in the context immediately preceding (Jer 12:7).

11. The same contrast between God's hatred and love is also found in Hosea: 3:1; 11:1; 14:5, so that there, too, the harsh, negative divine attitude towards his people is reversed and brought to a good solution.

12. A decade ago, Jan Assmann, kicked off a heated debate by his thesis that maintains that monotheistic religions would be "inherently violent" (*Die mosaische Unterscheidung oder der Preis des Monotheismus* [München: Carl Hanser, 2003]). More recently, Notger Slenczka has attacked the Old Testament in a similar vein and demanded its removal from academic teaching; for a criticism of such unfounded misinterpretations, see, among others, Rolf Schieder, ed., *Die Gewalt des einen Gottes: Die Monotheismusdebatte zwischen Jan Assmann, Micha Brumlik, Rolf Schieder, Peter Sloterdijk und anderen* (Berlin: Berlin University Press, 2014).

13. Janowski, *Ein Gott*; earlier works dealing with the problem are, e.g., Manfred Görg, *Der un-heile Gott: Die Bibel im Bann der Gewalt* (Düsseldorf: Patmos, 1995);

of the connection between religion—or rather, portrayals of God—and resulting human behavior, so that sometimes the Bible is held responsible for intolerance and violence.

(3) More fundamentally, and on a theoretical level, all human understanding is contextual. This hermeneutical principle is also valid for biblical texts, scrolls, and the Bible as a whole. Single signs or expressions, like words and phrases, need to be seen in an environment that establishes their meaning. This means that there can be no correct interpretation of a verse or a chapter without taking into account its connections, and that includes, at a minimum, the entire book in which it is found, and often much more, and not limiting investigation to certain passages, chapters, or sections.[14]

From the above, it should now be clear that on a practical, political (referring to its social relevance today), and theoretical level, it is necessary to go beyond doing *mere* exegesis solely of distinct passages, interpreting them within a limited perspective. One must incorporate a wider background and dedicate interest and effort to biblical theology. The flowering of recent publications is a sign that this need is widely felt. If any biblical exegesis is not inserted in theology, it risks being heavily flawed and runs the danger of misreading the texts because the necessary framework is missing.

Walter Dietrich and Christian Link, *Willkür und Gewalt*, vol. 1 of *Die dunklen Seiten Gottes*, 5th ed. (Neukirchen-Vluyn: Neukirchener Verlag, 2009).

14. The transmission of single scrolls, such as exist for Genesis, Exodus, etc., is a sign that they were conceived as a unity, no matter whether it is the result of a redactional process or was originally planned this way. For examples of the necessity to consider whole books, see above (1). For example, the links relating the book of Genesis to 2 Kings—e.g., God's promises to the forefathers to give them the land in Genesis—cannot be adequately understood unless one also takes into account their fulfilment in the book of Joshua. There are intended connections between them, and they require incorporation into one's interpretation of the respective texts—otherwise the portrayal of God could become flawed, in this case as one who makes many promises without actually carrying them out. Lohr's critique in his response in Baltimore misses the point: one must investigate individual sections *as well as* their insertion into a larger context. These two approaches do not exclude each other but are complementary (see also below §3.3).

3. Disputed Issues

The fields of biblical theology are so vast that I can address here only some fundamental questions. I will limit myself to seven areas and present them briefly.

3.1. Where to Begin[15]

In the past, *concepts* have often dominated the approaches. *Heilsgeschichte* was a dominant idea for Gerhard von Rad.[16] Preuß placed more emphasis on *Erwählung*, and he subsumed large parts of his two volumes under headings informed by *election*.[17] On the other hand, Bernhard Lang focuses on YHWH's *lordship*.[18] These and other authors have detected important themes and have overlaid these general ideas on the texts and books, using them as a sort of universal key to the understanding of the entire Bible.

Compared with this, and in contrast to it, it seems more appropriate to start with the texts and their variety. God's word, as communicated in the biblical books in a rich diversity, must have priority over human categories and theories, which, imposed on the individual texts, can narrow the wide spectrum of the Bible's messages.

An additional aspect of the first question touches on the *choice of text*. Responsible interpretation requires going back, as far as possible, to the "original." In the case of the Tanak, this is the Hebrew text of the MT, which in my opinion, even in disputed cases of other scrolls, offers the most reliable textual basis.[19] The LXX shows throughout all the signs of a

---

15. This question touches on the issue of the initial orientation for one's approach, not on the choice of specific texts (e.g., Gen 1, Isa 6, or Ps 2) with which to start.

16. Gerhard von Rad, *Theologie des Alten Testaments*, 7th ed., 2 vols. (München: Kaiser, 1978–1980). He often uses "Heilsgeschichte" (= salvation history; e.g., 1:135, 143) and "Heilsgeschehen" (= salvation events; 2:254, 380, etc.). This notion is taken from outside and applied to the Bible.

17. Preuß, *des Alten Testaments*: The title of §2 in part 1 of vol. 1 starts with "Erwählungsaussagen," and part 2 therein describes "JHWH als Subjekt des geschichtlich erwählenden Handelns." In vol. 2, part 3 deals with "Die Auswirkungen und das Weiterdenken der Urerwählung," and part 4 concentrates on "Folgen und Folgerungen der geschichtlich erfahrenen Erwählung."

18. Bernhard Lang, *Jahwe der biblische Gott: Ein Porträt* (München: Beck, 2002). All his five main sections start with "Herr" (= Lord, of wisdom, war, animals …).

19. E.g., the Books of Samuel and of Jeremiah, *pace* recent developments giving

translation, so that it cannot be taken as testimony for an originally different text, and the best Qumran manuscripts generally support the version of the MT.

3.2. What to Search For

What in recent years have been published as biblical theologies sometimes hardly deserve the name. Gerstenberger himself admits to concentrating on the "Sozialgeschichte Israels."[20] A. H. J. Gunneweg and Rainer Albertz have focused on the "Religionsgeschichte," whereas Bernhard Lang, Othmar Keel, and others have more been interested in the connections of the biblical God with the ancient Near East.[21] As important as the links with all these related fields and the respective studies are, they cannot form the center of what is called biblical theology. The legitimate application of this label is bound to the Bible and to how it speaks of God.

Another type of "deviation" from biblical theology is apparent in my own biography and in similarly oriented publications. Sweeney, in his introduction, distances biblical theology from *anthropology*.[22] It is true that all our talk of God in the Bible and elsewhere is tied to our human experience and that this must be reflected; however, human affairs and interests cannot be allowed to take center stage in biblical theology.[23]

In contrast to the orientations mentioned above, a biblical theology worthy of the name must concentrate on God and the way in which the Bible portrays God. As the central character and the most important figure

---

preference to the LXX. Sweeney, too, takes the Masoretic Text as basis for Jewish biblical theology and gives good reasons for doing so (*Tanak*, 28–30).

20. Gerstenberger, *Theologien im Alten Testament*, ch. 3.

21. See the respective (sub)titles of A. H. J. Gunneweg, *Biblische Theologie des Alten Testaments: Eine Religionsgeschichte Israels in biblisch-theologischer Sicht* (Stuttgart: Kohlhammer, 1993), and of Rainer Albertz, *Religionsgeschichte Israels in alttestamentlicher Zeit*, 2nd ed., 2 vols., GAT 8/1–2 (Göttingen: Vandenhoeck & Ruprecht, 1996–1997). See Lang, *Jahwe der biblische Gott*; see also the various publications of Othmar Keel, Christoph Uehlinger, and Silvia Schroer.

22. Sweeney, *Tanak*, 26: "Biblical theology is differentiated from biblical anthropology."

23. Joel N. Lohr, in his response, emphasized the divine commandments, yet there is no contradiction in that. God himself is more important than his precepts, and the obeisance to them is only a consequence of the relationship to him, a second step (see the passages in the next note), with minor weight.

in it, God therefore deserves the utmost attention. The Greek origin of the word *theology*, too, requires such a primary orientation on God.[24] In this approach lies also the hope of being able to perceive what is most important in the Bible.

3.3. How to Approach It

Who now believes in the once enthusiastically received theology of von Rad? His presentation of the "geschichtlichen" and "prophetischen Überlieferungen" is heavily dependent on theories that are outdated.[25] In a similar way, studies like those of Albertz, which use to a high degree redaction-critical models, literary-critical strata, or sources, carry the danger of being based too much on hypotheses; furthermore, such interpretations are widely disputed, even among colleagues inclined toward these approaches.

For these and other reasons, a more solid methodology is recommended. It must start with the text, observe all it says about God, collect the various enunciations, try to sift and to order them without leveling their differences, and take into account all relevant statements, at least within one book.[26] Only this combination of attention to the details (in singular phrases, expressions, verses) *together with* a global (encompassing a whole literary unity) perspective can lead to firm results.

In my research I have found several features especially helpful: to note the titles given to God, to detect what is unique (e.g., "king of the nations" in Jer 10:6) or rare, and to detect what is repeated and thus forms a focal point. In many books of the Bible there are passages or chapters where

---

24. I agree with Lohr that right behavior, submission to the divine will, is important, but it *follows* from knowing God. How God is, and is perceived, is a model for those believing in him, as Lev 11:45 ("holy"), Deut 10:18–19 ("love the stranger"), and similar constructions in the New Testament—as there are in Matt 5:48 (with "perfect") and Luke 6:36 (with "merciful"), applying the same expressions to God and his faithful—show.

25. These are the respective subtitles of the first and second volumes of von Rad, *Theologie des Alten Testaments*.

26. See above the example with God's hatred and love in Jeremiah and in Hosea. *Text* does not mean a reconstructed form of it or supposed layers but in its *final form*. Marvin A. Sweeney, in his chapter "What Is Biblical Theology?" in this volume refers to Bernard S. Childs and opts for the same orientation in dealing with the proposed topic.

theological ideas are concentrated (e.g., Deut 4; 10:12–22; 32).[27] Often these texts are also prayers (e.g., Exod 15; 1 Sam 2; Dan 9) and deserve special attention.

3.4. How Far Should the Study Extend?

This is a very decisive question, bearing on various delicate issues of which a few are mentioned below.

3.4.1. Theology in the Singular or Theologies in the Plural?

Who would mix an apple, a stone, and a car tire? What difference does it make if we talk about *the* theology of *the* Bible? Such a generalized way of speaking presupposes that all of its books contain nearly the same ideas and thus convey a similar message.

I do not deny the unity of the Bible as a canon or the interconnectedness of its respective parts; however, theologically, the various books differ quite widely, and, in my opinion, this must be respected more than has previously been the case. The book of Exodus shows a portrayal of God different from that of the book of Joshua.[28] Prophetic books such as Isaiah, Ezekiel, or Jonah vary in the ways in which they speak about God.[29] For these reasons, I think it is more appropriate to speak, even within the Bible, of theologies in the plural. This in no way suggests that there is more than one God; it only accounts for the large diversity of portrayals and presentations of YHWH in the various biblical scrolls.

---

27. Deut 32, e.g., is marked by the sevenfold theological use of צוּר "rock" (starting in 32:4).

28. In Exodus, God gives laws to the people and instructions for the sanctuary, themes that are dominant for many chapters in the second half of the book. These aspects are nearly absent from the book of Joshua, which, in turn, has the motif of God "giving rest," נוח in the hiphil, five times (1:13, 15; 21:44; 22:4; 23:1), more often than in any other biblical book, whereas in Exodus it occurs only once, in the divine promise in 33:14.

29. The book of Isaiah entitles YHWH twenty-six times as "the Holy One of Israel," which elsewhere is found only six times, and emphasizes this aspect, e.g., in 6:3, with the triple repetition of "holy" for him. The book of Ezekiel shows deep compassion for a female baby cast aside at birth (16:4–6) and portrays his splendor leaving the temple (various steps in 9:3 to 11:23). In the book of Jonah, God's compassion even encompasses foreigners known for their cruelty.

Practically, this requires a procedure that first takes into account the single books of the Bible and presents their theologies on their own merits.[30] Only afterward, in a second step, may links between the various theologies be established.[31]

Going further, one cannot stop with one book of the Tanak. *Biblical* theological research involves repeating the same procedure for every book, collecting observations about God on various levels.[32] The outcome is a rich variety in his portrayal, with several nuanced, distinct aspects in the individual books, and some common features connecting various books.[33] The Bible presents God in unlimited ways, corresponding to his essence, his freedom, and his universal character. Only the term *biblical theologies*, plural, can—and then only approximately—render justice to what he is.

3.4.2. Which Canon?

Marvin A. Sweeney and Dalit Rom-Shiloni, and similarly others, rightly insist on the difference between the Jewish Bible and the Christian Old Testament.[34] Must theologies of the Tanak and of the Old Testament therefore be different? In my view, no, for the following reasons.

---

30. Some books, however, e.g., those of the Torah or of the Deuteronomistic History, are interrelated, which means that investigation into their connections in the way they speak about God is required too. In the case of the Psalms, conversely, the individuality of every Psalm must be respected first, before bringing together similar divine features.

31. The motif of God's holiness may serve as an example: In God's invitation to the covenant in Exod 19:6, he offers the people the opportunity to become a "holy nation." The book of Leviticus continues on this line by exhorting the community to sanctify themselves and, by taking divine sanctity as a model and criterion for their own holiness (11:44–45), thus expands and emphasizes this motif.

32. See above the last paragraph in §3.3, indicating fruitful avenues for investigations.

33. Andrea L. Weiss, in her paper in this volume, speaks of the "multivocal nature of the Bible" and, quoting Jon D. Levenson, of "the unsystematic and polydox materials in the Hebrew Bible."

34. Sweeney, *Tanak*, 20–25. Dalit Rom-Shiloni, "Hebrew Bible Theology: A Jewish Descriptive Approach," *JR* 96 (2016): 165–84, republished in this volume, addresses two fundamental issues, the question of the borders of biblical theology, and of the terminology used for it, pointing out the differences from (usual) Christian conceptions that are based on presuppositions.

(1) To interpret a text requires first and foremost trying to understand it *as it was written*; it is not legitimate to apply foreign ideas or inappropriate categories to it. This means that even as a Christian I have to respect the "original intention" immanent in the text, without presuppositions, seeking to detect what the text wanted to say when and for whom it was written. I must not bring in anachronistically later developments to its interpretation. In this sense, there is no distinction between Jewish or Christian exegetical and theological research.

(2) The different *sequence* of the books of the Old Testament with respect to the Tanak is no real obstacle. On the contrary, there are good arguments for following the order of the Tanak, at least for the Torah and the Nevi'im, and I have done so myself.[35] For the Ketuvim there is no need to stick to their arrangement, as historically these biblical books have very different backgrounds, and their order differs even within the Jewish tradition.[36]

Generally speaking, coming first does not necessarily and *per se* imply increased significance. Is the last book of the Latter Prophets, Malachi, less important than, for example, the first book of the Former Prophets, Joshua? On the other hand, however, the position of the Torah at the front gives special weight to it, and this prominence of the first five books is widely respected in all confessions. The order of the books is less decisive than the appreciation and dedication shown to every individual book of Scripture and to all of them taken together. The sequence does not influence heavily the understanding of biblical theologies. It indicates, in part, a development in time and establishes a build-up in the knowledge of God.

(3) With regard to the *textual basis*, my remark above (in §3.1) giving priority to the MT is in accordance with many Jewish exegetes. In contrast, we can find today Jewish colleagues who favor the LXX in some cases.[37] Therefore, this border between Jewish and Christian exegesis no longer exists; the front line is among the confessions themselves.

---

35. Fischer, *Theologien des Alten Testaments*, 21–138, with justification on p. 20.

36. Various positions are indicated even for the Book of Jeremiah. According to b. B. Bat. 14b–15a, it ranks first among the Latter Prophets, immediately following after the book(s) of Kings.

37. Emanuel Tov favors, in several instances, the Greek version as representing supposedly an earlier form of the text (*Textual Criticism of the Hebrew Bible*, 2nd rev. ed. [Minneapolis: Fortress, 2001], esp. ch. 7).

(4) The different *number* of books regarded as Jewish Bible or Old Testament is no hurdle either. The Old Testament canon of the Protestant churches is equal to the Tanak. The Catholic Church accepts seven more books as canonical, the Greek Orthodox Church still more.[38] The large number of biblical books regarded as canonical is identical, is a common basis, and has decisive weight.

Thus the additional books *need not be a reason for division.* Their main theological emphasis corresponds with that of the other biblical scrolls, and their interpretation is normally based on them. They are less frequently dealt with, although recently they have received more attention.[39] They do not essentially change the portrayal of God but may lay additional weight on some particular aspects that are already known.[40]

3.4.3. The Relationship with the New Testament

This is probably the most critical issue, resulting from the different conceptions of the canon. It is true that up to now Christian Old Testament theology was often biased. Many Christian interpreters throughout history have regularly seen texts and ideas of the Hebrew Bible almost exclusively in the light of Jesus and the New Testament, and they relativized it from

---

38. The so-called deuterocanonical books, accepted in the Catholic Church in addition to the Hebrew Bible, are Judith, Tobit, 1 and 2 Maccabees, Wisdom, Sirach, and Baruch. The Orthodox Churches regard still more books as canonical, e.g., 1 Ezra, 3 and 4 Maccabees, and Psalms of Solomon.

39. The commentaries on the book of Baruch by Odil Hannes Steck (Odil Hannes Steck, Reinhard Gregor Kratz, and Ingo Kottsieper, *Das Buch Baruch, der Brief des Jeremia, Zusätze zu Ester und Daniel*, ATD 5 [Göttingen: Vandenhoeck & Ruprecht, 1998]) and on the book of Wisdom by Helmut Engel (*Das Buch der Weisheit*, NSKAT 16 [Stuttgart: Katholisches Bibelwerk, 1998]) are examples that have fostered a great deal of interest and research in their respective areas since their publication.

40. The book of Tobit, e.g., excels in God's sending of his messenger/angel (Tob 5–12), picking up a motif present since Gen 16. For the book of Baruch, God's identification as the "Eternal One" is specific (eight times, from Bar 4:10 onward; see Ps 90:2; 92:9; 93:2, etc.), and its extended confessional prayer (Bar 1:15–3:8) follows along the lines of similar texts, like Neh 9 and Dan 9. The dedication of the temple mentioned in Ps 30:1 finds an echo in 1 Maccabees, with the cleansing of the temple and the dedication of the altar (4:36–59).

this perspective.[41] This has received ever more criticism in recent years, and rightly so, in Jewish as well as in Christian circles.[42]

In contrast to such a depreciation of the Tanak—and at the same time also of the Old Testament, the first part of their own Bible—among Christian theologians as being only of secondary importance, these biblical books forming the Jewish Bible are God's primary revelation. As such, they remain the indispensable foundation for every biblical theology and must be regarded and respected in their own right. To judge them from outside is biased and unhelpful. Still more, it is dangerous to devalue God's first words and thus one's own roots.

A *hermeneutical decision* is connected with this issue. Methodologically, it is not sound to interpret a text with concepts foreign to it or criteria taken from outside; rather, every utterance must first be understood in the way it was originally meant (see also above in §3.4.2, point 1). This implies that a responsible reading of, for example, Isa 7:14 must first bring forth the meaning it has within the book of Isaiah and its time. It is not legitimate to connect the interpretation of this passage, right from the start, with its quotation in Matt 1:23. However, in a second step, clearly to be distinguished from the exegetical analysis of Isa 7:14, the citation in the Gospel of Matthew may be adduced as part of the *Wirkungsgeschichte*. This can be done, but it need not be.[43]

---

41. This procedure takes later developments as a measure by which to evaluate earlier positions. Such a "projecting backward" leads to unfair judgments and, from a historical perspective, is irresponsible.

42. For Jewish criticism, see recently Sweeney, *Tanak*, 10, who calls it "vilification" (*Tanak*, 10), and Rom-Shiloni, who notes that terminology of "supersessionism" is based on illegitimate "retrojection" ("Hebrew Bible Theology," 172–73). One of the most outspoken Christian critics was Erich Zenger. In his influential introduction to the Old Testament he challenged problematic understandings of the relationship between the two Testaments; he strongly opposed the idea of seeing the New Testament as standing in "contrast" to the Old Testament, as relativizing it, or as taking it as an evolution of the former one, surpassing and outdating it (Zenger et al., *Einleitung in das Alte Testament*, ed. Christian Frevel, 8th rev. ed., KST 1 [Stuttgart: Kohlhammer, 2012], 17–19). Christoph Dohmen, Norbert Lohfink, and others have argued similarly in various publications.

43. Generally, many New Testament passages highly appreciate the Tanak; examples are Matt 5:17–18, Luke 24:44–45, and Rom 11:16–18, among others. There is no opposition or rivalry between the biblical God and Jesus.

3.5. What Is the Role of Faith?

Some exegetes regard their profession as mere literary analysis of some ancient texts or as a kind of *Religionswissenschaft* dealing with a limited corpus, namely, old Hebrew literature. As every understanding presupposes a common "horizon," there must be some sort of affinity between the biblical text and its interpreters.[44] If now the biblical books are based in faith communities and describe their experiences with God, a similar belief in those interpreting them is in no way an obstacle but rather a helpful qualification for sensing the real character and the profound message of the texts of the Bible.

Recently this has been acknowledged more and more. Walter Brueggemann's insistence on "testimony," Friedhelm Hartenstein's perception of the Old Testament as "geglaubte Geschichte," Reinhard Feldmeier and Hermann Spieckermann's portrayal of YHWH as "Gott der Lebendigen," and many other contributions in the past years clearly demonstrate the central role of faith in biblical theology.[45]

---

44. This principle has been amply described by Hans-Georg Gadamer and further developed by Emerich Coreth. Their observations are not only valid for philosophical reasoning but apply generally for all areas and dimensions of understanding. See Gadamer, *Wahrheit und Methode: Grundzüge einer philosophischen Hermeneutik* (Tübingen: Mohr, 1960), translated into English as Gadamer, *Truth and Method*, trans. Garrett Barden and John Cumming (London: Sheed & Ward, 1975); Coreth, *Grundfragen der Hermeneutik: Ein philosophischer Beitrag* (Freiburg: Herder, 1969).

45. See the titles of the first four parts of Brueggemann, *Theology of the Old Testament*: "Israel's Core Testimony"; "Israel's Countertestimony"; "Israel's Unsolicited Testimony"; and "Israel's Embodied Testimony." Friedhelm Hartenstein, "JHWH's Wesen im Wandel: Vorüberlegungen zu einer Theologie des Alten Testaments," *TLZ* 137 (2012): 3–20, here 4, quoting Jan C. Gertz. On pp. 8–10, picking up ideas of Paul Ricœur's "Hermeneutik des Zeugnisses" (in *An den Grenzen der Hermeneutik: Philosophische Reflexionen über die Religion*, ed. Veronika Hoffmann [Freiburg: Alber, 2008]: 7–40), he qualifies the Bible's way of speaking as "Glaubensaussagen" and "Bekenntnis." Steven Kepnes, in his excellent presentation given at the Society of Biblical Literature conference in Atlanta on November 23, 2015, has stressed the essential role of faith and of a believing community for the understanding of the Bible. "Gott der Lebendigen" is in English "the God of the living"; see Reinhard Feldmeier and Hermann Spieckermann, *Der Gott der Lebendigen: Eine biblische Gotteslehre*, Tobith 1 (Tübingen: Mohr Siebeck, 2011), 2; see God's own teaching ("Lehre durch Gott selbst") as a source for the Bible and the faith rooted in it.

In fact, one's own belief is methodologically a key to it. How can one talk about the biblical God without an inner knowledge of God? How can one feel the unlimited force and fascinating beauty of the biblical texts if one has no sensitivity to what makes them so special and unique? A personal experience of faith and even a longing for God (e.g., Pss 42; 63) provide an apt resonance chamber within which biblical texts and the ways in which they speak of God can resound, and where interpreters may come into harmony with them.[46]

3.6. Descriptive or Also Critical?

Why is it not sufficient to render the results of the theological analyses by listing the main ideas or by paraphrasing them in one's own words? The task of describing the findings of the research is only the initial step. Discussion, reflection, and critique must necessarily follow, as is shown by the example above of Jer 12:8 in contrast to Jer 31:3 and affirmed by colleagues such as Rom-Shiloni.[47]

It does not suffice simply to enumerate the tensions, discrepancies, and even contradictions to be found in the vast variety of the Bible's depictions of God. To set one concept beside another one without clarifying their relationship would not account for their different positioning and importance. In fact, there are passages bearing more relevance than others.[48] Furthermore, the *dynamic* of a literary work also helps one to discern the significance of individual expressions; in the case of Jeremiah,

---

46. The Dogmatic Constitution *Dei Verbum* of the Second Vatican Council (1965) expresses this in the following way: "Holy Scripture must be read and interpreted in the sacred spirit in which it was written" (12). Lohr, in his response to my paper in Baltimore, referring to Gershom Ratheiser, emphasized the role of an observant life and a practical sympathy for the Bible's commandments. Yet this is no contrast to the role of faith here, as I only want to show how its epistemological function for understanding the Bible and as true faith will lead to a corresponding daily pattern of behavior.

47. Rom-Shiloni, although insisting on the "descriptive" aspect, as given in her title "Hebrew Bible Theology: A Jewish Descriptive Approach," also reflects on the various modes of biblical theologies throughout her entire paper and calls her procedure a "descriptive critical approach" (172).

48. E.g., God's long revelation on Mount Sinai in the book of Exodus weighs more than the Pharaoh's short statement about him in Exod 9:27. Additionally, as is clear in this case, what God himself is saying has a higher authority than how others describe him.

the passage in 31:3 relativizes the earlier one in 12:8, attributing to it only limited value. Finally, the biblical books not only contain divine revelation but are also written down in human words and ideas that may differ from what God wants or change within the stream of history.[49] Thus biblical theologies, while accepting the paramount authority of the Tanak, must also be attentive to its human limitations and weaknesses.

3.7. Is There a Core to the Biblical Theologies?

There has been a long search for a *Mitte*, a kernel in the Bible's portrayal of God, with various suggestions being offered.[50] In my view, those seeing YHWH's self-definition in the *Gnadenrede* on Mount Sinai in Exod 34:6–7 as the key are on the right track.[51] There God reveals himself to be both merciful and just, with mercy predominating. This idea is repeated various times throughout the Bible, and there is no book in it that as a whole would oppose it.[52] Thus mercy and justice also become keys for human behavior.

This step, of showing the concurring main features, the characteristics, in some way the *unity* within the manifold ways in which the biblical books talk about God, is necessary too. It does conform to the central confession of biblical faith: that YHWH is אחד—"one" and "unique" (Deut 6:4). It is the task of biblical theologians to elucidate both aspects: God's unfathomable richness, resulting in the vast diversity of talk about him, and his being at the same time *one*.

---

49. Both dimensions, the divine and the human, are sometimes combined within a short section of text (see Deut 1:1, 3; Jer 1:1–2 [MT]), thus making the audience aware of the double character of the following.

50. For an overview of various (German) approaches, see Mark W. Elliott, *The Reality of Biblical Theology*, RD 39 (Frankfurt: Lang 2007), 106–17. For a new suggestion, see Oeming, "Viele Wege zu dem Einen," whose subtitle uses the term "transzendente Mitte," which he exemplifies on pp. 92–95.

51. The term *Gnadenrede* has been coined by Matthias Franz in *Der barmherzige und gnädige Gott: Die Gnadenrede vom Sinai (Exodus 34,6–7) und ihre Parallelen im Alten Testament und seiner Umwelt*, BWANT 160 (Stuttgart: Kohlhammer 2003). Because of the variations in the expression (see Pss 86:15; 103:8; 145:8, etc.), it is more appropriate than the term "Gnadenformel," which had earlier been introduced by Spieckermann.

52. Although it may be contested for a limited time or for a certain situation, as in Ezek 9:10 and Jer 13:14, there is no biblical scroll that at the end or in its dynamic would deny God's mercy.

4. Results

Looking back over the above comments, biblical theology appears in a new light.

There are many good reasons why it is necessary for exegetes to make a strong commitment to biblical theology. This task can no longer be done in the singular; rather the variety of ways in which the Bible speaks about God demands that we consider plural biblical *theologies*.

Hermeneutical decisions with respect to contextual reading, the role of the interpreter, the interpreter's stance and interests, and a critically reflective methodology are essential for a correct and fruitful approach to biblical themes and theology.[53]

Biblical theologies should put their focus on God. Related fields, like the history of Israel, science of religion, and social sciences, may contribute and should be taken into account but should never be allowed to take priority over the concentration on God.

Although often, in the past, Christian Old Testament theologies have differed from theologies of the Jewish Bible, this need not be so. There is no inherent opposition between them, and Christian interpreters should unquestionably, as a first step, read the Hebrew Bible in a similar way to their Jewish colleagues.

A faith perspective is an appropriate stance from which to approach God's word, and this is true, too, for the study of biblical theologies. However, it needs a critical attitude as a complement. Belief without critical distance tends to become blind; too sharp a criticism of the Bible without an inner sympathy for it risks missing fundamental issues.

Central to YHWH's character as portrayed in the Bible are his mercy and justice. This has enormous relevance for today, and for the whole world. Biblical theology has the opportunity and the mission to exert an influence in this direction, making the earth more divine and at the same time more human.

---

53. A good example is Kessler, *Old Testament Theology*, who in his first three chapters discusses at length the relevant issues and various stances taken with regard to them (1–107).

Bibliography

Albertz, Rainer. *Religionsgeschichte Israels in alttestamentlicher Zeit.* 2nd ed. 2 vols. GAT 8/1–2. Göttingen: Vandenhoeck & Ruprecht, 1996–1997.

Assmann, Jan. *Die mosaische Unterscheidung oder der Preis des Monotheismus.* München: Carl Hanser, 2003.

Brueggemann, Walter. *Theology of the Old Testament: Testimony, Dispute, Advocacy.* Minneapolis: Fortress, 1997.

Childs, Brevard S. *Biblical Theology of the Old and New Testaments: Theological Reflection on the Christian Bible.* Minneapolis: Fortress, 1993.

Coreth, Emerich. *Grundfragen der Hermeneutik: Ein philosophischer Beitrag.* Freiburg: Herder, 1969.

Dietrich, Walter, and Christian Link. *Willkür und Gewalt.* Vol. 1 of *Die dunklen Seiten Gottes.* 5th ed. Neukirchen-Vluyn: Neukirchener Verlag, 2009.

Elliott, Mark W. *The Reality of Biblical Theology.* RD 39. Frankfurt: Lang 2007.

Engel, Helmut. *Das Buch der Weisheit.* NSKAT 16. Stuttgart: Katholisches Bibelwerk, 1998.

Feldmeier, Reinhard, and Hermann Spieckermann. *Der Gott der Lebendigen: Eine biblische Gotteslehre.* Tobith 1. Tübingen: Mohr Siebeck, 2011.

Fischer, Georg. "Biblical Theology in Transition—an Overview of Recent Works, and a Look Ahead at How to Proceed." Pages 79–90 in *Biblical Theology: Past, Present, and Future.* Edited by Carey Walsh and M. W. Elliott. Eugene, OR: Wipf & Stock, 2016.

———. *Theologien des Alten Testaments.* NSKAT 31. Stuttgart: Katholisches Bibelwerk Stuttgart, 2012.

Franz, Matthias. *Der barmherzige und gnädige Gott: Die Gnadenrede vom Sinai (Exodus 34,6–7) und ihre Parallelen im Alten Testament und seiner Umwelt.* BWANT 160. Stuttgart: Kohlhammer 2003.

Gadamer, Hans-Georg. *Truth and Method.* Translated by Garrett Barden and John Cumming. London: Sheed & Ward, 1975.

———. *Wahrheit und Methode: Grundzüge einer philosophischen Hermeneutik.* Tübingen: Mohr, 1960.

Gamper, Arnold. *Gott als Richter in Mesopotamien und im Alten Testament: Zum Verständnis einer Gebetsbitte.* Innsbruck: Wagner, 1966.

Gerstenberger, Erhard S. *Theologien im Alten Testament: Pluralität und Synkretismus alttestamentlichen Gottesglaubens.* Stuttgart: Kohlhammer, 2001.

Görg, Manfred. *Der un-heile Gott: Die Bibel im Bann der Gewalt.* Düsseldorf: Patmos, 1995.

Greenberg, Moshe. *Ezekiel 1–20.* AB 22. New York: Doubleday, 1983.

Gunneweg, A. H. J. *Biblische Theologie des Alten Testaments: Eine Religionsgeschichte Israels in biblisch-theologischer Sicht.* Stuttgart: Kohlhammer, 1993.

Hartenstein, Friedhelm. "Jhwhs Wesen im Wandel." *TLZ* 137 (2012): 3–20.

———. "JHWH's Wesen im Wandel: Vorüberlegungen zu einer Theologie des Alten Testaments." *TLZ* 137 (2012): 3–20.

House, Paul R. *Old Testament Theology.* Downers Grove, IL: InterVarsity, 1998.

Janowski, Bernd. *Ein Gott, der straft und tötet? Zwölf Fragen zum Gottesbild des Alten Testaments.* Neukirchen-Vluyn: Neukirchener Verlag, 2013.

Kessler, John. *Old Testament Theology: Divine Call and Human Response.* Waco, TX: Baylor University Press, 2013.

Lang, Bernhard. *Jahwe der biblische Gott: Ein Porträt.* München: Beck, 2002.

Moberly, R. W. L. *Old Testament Theology: Reading the Hebrew Bible as Christian Scripture.* Grand Rapids: Baker Academic, 2013.

Oeming, Manfred. "Viele Wege zu dem Einen: Die 'transzendente Mitte' einer Theologie des Alten Testaments im Spannungsfeld von Vielheit und Einheit." Pages 83–108 in *Viele Wege zu dem Einen: Historische Bibelkritik—die Vitalität der Glaubensüberlieferung in der Moderne.* Edited by Stefan Beyerle, Axel Graupner, Udo Rüterswörden, and Ferdinand Ahuis. BThSt 121. Neukirchen-Vluyn: Neukirchener Verlag, 2012.

Preuß, Horst Dietrich. *Theologie des Alten Testaments.* 2 vols. Stuttgart: Kohlhammer, 1991–1992.

Rad, Gerhard von. *Theologie des Alten Testaments.* 7th ed. 2 vols. München: Kaiser, 1978–1980.

Ricœur, Paul. "Hermeneutik des Zeugnisses." Pages 7–40 in *An den Grenzen der Hermeneutik: Philosophische Reflexionen über die Religion.* Edited by Veronika Hoffmann. Freiburg: Alber, 2008.

Rom-Shiloni, Dalit. "Hebrew Bible Theology: A Jewish Descriptive Approach." *JR* 96 (2016): 165–84.

Schieder, Rolf, ed. *Die Gewalt des einen Gottes: Die Monotheismusdebatte zwischen Jan Assmann, Micha Brumlik, Rolf Schieder, Peter Sloterdijk und anderen.* Berlin: Berlin University Press, 2014.

Schmid, Konrad. *Gibt es Theologie im Alten Testament: Zum Theologiebegriff in der alttestamentlichen Wissenschaft.* Theologische Studien 7. Zürich: TVZ, 2013.

Steck, Odil Hannes, Reinhard Gregor Kratz, and Ingo Kottsieper. *Das Buch Baruch, der Brief des Jeremia, Zusätze zu Ester und Daniel.* ATD 5. Göttingen: Vandenhoeck & Ruprecht, 1998.

Sweeney, Marvin A. *Tanak: A Theological and Critical Introduction to the Jewish Bible.* Minneapolis: Fortress, 2012.

Tov, Emanuel. *Textual Criticism of the Hebrew Bible.* 2nd rev. ed. Minneapolis: Fortress, 2001.

Zenger, Erich, et al. *Einleitung in das Alte Testament.* Edited by Christian Frevel. 8th rev. ed. KST 1. Stuttgart: Kohlhammer, 2012.

What Is Biblical Theology?
With an Example on Divine Absence
and the Song of Songs

Marvin A. Sweeney

1. Introduction

Biblical theology has changed markedly in the years since World War II, when biblical theologians such as Walther Eichrodt and Gerhard von Rad wrote their magisterial works.[1] When viewed from the perspective of contemporary theology, each has its problems. Eichrodt dismissed the theological significance of Judaism and opted for an essentially Christian supersessionist perspective when he misrepresented Judaism as a legalistic system of observance devoid of the divine will, expressing his view of "Judaism's torso-like appearance ... in separation from Christianity."[2] Von Rad avoided anti-Jewish statements but nevertheless constructed a progression of *Heilsgeschichte* or "salvation history" that had no place for Judaism. In addition, both scholars neglected books of the Hebrew Bible, such as Esther and Song of Songs, neither of which mentions G-d, thereby dismissing books of sacred Scripture that appear in both the Jewish and the Christian Bibles. Neither addressed the theological issues raised by the Shoah, in which Germany and its sympathizers deliberately murdered

---

1. Walther Eichrodt, *Theology of the Old Testament*, trans. J. A. Baker, OTL, 2 vols. (Philadelphia: Westminster; London: SCM, 1961–1967); Gerhard von Rad, *Old Testament Theology*, trans. David M. G. Stalker, 2 vols. (New York: Harper & Row, 1962–1965); see also the response of Jon D. Levenson, "Why Jews Are Not Interested in Biblical Theology," in *The Hebrew Bible and Historical Criticism: Jews and Christians in Biblical Studies* (Louisville: Westminster John Knox, 1993), 33–61, to both of these works.

2. Eichrodt, *Theology of the Old Testament*, 1:26.

some six million Jews, even though both had lived through that sordid period in human history.

But biblical theology has changed, insofar as the field has learned to take account of both Judaism and Christianity as well as theological issues such as the absence of G-d, particularly in the aftermath of the Shoah or Holocaust. This paper therefore addresses two issues. The first is a theoretical discussion of what constitutes biblical theology in the contemporary interreligious world of Judaism and Christianity. The second is an illustration of how biblical theology might be conceived in relation to the question of divine absence and the Song of Songs in the contemporary post-Shoah and interreligious world.

2. What Is Biblical Theology?

Biblical theology is the systematic theological exposition of the Bible.[3] Because the Bible appears in a variety of forms in both Judaism and Christianity, it is imperative that interpreters consider the context in which biblical theology is pursued. In Judaism, the Bible comprises the Tanak, twenty-four books of the Bible written in Hebrew and Aramaic that are organized into three major sections: the Torah or Instruction; the Nevi'im or Prophets, including both the Former and the Latter Prophets; and the Ketuvim or the Writings. In Christianity, the Bible comprises both the Old Testament and the New Testament, although the number and order of books may vary within these two major rubrics. In Roman Catholicism, there are forty-six books of the Old Testament and twenty-seven books in the New Testament, for a total of seventy-three. In Protestant Christianity, there are thirty-nine books of the Old Testament, twenty-seven of the New Testament, and seven of the Apocrypha. Other traditions, such as the Slavonic, Armenian, and Ethiopian, may include other books. Because Christianity considers the various versions of the Bible to be witnesses to the true Bible, the Christian Bible appears in a variety of forms and languages, such as Hebrew, Greek, Aramaic, Syriac, Latin, Ethiopian, Slavonic, Armenian, and others.

From its inception in the eighteenth century through the late twentieth century, biblical theologians have attempted to define a consistent

---

3. Marvin A. Sweeney, "Biblical Theology. I. Hebrew Bible/Old Testament," *EBR* 3:1137–49, esp. 1137.

and unified principle or center (*Mitte*) around which to organize a biblical theology.[4] Proposals included variations of the G-d-man-salvation paradigm, covenant, *Heilsgeschichte* (salvation history), and others, but no one concept proved adequate to account for the entire Bible. Following the collapse of biblical theology in the late twentieth century, several new models or dimensions have emerged, such as the canonical form of the Bible, the dialogical character of the Bible, and the question of the theological integrity of the Bible. I would like to consider each of these dimensions.

2.1. The Canonical Forms of the Bible

The first dimension is the canonical form of the Bible. Much of the first two centuries of modern critical biblical scholarship was spent in efforts to unravel the compositional history of the Bible in order to identify the earliest—and therefore the most authentic—layers of the biblical text. Such early texts would then serve as the basis for reconstructing the allegedly authentic message of the Bible. But as such work progressed, scholars became increasingly uncomfortable with assertions about biblical theology that were based upon a reconstructed text that was never actually recognized in the churches or synagogues as the Bible.

Fundamentalists had long advocated basing their interpretation of the Bible on the final form of the biblical text, but when Brevard S. Childs proposed a canonical biblical theology that would base its interpretation on both the final form of the biblical text and its historical dimensions, he provoked an uproar of protests in some circles and a sigh of relief in others.[5] Childs proposed that the final form of the biblical text should serve as the basis for theological interpretation, not because the biblical text did

---

4. For discussion of biblical theology, see Sweeney, "Biblical Theology"; Sweeney, *Tanak: A Theological and Critical Introduction to the Jewish Bible* (Minneapolis: Fortress, 2012), 3–41; Gerhard Hasel, *Old Testament Theology: Basic Issues in the Current Debate* (Grand Rapids: Eerdmans, 1991); John H. Hayes and Frederick Prussner, *Old Testament Theology* (Atlanta: John Knox, 1985); Hans-Joachim Kraus, *Die biblische Theologie* (Neukirchen-Vluyn: Neukirchener Verlag, 1970); Leo G. Perdue, *The Collapse of History*, OBT (Minneapolis: Fortress, 1994); Perdue, *Reconstructing Old Testament Theology*, OBT (Minneapolis: Fortress, 2005).

5. Brevard S. Childs, *Old Testament Theology in a Canonical Context* (Minneapolis: Fortress, 1985); Childs, *Biblical Theology of the Old and New Testaments* (Minneapolis: Fortress, 1993); for critique, see James Barr, *The Concept of Biblical Theology* (Minneapolis: Fortress, 1999).

not presuppose a compositional history, but because the final form of the biblical text was the form in which the church had received the text and interpreted it throughout its own history. Childs did not entirely eschew the diachronic dimensions of the text; indeed, he frequently viewed the process by which the final form of the biblical text was achieved to be a source of theological insight as well, and in many cases it is debatable whether he fully escaped his own historical-critical background when interpreting the final form of the biblical text. But his essential goal was to uncover the *res*, or essence, of the biblical text that was embedded therein.

Childs's proposal offered a new dimension for biblical theology, which was especially so important because historical criticism had, in fact, been employed to privilege Protestant self-understanding and to polemicize against Jewish and Roman Catholic self-understandings. An example would be Julius Wellhausen's privileging of the J source in the Pentateuch, with its face-to-face "prophetic" encounter between G-d and humans, as the earliest and therefore most authentic understanding of the Pentateuch versus the place of the Priestly source, with its alleged interests in law and ritual, at the end of a largely degenerative process.[6] A canonical reading of the Pentateuch, for example, had the potential to correct the theological biases of Wellhausen's work if properly pursued.

But there were also problems with Childs's proposal that went beyond the simple dichotomy between historical or diachronic and canonical or synchronic reading strategies. For one, Childs did not account for the variety of canonical forms and versions extant for the Christian Bible.[7] Childs employed the Hebrew MT as the basis for his final canonical form of the Bible, which was apparently a nod to his understanding of the historical priority and authority of the text. He also included classical Jewish readings of the Bible together with those of Christian interpreters as part of his discussion of the canonical form of the text. But Christianity did and does not read the MT as the primary form of the Bible; Christianity reads the Greek LXX in its manifest forms, the Syriac Peshitta, the Latin Vulgate, and other versions all as witnesses to its understanding of the true form of the Bible revealed by G-d to humankind. Furthermore, Childs presumed

---

6. Julius Wellhausen, *Die Composition des Hexateuch* (Berlin: Georg Reimer, 1889); Wellhausen, *Prolegomenon to the History of Ancient Israel* (New York: Meridian, 1957).

7. See James A. Sanders, *Torah and Canon* (Philadelphia: Fortress, 1984); Sanders, *Canon and Community* (Philadelphia: Fortress, 1972).

a flat or singular understanding of the *res*, or truth, embedded within that text that did not account for its variety of forms, languages, and contexts for interpretation, including both the differences between Judaism and Christianity and the differences within Judaism and Christianity.

Consequently, biblical theology must account for the variety of canonical forms of the Bible and the contexts in which it is read. In my own work, I have distinguished between the canonical forms of the Tanak in Judaism and the Old Testament and New Testament in Christianity as a basis for theological interpretation.[8] In Judaism, the tripartite division of the Tanak into the Torah, Prophets, and Writings entails a theological dimension in which the Torah portrays the ideals of ancient Israel and its life in the land of Israel, the Prophets portray the disruption of those ideals as Israel and Judah are taken away from the land of Israel to Assyrian and Babylonian exile, and the Writings portray the attempt to reestablish ideal Jewish life in the land of Israel under foreign rule. The Christian Bible likewise points to its own theological view of history in which the earlier or old covenant/testament of Moses based on torah/law is revealed followed by the revelation of the new covenant/testament of Jesus Christ. As I have constructed the Christian canon, the four-part structure of the Old Testament points to progression through history: the Pentateuch takes up humanity's earliest history, the historical books take up Israel's later history, the wisdom and poetic books point to ahistorical questions of faith and knowledge, and the prophetic books point to the future. The New Testament has a similar structure, including the earliest history of Christ's revelation in the Gospels, the later history of the early church in Acts, ahistorical questions of faith and knowledge in the Epistles, and a view of the future return of Christ in the Apocalypse. Other constructions of the Christian canon are, of course, extant, but this provides an example of how a canonical principle of interpretation might work in the construction of a distinctive Christian biblical theology.

2.2. The Dialogical Dimension of the Bible

The second dimension of biblical theology I would like to consider is the dialogical dimension of the Bible.[9] Biblical theologians justifiably presume

---

8. Sweeney, *Tanak*, 20–36.

9. Sweeney, *Tanak*, 2036; cf. Walter Brueggemann, *Old Testament Theology* (Minneapolis: Fortress, 1997).

that the Bible represents divine truth, whatever their own particular religious tradition might be, but the nature of that truth raises issues. For the most part, interpreters presume that the truth represented by the Bible is intellectually consistent and without contradiction. Such a view, of course, led to the many attempts noted above to define a single principle around which to conceive or organize a biblical theology.

But the pluralistic nature of the Bible's contents extends not only to the many textual versions and canonical forms in which the Bible appears but to its basic contents as well. Eichrodt attempted to define a biblical theology based upon the concept of covenant but failed in his attempt because not all of the books of the Bible are concerned with covenant.[10] Von Rad likewise attempted to define a biblical theology based on the concept of *Heilsgeschichte*, or salvation history, but the Bible is likewise not entirely concerned with history.[11] Having completed his *Old Testament Theology*, criticism compelled him to write his *Wisdom in Israel* to account for the ahistorical wisdom literature, but even this volume attempted to interpret the wisdom literature through a historical lens.[12]

But von Rad's work also opened the door to a more pluralistic reading of the Bible even if he did not fully achieve it himself. One of his major accomplishments was the recognition that each of the prophets had a distinct message, based upon the distinct institutional tradition on which the prophet was based. Isaiah was a royalist based in the Davidic covenant. Jeremiah presupposed the Mosaic covenant tradition based on torah. Ezekiel was a Zadokite priest based in the Jerusalem temple. Such observations did not prevent von Rad from misreading many prophets. His treatment of Micah, for example, folds the prophet from Moresheth-Gath into the Isaian tradition, not recognizing that Micah, who was hardly a Davidic supporter, called for the destruction of Jerusalem, something that Isaiah never did.

Nevertheless, von Rad's recognition of the unique institutional identities of the prophets paved the way for the recognition of an essential dimension of the prophetic literature: the prophets disagree among

---

10. Eichrodt, *Theology of the Old Testament*.

11. Von Rad, *Old Testament Theology*.

12. Gerhard von Rad, *Wisdom in Israel* (Nashville: Abingdon, 1972); cf. Rolf P. Knierim's attempt to address this issue in "Cosmos and History in Israel's Theology," *The Task of Old Testament Theology* (Grand Rapids: Eerdmans, 1995), 171–224.

themselves concerning the nature of YHWH's action in the world.[13] The book of Isaiah, founded in the Davidic tradition, ultimately gives up the notion of a Davidic monarch and instead identifies the nation Israel as the recipient of the Davidic promise and King Cyrus of Persia as YHWH's temple builder, messiah, and regent for the true King, YHWH. Jeremiah, although frequently citing his senior colleague Isaiah, ultimately argues that Jerusalem will come under judgment as well, just as the Northern Kingdom of Israel did in Isaiah's day. As a priest, he calls for observance of Mosaic torah rather than faith in the Davidic promise and indeed redefines the Davidic covenant to include the city of Jerusalem and the Levitical priesthood, at least in the MT form of the text. Ezekiel the Zadokite priest holds to the sanctity of the Jerusalem temple as his central concern for understanding YHWH's actions in the world and maintains the continuity of the house of David, noting that the Davidic monarch or prince will be among those who worship YHWH at the restored temple.

We may observe other differences elsewhere. The Former Prophets maintain that Israel and Judah were destroyed in large part because of the charge that the people failed to observe YHWH's torah, but they place special blame on the monarchs King Jeroboam ben Nebath of Israel and King Manasseh ben Hezekiah of Judah for the respective destructions of Israel and Judah years after their deaths.[14] Chronicles disagrees and portrays Jeroboam ben Nebath as a king of little consequence and Manasseh ben Hezekiah as a repentant monarch who returns to YHWH in his later years. Josiah defies the word of G-d in Chronicles and dies as a result, whereas in Kings he is the ideal Davidic monarch. According to Chronicles, it is the people, their leaders, and the priests who defiled the temple, resulting in its destruction in their own generation; it was not the fault of monarchs who died decades or centuries before the disaster. Contrary to other biblical books, Esther and Song of Songs do not even mention G-d, which in the minds of many raises questions as to whether they are even theological books.

Given the fundamental disagreement so frequently apparent among biblical books, interpreters must recognize that the Bible does not posit a consistent understanding of truth, at least not in the way that rational theology or philosophy might envision. Rather, the Bible posits a variety

---

13. See my discussion of Isaiah, Jeremiah, and Ezekiel, in Sweeney, *Tanak*, 265–343.

14. See my discussion in *Reading the Hebrew Bible after the Shoah: Engaging Holocaust Theology* (Minneapolis: Fortress, 2008), 64–83.

of truths about divine action—or absence—in the world and the expected human response. Do we have faith in YHWH's eternal promise to the house of David and the city of Jerusalem? Do we observe Mosaic torah? Do we engage the sanctity of the Jerusalem temple? Do we attribute our problems to past generations? Or do we look to our own generation to identify our problems? Do we act in the world when G-d does not? All of these options and more appear within the books of the Bible text, and insofar as they are all sacred Scripture, they are all true.

But this is the point at which we must recognize the dialogical nature of the Bible. The books of the Bible disagree among themselves and sometimes even within themselves as each of the biblical writings posits its understanding of G-d, Israel/Judah, creation, the nations, the various institutions of Israel/Judah, and so on in an effort to discern divine truth in the world in which we live. With their differing viewpoints, the books of the Bible are in dialogue with each other, often disagreeing, but each represents a particular viewpoint or viewpoints that must be engaged to understand the full range of truth that is presented therein. Each offers its own particular insight, even when it disagrees with or challenges the insights of other biblical writings. We may no longer be selective, reading Isaiah instead of Ezekiel, Kings instead of Chronicles, the prophets instead of the wisdom literature, and so on. Such a viewpoint aids readers in better understanding G-d and our relationship with G-d who cannot be reduced to a single principle or perspective, and such an understanding of the dialogical character of the Bible corresponds well with a canonical model in which the various canonical forms of the Bible differ from one another and disagree.

2.3. The Question of Theodicy

Finally, we must recognize the role of the question of theodicy in biblical theology. Modern experience with the Shoah is a key issue here because it raises questions of divine power, presence, and integrity in a way that past generations of scholars did not fully engage.[15] Past generations of interpreters have presumed divine righteousness and presence in their theological understandings of the Bible, but they did so while privileging the historical books and the prophets and frequently ignoring or brushing

---

15. Sweeney, *Reading the Hebrew Bible after the Shoah.*

aside books such as Job, Esther, Lamentations, and others that did not fit well into a theocentric worldview in which G-d was always present, powerful, and righteous. Such views likewise influenced the way in which we read even the most central of books, such as Isaiah or Psalms.

Isaiah is a case in point.[16] Isaiah is one of the most cited prophets in both Jewish and Christian tradition, but the call vision in Isa 6 raises troubling questions about YHWH's actions in the world. Here Isaiah is commanded to render the people blind, deaf, and dumb to ensure that they do not repent, so as to enable YHWH to carry out a program of punishment, exile, and restoration over the course of several centuries to be recognized as the true sovereign of creation. Isaiah presents a teleologically based understanding of YHWH's actions in the world in which YHWH's role as sovereign of all creation is ultimately to be recognized throughout all creation. Most interpreters have viewed such an agenda as an expression of supreme theological importance and character, but one can only maintain such a viewpoint if one is around at the end of the process. When considered from an ontological moral viewpoint, YHWH's commission to Isaiah is sinful, insofar as it will deliberately sacrifice generations of Jews for the greater glory of G-d. Modern theological discussion of the Shoah rejects such an understanding of the murder of some six million Jews in the twentieth century, but biblical theologians have been slow to recognize that Isaiah calls for precisely such a model.

Isaiah is sacred Scripture, so we must ask: What are we to learn from this? Whereas past interpreters might see Isaiah's commission as a test of faith, post-Shoah interpreters might see another dimension: YHWH presents Isaiah with a course of action to which he must stand up and reject. Isaiah does not do so, and by the end of the book of Isaiah the ideals of the nations streaming to Zion to learn the torah of YHWH have not been achieved. Isaiah ends with a portrayal of the bodies of the wicked strewn about; perhaps if Isaiah had stood up to YHWH and said "No!" like Moses in the wilderness, or Amos upon seeing the locusts and the fire, or Job when confronted with punishment that made no sense, or Bat Zion demanding that YHWH look at what was done to her, the book of Isaiah might have arrived at a different conclusion in which the goals of the book had been achieved. Perhaps the prophet shows us what not to do; indeed, what might have happened in World War II if enough people had stood up

---

16. Sweeney, *Reading the Hebrew Bible*, 84–103.

and said "No!" to Adolf Hitler in Nazi Germany or Hideki Tojo in Imperial Japan? Or on a lesser scale, what might happen when we challenge authority that is exercised illegitimately or for immoral purpose?

Such an example shows that a critical questioning of even G-d is part and parcel of biblical theology. We cannot presume righteousness even at the highest levels of authority. Like Esther in a time of threat, we must learn to act on our own when G-d does not appear, and like Eve in the garden, we must learn to exercise our own intellects and moral capacities when G-d is not always present to tell us what to do. That, too, is a task of biblical theology and it is one that emerges when we recognize that we, too, must learn to act as moral agents or as true stewards of creation in the world that has been entrusted to us.

3. The Absence of G-d in the Song of Songs

The Song of Songs is one of the most controversial books in the Hebrew Bible insofar as it lacks any explicit reference to G-d and employs sexual and sensual imagery to depict graphically a sexual liaison between two human lovers.[17] Song of Songs was nearly banned from the Hebrew Bible in Jewish tradition due to a dispute among the sages concerning its status, apparently due to its sexual motifs and mystical allusions, as recorded in m. Yad. 3:5. But R. Akiva ben Joseph, one of the most revered of the rabbinic sages, came to the rescue of the Song of Songs by declaring, "G-d forbid! No man in Israel ever disputed the Song of Songs (that he should say) that it does not render the hands unclean [i.e., hold sacred status as Scripture], for all the ages are not worth the day on which the Song of Songs was given to Israel; for all the Writings [i.e., Ketuvim] are holy, but the Song of Songs is the Holy of Holies."[18] Rabbi Johanan ben Joshua then

---

17. For major commentaries and studies, see David M. Carr, *The Erotic Word: Sexuality, Spirituality, and the Bible* (Oxford: Oxford University Press, 2003); J. Cheryl Exum, *Song of Songs: A Commentary*, OTL (Louisville: Westminster John Knox, 2005); Michael Fishbane, *Song of Songs*, JPSBC (Philadelphia: Jewish Publication Society, 2015); Othmar Keel, *The Song of Songs*, ContC (Minneapolis: Fortress, 1994); Tremper Longman III, *Song of Songs*, NICOT (Grand Rapids: Eerdmans, 2001); Roland E. Murphy, *The Song of Songs*, Hermeneia (Minneapolis: Fortress, 1990); Marvin H. Pope, *Song of Songs*, AB 7C (Garden City, NY: Doubleday, 1977); Phyllis Trible, *G-d and the Rhetoric of Sexuality*, OBT (Philadelphia: Fortress, 1978).

18. Translation from Herbert Danby, *The Mishnah* (Oxford: Oxford University Press, 1977), 781–82.

ruled in favor of accepting Song of Song as sacred Scripture in keeping with the views of Shimon ben Azzai, who cited a tradition from R. Eleazar ben Azariah. In the aftermath of this decision, the Song of Songs has been interpreted allegorically as a depiction of the relationship between G-d and Israel in the wilderness following the exodus from Egypt. The book is therefore read and studied at Passover. Christian tradition takes a similar approach by reading Song of Songs allegorically as a depiction of the relationship between Christ and the church. More commentaries have been written on Song of Songs than any other book of the Hebrew Bible.

But the decision to read Song of Song allegorically in both Jewish and Christian traditions points to the fundamental problem of the book. G-d is absent in the Song of Songs. Because Jewish and Christian readers of the book are generally believers in G-d—and I count myself among them—they have chosen a hermeneutical standpoint that deliberately reads G-d or Christ into the text despite the fact that neither G-d nor Christ are at all mentioned in the book. Some point to the Hebrew term שלהבתיה, "an intense flame," in Song 8:6 as evidence of the presence of G-d in the book because its last syllable, יה, employs the first component of the holy name of G-d, but the syllable functions only as a means to intensify the imagery of the flaming fire depicted in the word.[19] Indeed, even the decision of the Theology of the Hebrew Scripture Section to label the theme of this session as "The Hiddenness of G-d" presupposes the belief that the presence of G-d lies within the Bible—and therefore within each of its books—insofar as they are read as sacred Scripture that communicates the will or the word of G-d.

But such an approach obscures the reality of the text: G-d is indeed absent in the text of the Song of Songs, and assertions to the contrary, however subtly expressed, undermine our ability to interpret this singular feature. Song of Songs is not alone in this absence; G-d is also absent in the Hebrew MT version of the book of Esther—and this, too, has provoked controversy in Esther's interpretation.[20] But Esther is frequently read in relation to the problems of divine presence instigated

---

19. E.g., Exum, *Song of Songs*, 253–54; Longman, *Song of Songs*, 212–13; Murphy, *Song of Songs*, 192–93, 197–98.

20. See my paper, Marvin A. Sweeney, "Absence of G-d and Human Responsibility in the Book of Esther," in *Exegetical and Theological Studies*, vol. 2 of *Reading the Hebrew Bible for a New Millennium*, ed. Wonil Kim et al., SAC (Harrisburg, PA: Trinity Press International, 2000), 264–75; Sweeney, *Tanak*, 441–44.

by the reality of the Shoah with questions as to whether G-d was truly present, engaged, or even moral in the face of the genocide.[21] Song of Songs, however, presupposes no such scenario of potential or realized genocide. Song of Songs presupposes the sensuality, passions, and pure joy of human sexuality—apart from the presence of G-d—and it is this that demands our attention.

We will therefore proceed by analyzing the formal characteristics of the Song of Songs, its literary structure, genre, and settings, in an effort to ascertain the purposes of the book.[22] We will then turn to consider its purposes in relation to the motif of the absence of G-d and its place within the Hebrew Bible.

3.1. Formal Analysis of the Song of Songs

A formal analysis of the Song of Songs is essential to determine the organization of its contents in order to discern its interpretation. Song of Songs begins in 1:1 with a superscription that presents both the title of the book and the identification of its author: שיר השירים אשר לשלומה, "the Song of Songs, which is Solomon's." The attribution to Solomon signals both the artistic character of the work and its sexual concerns, insofar as Solomon is remembered as the wisest of Israel's monarchs and one who authored 1,005 songs and married some seven hundred wives and three hundred concubines (1 Kgs 5:9–13; 11:1–5). Although the Kings narrative is constructed as a means to critique Solomon for apostasy, the number of his wives actually testifies to his wisdom in international relations, insofar as ancient treaties among nations were sealed with a marriage between the royal houses of each nation, as well as his stellar reputation as a lover of women, as seen from the standpoint of those who value quantity.[23] The superscription thereby suggests to the reader that the book conveys both artistic beauty and passion concerning love.

---

21. E.g., Emil Fackenheim, *The Jewish Bible after the Holocaust: A Rereading* (Bloomington: Indiana University Press, 1990), 87–92; Sweeney, *Reading the Hebrew Bible after the Shoah*, 219–22.

22. For discussion of method, see Marvin A. Sweeney, "Form Criticism," in *To Each Its Own Meaning: Biblical Criticisms and Their Application* (Louisville: Westminster John Knox, 1999), 58–89.

23. On Kings as critique of Solomon, see Marvin A. Sweeney, *1 and 2 Kings: A Commentary*, OTL (Louisville: Westminster John Knox, 2007), 62–186.

Although scholars continue to disagree concerning the literary structure and interpretation of the Song of Songs, Phyllis Trible has presented one of the most cogent and suggestive analyses of the formal characteristics of the book.[24] She asks the most fundamental form-critical questions of the work: Who is speaking? To whom? About what? To identify three fundamental characters, apart from the narrator in the superscription of the book, whose interaction provides the foundation for determining the formal structure and organization of the Song of Songs. The fundamental characters include the female lover, who plays the dominant role in initiating the dialogue of the book and moving the plot forward; the male lover, who serves as counterpoint and complement to the female lover; and the daughters of Jerusalem or Zion, who are addressed at the conclusion of each major movement of the text. Although the daughters of Jerusalem or Zion do not have voice in the text, many interpreters maintain that they are a chorus of women who play a key role in the performance of the Song by giving voice to a chorus whose words do not appear in the text. Insofar as the addresses to the daughters of Jerusalem/Zion appear in Song 2:7; 3:5; 5:8; and 8:4, the five constituent subunits or movements in the text include Song 1:2–2:7; 2:8–3:5; 3:6–5:8; 5:9–8:4; and 8:5–14. Each expresses a specific set of concerns that gives expression to the literary tension of the text and advances the plot, thereby leading ultimately to its culmination in Song 8:5–14.

Song 1:2–2:7 constitutes the first subunit or movement of the Song of Songs insofar as it presents the woman's expression of desire for her male lover. She is the speaker throughout, and she speaks in a sequence of stanzas that combine first-person assertions about her own qualities with second-person addresses to her male lover that both portray his qualities and rhetorically appeal for his response. She begins in Song 1:2–4 with an appeal for her lover's kisses and observations of his sweet fragrance that prompt the maidens to love him, and she concludes with a proposition that they go off together to make love. She describes herself as dark and beautiful in Song 1:5–8, employing nouns based on the root שחר, which typically conveys efficacy insofar as black represents the combination of

---

24. Trible, *G-d and the Rhetoric of Sexuality*, 144–65; cf. Sweeney, *Tanak*, 425–29; contra Roland E. Murphy, *Wisdom Literature: Job, Proverbs, Ruth, Canticles, Ecclesiastes, Esther*, FOTL 13 (Grand Rapids: Eerdmans, 1981), 98–124, who treats the book as a series of individual units.

all colors and their power of expression.[25] As she speaks of her unguarded vineyard, here understood as an invitation, she asks him where he grazes his sheep so that she might follow him and join him. Finally, in Song 1:9–2:7 she employs hints of the *waṣf* form to describe both herself and her lover, often in very explicit and yet concealed terms, such as her reference to him as a bundle of myrrh between her breasts in Song 1:13 or his flag of love over her in the wine house in Song 2:4, as she anticipates their union.[26] The subunit concludes with her adjuration to the maidens of Jerusalem in 1:7 not to awaken or arouse love until it desires, apparently an adjuration to follow through with what they might start.

Song 2:8–3:5 then turns to the approach of the male lover, which suggests the impending consummation of the union between the woman and the man. She employs faunal imagery to describe his approach in Song 2:8–13 as a gazelle or a young stag leaping over mountains and hills to come to her. She then portrays him gazing through the window at her and bidding her to join him as spring blossoms in the land. She addresses him as her dove in Song 2:14, asking to see his face and hear his voice. In Song 2:15–17 she declares that "my beloved is mine, and I am his," prior to Song 3:1–5, in which she rises from her bed to find her lost love, who is not with her. The stanza ends in tension, as she once again adjures the daughters of Jerusalem by the gazelles and the rams of the field not to arouse love until it desires.

Song 3:6–5:8 turns to the loss of the male lover in an expression of narrative tension that threatens the consummation of the relationship expected by both the woman and the reader. She begins the subunit in Song 3:9–11 with an image of King Solomon upon his palanquin and calls upon the daughters of Zion and Jerusalem to go out and see King Solomon decked out in the crown his mother gave him on his wedding day. The image apparently expresses her desire for union with her lost lover. Song

---

25. See also Isa 8:20, in which שׁחר refers to "dawn" and the efficacy of creation as well as Isa 47:11, in which שׁחרה refers to the magical powers of the daughter of Babylon. For discussion, see Marvin A. Sweeney, "A Philological and Form-Critical Reevaluation of Isaiah 8:16–9:6," in *Reading Prophetic Books: Form, Intertextuality, and Reception in Prophetic and Post-Biblical Literature*, FAT 2/89 (Tübingen: Mohr Siebeck, 2014), 35–49, esp. 39–40; cf. Pope, *Song of Songs*, 307–18.

26. For discussion of the *waṣf* form, see esp. Pope, *Song of Songs*, 54–59; Longman, *Song of Songs*, 50–52; Murphy, *Song of Songs*, 47–48; Marvin H. Fox, *The Song of Songs and Ancient Egyptian Love Poetry* (Madison: University of Wisconsin Press, 1999).

4:1–7 then turns to a *waṣf*, spoken by the man, in which he describes her beauty with faunal images: "Your two breasts are like two fawns, twins of a gazelle, grazing among the lilies." He turns in Song 4:8–11 to claims that she has captured his heart and that sweetness drops from her lips. In Song 4:12–5:1 he describes her as his bride, a locked garden, and a well of living water from which he would presumably drink, but in 4:16 the woman speaks again, asking the winds to blow and spread the fragrance of the garden so that he might enjoy its fruits. By Song 5:1, the man claims that he has entered as an unidentified voice calls upon the lovers to eat and drink of love. In Song 5:2–8, the woman awakens from her dream believing that her lover is at the door, but when she opens it, he is gone. When she goes out to search for him in the night, the city guards abuse her. She concludes with an adjuration to the daughters of Jerusalem asking them to tell her beloved, if they meet him, that she is faint with love.

Song 5:9–8:4 then moves to resolution with a portrayal of the union of the two lovers. Song 5:9 begins with the voice of the daughters of Jerusalem asking the woman how and why her lover is better than another that she adjures them as she has done. She responds with a *waṣf* in Song 5:10–16 in which she describes her man as having a head of the finest gold with curly black locks, eyes like doves, a torso like a tablet of ivory, and a deliciously sweet mouth. The maidens agree to help her search in Song 6:1–3, as the woman reiterates that her beloved is hers. Song 6:4–11 then follows with a *waṣf* sung by the man in which he describes the woman's hair like a flock of goats, a phrase that must have been intended to melt any Judean woman's heart! In Song 6:10 he regains his poise by asking, "Who is this that shines like the dawn, beautiful like the moon, radiant like the sun, awesome like banners?" In Song 6:11 he goes down to the garden of nut trees to look for his love. In Song 7:1–10 the daughters of Jerusalem address her as the Shulemite, a reference to a village known for its beautiful women, and call for the woman to turn back so that they might describe her beauty with another *waṣf*. She responds in Song 7:11 with her insistent declaration, "I am my beloved's, and for me is his desire." She then invites him to join her in the vineyards, where she gives herself to him. She concludes in Song 8:4 with her well-known adjuration to the daughters of Jerusalem: "Do not awaken or arouse love until it desires."

Song 8:5–14 is a frequently misunderstood conclusion to the book. Some see this section as a series of disconnected additions to the text, but the imagery presented and the interrelationships of the individual images indicate a concern with communicating the significance of the relationship between the woman and the man.[27] It thereby provides hints as to the purpose of the Song of Songs.

The first image in Song 8:5 presents a rhetorical question that asks who it is coming up from the wilderness leaning upon her beloved. The answer is obviously the woman. She tells her lover that she aroused him under the apple tree where her mother conceived him. This segment draws upon the bridal motif so well known in the Prophets in which Israel is the bride and YHWH is the groom. Here it subtly signals that the lovers are to be identified with Israel and YHWH, but it also points to the impending sexual union as an act that will result in the conception of a child, indicating that the union will have ongoing results in the creation of a human being.

Song 8:6–7 then turns to the imagery of the woman's role as a seal upon the heart of the man. The seal (Hebrew חותם) refers to the signet ring used to seal and sign a document in the ancient Israelite/Judean world, thereby signing a contract that binds two parties into a lasting relationship.[28] It can be used for political and business purposes, but the present context suggests a marriage relationship. The woman's statements that "love is as strong as death" and that "passion/zeal is as hard as Sheol" points to the intensity and presumed permanence of the relationship as a blazing flame that cannot be quenched.[29] Her last comment points to the futility and ridiculousness of anyone who thinks that he or she can buy such love with money.

Song 8:8–10 presents the little sister with no breasts who is yet too young for marriage but nevertheless can become engaged. It is not uncommon for young girls to be engaged for marriage by their parents long before they reach a suitable age. The imagery of a wall overlaid with silver is inherently defensive and lends itself to the understanding that she is no longer available for relationships with other young men.[30] The imagery of the door paneled in cedar indicates that someone will be able to enter, presumably the young man to whom she is engaged. Her final statement, "I am a wall, my breasts are like towers; so I am in his eyes as one who finds

---

27. For the view of this section as disconnected additions, see, e.g., Murphy, *Song of Songs*, 195.

28. See Exum, *Song of Songs*, 250–51; Keel, *Song of Songs*, 271–72; Longman, *Song of Songs*, 209–10.

29. Exum, *Song of Songs*, 251–53.

30. See Exum, *Song of Songs*, 254–59.

peace," portrays the manner in which her fiancé gazes upon her as he waits for the time of their marriage.

Song 8:11–12 presents the statement of the girl concerning Solomon's need to post guards over his vineyard, in this case, a subtle reference to the girl to whom he is betrothed. She mentions the thousand shekels of silver that a man would pay for her, but she is not for sale. Solomon can keep his money, but he must pay his guards.

Finally, Song 8:13–14 portrays the young woman sitting in the garden where someone might hear. She asks to hear the voice of her beloved and proposes that they flee to the hills, where they may consummate their relationship in private. The book thus ends in anticipation of the sexual union that has functioned as the fundamental premise of the plot throughout.

The formal structure of the book, an allegorical dramatization of relationship between two lovers, then appears as follows:

I.	Superscription: Solomon's Song of Songs	1:1
II.	Dramatization in five episodes	1:2–8:14
	A. Woman expresses desire for her male lover	1:2–2:7
	B. Approach of the male lover	2:8–3:5
	C. Loss of the male lover	3:6–5:8
	D. Reunion of the two lovers	5:9–8:4
	E. Consummation	8:5–14

This analysis of the Song of Songs points to its fundamental character as a love song in which a woman anticipates her union or marriage with a man who is to become her husband. Such a conclusion should surprise no one. When we consider the setting for the performance of such a song, a wedding is the first thing that must come to mind. Indeed, the narrative account in Judg 21:19–24 concerning the Benjaminite men who would lie in wait to claim their brides from the maidens dancing in the vineyards at the Shiloh sanctuary provides a suitable setting for such a song. The portrayal of the event is polemical, insofar as Israel had nearly destroyed Benjamin for its role in the rape and murder of the Levite's concubine in Judg 19–21, so the Benjaminites must seize their brides as if to rape them because Israel had vowed not to give its daughters to Benjamin.[31] But the temple setting and

---

31. Marvin A. Sweeney, *King Josiah of Judah: The Lost Messiah of Israel* (Oxford: Oxford University Press, 2001), 110–25; Sweeney, "Davidic Polemics in the Book of Judges," *VT* 47 (1997): 517–29.

the dancing in the vineyards portends the celebration of a sacred festival, perhaps Sukkot, which celebrates the fruit harvest of grapes and other produce prior to the onset of the fall rains. Such a setting might serve as the occasion for an engagement and subsequent wedding, but it also points to the mythologized portrayal of the relationship between YHWH and Israel as groom and bride, insofar as YHWH the groom provides the rains that produce grapes for the bride, Israel. A work such as the Song of Songs would easily serve a dual purpose as a wedding or engagement song for young lovers as well as a liturgical song to celebrate a holiday that marks YHWH's provision of fruit or food for the people. When read from this perspective, Song of Songs is a joyous song that celebrates the impending marriages between young men and women, as well as the harvest of fruit that follows from the relationship between YHWH and Israel.

3.2. The Absence of G-d

But there is another dimension to the Song of Songs that pertains to the motif of the absence of G-d in the text. Despite our best efforts to read G-d into the Song of Songs, G-d remains entirely absent in the text of the Song of Songs, and the human characters emerge as the main and only characters in the book. This has important ramifications for the interpretation of the Song of Songs.[32]

First, the human characters of the Song of Songs, including the woman, the man, and the daughters of Jerusalem/Zion, are the only figures in the book who will serve its narrative agenda. In this case, we do not see in the narrative the need to overcome the challenges of foreign invasion, religious apostasy, the observance of divine torah, or any of the major crises and challenges that so frequently fill the pages of the Hebrew Bible. Instead, the characters of the Song of Songs have only the happy task of consummating a sexual union. But as the above analysis has shown, the projected sexual consummation envisioned in the Song has wider ramifications. For one, the Song does not simply envision the sexual union itself; it envisions the sexual union in the context of a wedding between the woman and the man. As for the daughters of Jerusalem/Zion, they are not simply a necessary sounding board for the woman; they perhaps must be considered as her attendants as she prepares for her wedding.

---

32. See esp. Carr, *Erotic Word*, who points to the role of sexuality in human spirituality.

Second, the human characters of the Song of Songs have only themselves on whom to rely. They cannot or do not depend on G-d to resolve the tensions that emerge within the narrative progression of the text; they can rely only on themselves to resolve those tensions. More specifically, it is the woman who must find the way to overcome the obstacles that she encounters. She does so by establishing relationships with the other characters of the book. She speaks repeatedly to the daughters of Jerusalem/Zion, adjuring them not to awaken love until it desires. Her adjurations serve as a form of chorus or perhaps an interlude that marks the various movements of the Song and its plot, but they also function as a means to establish the daughters of Jerusalem/Zion as her fictive audience. In this capacity, they become her sounding board as she pours out her emotions and feelings concerning her male counterpart. Although they rarely speak, they serve as her support group and enable her to muster the will and determination to persist in her goal: to wed and bed the man in the narrative. In this regard, they are essential to her efforts. She repeatedly expresses her fears and doubts together with her desires, and the daughters of Jerusalem/Zion, simply by serving as her audience, enable her to overcome those fears and doubts so that she might persist through the realization of her goals.

The woman must also establish her relationship with the man. Granted, the relationship is rather one-dimensional. She speaks only of her passion for him and her perceptions of his attractiveness; the man is no different. The reader learns little about him other than that he, too, finds her attractive and wants the union to take place, but he reveals little more. When he disappears, neither the woman nor the reader knows where he goes. Maybe he has another woman? Maybe he has a job, a profession, or a business? Maybe he is a drunk or a gambler? Maybe he got cold feet? Neither the woman nor the reader will ever know where he is when he is gone, but indeed, it doesn't matter. This narrative is told from the perspective of the woman, and she does not need to know what he is doing. Her need is to have him return to her so that they might proceed. His needs do not really count apart from hers. Here it is wise to remember that, even in antiquity, the wedding is all about the bride!

Third is the question of what happens on the morning—or the lifetime—after the consummation of the sexual relationship. By establishing relationships with the other human characters in the book, the woman in the Song of Songs overcomes the obstacles that bar her from achieving her goal: the consummation of the union with the man, or more properly, her marriage to the man. But although the book and the reader are fixated on the sexual union, that union has wider implications as well. Sexual union in the ancient world generally entails childbirth, both as a biological and as a social reality. Contemporary means of contraception have enabled modern humans to pursue sexual relations purely for pleasure, but the absence or limits of effective contraception in the ancient world pointed to the expectation that the birth of children would follow from sexual intercourse. Contraception has always been available since antiquity, even if its effectiveness has not always been assured, but the social expectation of sexual relations—and of weddings in particular—is that they lead to childbirth. This reality points to another dimension of the Song of Songs: the human characters in the narrative, specifically the woman and the man, are in a position to act as creators in producing human life. Childbirth is not mentioned specifically as an outcome of the sexual union in the Song of Songs, but it is hinted at when the woman speaks of taking her lover to the garden where his mother gave birth to him. Even if it is mentioned only in an ancillary way, the creative powers of the woman and the man in their relationship with each other grants to them a degree of creative power otherwise enjoyed and exercised by G-d. In this respect, the human characters of the Song of Songs partner together to consummate their relationship, but they also partner together with G-d to continue or to complete the creation that G-d has initiated outside of the book.

Fourth is a continuation of what happens on the morning or lifetime after the sexual union. When children are born as a result of the sexual union, what are the woman and the man to do with them? Their task is to feed and clothe them, raise them, educate them, and form them into adult human beings who will someday engage in sexual union and marriage to continue the cycle of creation and life that the original relationship between the woman and the man initiated. Although sexual union and the wedding are the end result of the narrative progression of the Song of Songs, the union is only the beginning of the postnarrative life that such union entails. Again, the human characters of the Song of Songs as a result of the relationship that they create through their sexual union will function as creators akin to G-d when they raise the children that result from their sexual union. In this respect, Trible is correct to point to Gen 3 as the intertextual corollary to the Song of Songs.[33] The woman in Gen 3 will give

---

33. Trible, *G-d and the Rhetoric of Sexuality*, 72–143.

birth to children as a result of her sexual desire for the man—and his for her, although this dimension is not acknowledged in the text of Gen 3. It is therefore important to note that this role for women (and men) emerges only after the woman acquires knowledge or wisdom in the Gen 3 narrative by eating from the tree of the knowledge of good and evil. Women are the first teachers of their children, if only by virtue of the fact that they must be around their infants when they are young to provide them with food. It is the women who play the key role, therefore, in forming the personality and worldview of their children, thereby preparing them for their lives as adults who will someday have children of their own and raise and educate them in turn.

3.3. Song of Songs as an Expression of Biblical Theology

Altogether, this analysis of the Song of Songs and the motif of the absence of G-d in the Song points to a key dimension of the text. Human beings are not simply sexual beings in the Song of Song. Through their relationships with each other, they emerge as creator figures on a par with G-d insofar as their sexual union enables them to become creators of new human beings with all that entails, that is, raising and educating the children that are born so that they, too, can become effective human beings and partners with G-d—and each other—in continuing and completing the creation that G-d initiated.

That is why R. Akiva declares the Song of Songs to be the Holy of Holies in sacred Scripture. Insofar as Song of Songs envisions such a creative role for human beings resulting from their sexual capacities, the book became foundational together with Ezekiel and other texts in the development of Jewish mysticism during the Second Temple period, the Rabbinic period, and beyond.[34] Indeed, Song of Songs plays a key role in the development of the *merkabah* tradition, particularly the Sefer Yetzirah and the Shiur Qomah that respectively examine the creative power of divine and human speech and the human perception of the divine presence in the world.[35]

---

34. For the creative role of human beings through sex, see Carr, *Erotic Word*, 139–51. For a survey of the influence of Song of Songs on later Jewish literature and thought, see Fishbane, *Song of Songs*, 245–304.

35. A. Peter Hayman, *Sefer Yeṣira: Edition, Translation, and Text-Critical Commentary*, TSAJ 104 (Tübingen: Mohr Siebeck, 2004); Martin Cohen, *The Shiʿur Qomah: Liturgy and Theurgy in Pre-Kabbalist Jewish Mysticism* (Lanham: University

These books in turn played key roles in the development of the kabbalistic tradition that turned to the examination of the personality of G-d and the recognition that the presence of G-d abides in each and every one of us, beginning with our sexual characters and capacities.[36]

4. Biblical Theology in Transition

Biblical theology has changed markedly since the collapse of the field in the late twentieth century. It is a field that must learn to engage the entire Bible but at the same time to recognize that the Bible appears in different canonical and versional forms. It is a field that must learn to recognize that all of its books require engagement, not just the ones that we select because they are most compatible with our own theological world views. It is a field that must recognize that the Bible lessons are not always to be emulated; sometimes the Bible shows us courses of action or thought that must be challenged as we human beings must learn fully to distinguish between good and evil—especially when the evil comes from G-d. There are a host of other issues to discuss, such as the roles of law and ritual as expressions of sanctity, the continuing validity of G-d's eternal covenant with Israel and its implications for Christian theology, a reevaluation of the New Testament claims of a loving G-d when measured against the destruction of Jerusalem in 70 CE, and others. For now, we are just beginning.

Bibliography

Barr, James. *The Concept of Biblical Theology*. Minneapolis: Fortress, 1999.

Brueggemann, Walter. *Old Testament Theology*. Minneapolis: Fortress, 1997.

Carr, David M. *The Erotic Word: Sexuality, Spirituality, and the Bible*. Oxford: Oxford University Press, 2003.

Childs, Brevard S. *Biblical Theology of the Old and New Testaments*. Minneapolis: Fortress, 1993.

Press of America, 1983); Cohen, *The Shiʿur Qomah: Texts and Recensions* (Tübingen: Mohr Siebeck, 1985); Marvin A. Sweeney, "Dimensions of the Shekhinah: The Meaning of the *Shiur Qomah* in Jewish Mysticism, Liturgy, and Rabbinic Thought," *HS* 54 (2013): 107–20.

36. Gershom Scholem, *Major Trends in Jewish Mysticism* (New York: Schocken, 1941).

———. *Old Testament Theology in a Canonical Context*. Minneapolis: Fortress, 1985.

Cohen, Martin. *The Shiʿur Qomah: Liturgy and Theurgy in Pre-Kabbalist Jewish Mysticism*. Lanham: University Press of America, 1983.

———. *The Shiʿur Qomah: Texts and Recensions*. Tübingen: Mohr Siebeck, 1985.

Danby, Herbert. *The Mishnah*. Oxford: Oxford University Press, 1977.

Eichrodt, Walther. *Theology of the Old Testament*. Translated by J. A. Baker. OTL. Philadelphia: Westminster; London: SCM, 1961–1967.

Exum, J. Cheryl. *Song of Songs: A Commentary*. OTL. Louisville: Westminster John Knox, 2005.

Fackenheim, Emil. *The Jewish Bible after the Holocaust: A Rereading*. Bloomington: Indiana University Press, 1990.

Fishbane, Michael. *Song of Songs*. JPSBC. Philadelphia: Jewish Publication Society, 2015.

Fox, Marvin H. *The Song of Songs and Ancient Egyptian Love Poetry*. Madison: University of Wisconsin Press, 1999.

Hasel, Gerhard. *Old Testament Theology: Basic Issues in the Current Debate*. Grand Rapids: Eerdmans, 1991.

Hayes, John H., and Frederick Prussner. *Old Testament Theology*. Atlanta: John Knox, 1985.

Hayman, A. Peter. *Sefer Yeṣira: Edition, Translation, and Text-Critical Commentary*. TSAJ 104. Tübingen: Mohr Siebeck, 2004.

Keel, Othmar. *The Song of Songs*. ContC. Minneapolis: Fortress, 1994.

Knierim, Rolf P. "Cosmos and History in Israel's Theology." *The Task of Old Testament Theology*. Grand Rapids: Eerdmans, 1995.

Kraus, Hans-Joachim. *Die biblische Theologie*. Neukirchen-Vluyn: Neukirchener Verlag, 1970.

Levenson, Jon D. "Why Jews Are Not Interested in Biblical Theology." Pages 33–61 in *The Hebrew Bible and Historical Criticism: Jews and Christians in Biblical Studies*. Louisville: Westminster John Knox, 1993.

Longman, Tremper, III. *Song of Songs*. NICOT. Grand Rapids: Eerdmans, 2001.

Murphy, Roland E. *The Song of Songs*. Hermeneia. Minneapolis: Fortress, 1990.

———. *Wisdom Literature: Job, Proverbs, Ruth, Canticles, Ecclesiastes, Esther*. FOTL 13. Grand Rapids: Eerdmans, 1981.

Perdue, Leo G. *The Collapse of History*. OBT. Minneapolis: Fortress, 1994.

———. *Reconstructing Old Testament Theology*. OBT. Minneapolis: Fortress, 2005.

Pope, Marvin H. *Song of Songs*. AB 7C. Garden City, NY: Doubleday, 1977.

Rad, Gerhard von. *Old Testament Theology*. Translated by David M. G. Stalker. New York: Harper & Row, 1962–1965.

———. *Wisdom in Israel*. Nashville: Abingdon, 1972.

Sanders, James A. *Canon and Community*. Philadelphia: Fortress, 1972.

———. *Torah and Canon*. Philadelphia: Fortress, 1984.

Scholem, Gershom. *Major Trends in Jewish Mysticism*. New York: Schocken, 1941.

Sweeney, Marvin A. *1 and 2 Kings: A Commentary*. OTL. Louisville: Westminster John Knox, 2007.

———. "Absence of G-d and Human Responsibility in the Book of Esther." Pages 264–75 in *Exegetical and Theological Studies*. Vol. 2 of *Reading the Hebrew Bible for a New Millennium*. Edited by Wonil Kim, Deborah Ellens, Michael Floyd, and Marvin A. Sweeney. SAC. Harrisburg: Trinity Press International, 2000.

———. "Biblical Theology. I. Hebrew Bible/Old Testament." *EBR* 3:1137–49.

———. "Davidic Polemics in the Book of Judges." *VT* 47 (1997): 517–29.

———. "Dimensions of the Shekhinah: The Meaning of the *Shiur Qomah* in Jewish Mysticism, Liturgy, and Rabbinic Thought." *HS* 54 (2013): 107–20.

———. "Form Criticism." Pages 58–89 in *To Each Its Own Meaning: Biblical Criticisms and Their Application*. Louisville: Westminster John Knox, 1999.

———. *King Josiah of Judah: The Lost Messiah of Israel*. Oxford: Oxford University Press, 2001.

———. "A Philological and Form-Critical Reevaluation of Isaiah 8:16–9:6." Pages 35–49 in *Reading Prophetic Books: Form, Intertextuality, and Reception in Prophetic and Post-Biblical Literature*. FAT 2/89. Tübingen: Mohr Siebeck, 2014.

———. *Reading the Hebrew Bible after the Shoah: Engaging Holocaust Theology*. Minneapolis: Fortress, 2008.

———. *Tanak: A Theological and Critical Introduction to the Jewish Bible*. Minneapolis: Fortress, 2012.

Trible, Phyllis. *G-d and the Rhetoric of Sexuality*. OBT. Philadelphia: Fortress, 1978.

Wellhausen, Julius. *Die Composition des Hexateuch*. Berlin: Georg Reimer, 1889.

———. *Prolegomenon to the History of Ancient Israel*. New York: Meridian, 1957.

Biblical Theology in Context(s):
Jewish, Christian, and Critical Approaches to the Theology of the Hebrew Bible

Julia M. O'Brien

The essays in this collection reflect the reality that different understandings of biblical theology focus on different aspects of the interpretative process. In my contribution to the conversation, I highlight the contextual nature of interpretation and suggest implications for ways in which biblical theology is currently practiced. The following definition will ground and frame my discussion:

> Biblical theology is a contextual enterprise in which readers functioning within particular socially located contexts engage texts composed in other socially located contexts in the search for a deeper understanding of human existence.

1. The Context of Readers

A key claim of postmodern biblical interpretation is the illusory nature of objectivity. The "critical" methods developed in continental Europe, Great Britain, and the United States in the seventeenth through the early twentieth century in the attempt to bring Enlightenment sensibilities to biblical study claimed simply to describe the text itself and/or to investigate its prehistory without presupposition. Early practitioners of these methods such as Baruch Spinoza, Jean Astruc, and Hermann Samuel Reimarus proclaimed their freedom from confessional constraints and their willingness to submit only to the dictates of human logic. In turn, biblical theology became defined as an essentially descriptive task, as the scholar-as-anthropologist reported on the explicit and implicit claims that ancient texts make about the deity, humans, and the world in which they intersect.[1]

Post-Enlightenment biblical scholars have demonstrated—often in painstaking detail—just how *subjective* earlier generations of biblical theologians actually were, exposing the influence of various social, religious, and political contexts on the claims that theologians had "discovered" in the text. Julius Wellhausen's identification and positive valuation of "primitive religion," along with his devaluation of ritual in "late Judaism," has been repeatedly linked to the ideologies of German anti-Judaism and a pervasive anti-institutional, anticlerical bias.[2] Walther Eichrodt's identification of covenant as the unifying theme of the Hebrew Bible and his insistence that the prophets conveyed not universal ethics but the specific, even idiosyncratic, demands of Israel's God are seen to reflect the teaching of the Reformed Church to which he belonged, one that had long preached the Bible in light of covenant theology and whose key theological doctrine is divine sovereignty. The influence of Karl Barth's insistence on the radical uniqueness of the biblical message and the Christ event have been traced in the writings of Walther Eichrodt and Gerhard von Rad.[3] Burke O. Long's scathing exposé of William F. Albright and his protégés underscores the ways in which a scholar who insisted on his own objectivity continued to be shaped by his conservative Christian upbringing.[4] The unnamed assumptions that inform the work of the Christian Biblical Theology Movement of the mid-twentieth century, of Brevard S. Childs, of Walter Brueggemann, and of other influential figures in the field of biblical theology have been explored as well.[5]

It is for this reason that I believe the rise of socially located readings of biblical texts and theologies have been so important and why I think the sharpness of their critique of Enlightenment methods is warranted.

---

1. An example of this perspective can be found in James Barr, *The Concept of Old Testament Theology: An Old Testament Perspective* (Minneapolis: Fortress, 1999).

2. See, for example, Diane Banks, *Writing the History of Israel*, LHBOTS (New York: T&T Clark, 2006).

3. Julia M. O'Brien, *Challenging Prophetic Metaphor: Ideology and Theology in the Prophets* (Louisville: Westminster John Knox, 2008), ch. 1.

4. Burke O. Long, *Planting and Reaping Albright: Politics, Ideology, and Interpreting the Bible* (University Park: Pennsylvania State University Press, 1997).

5. See O'Brien, *Challenging Prophetic Metaphor*, ch 1. See also Harold C. Washington, "Violence and the Construction of Gender in the Hebrew Bible: A New Historicist Approach," *BibInt* 5 (1997): 324–63.

Feminist, queer, womanist, mujerista, and Asian American approaches, along with disability studies and other "interested" readings, have demonstrated not only that texts can be *applied* differently depending on one's interests but also that they actually *say* different things depending on who is listening. For example, both Dennis T. Olson (writing in the *Theological Bible Commentary*) and Judy Fentress-Williams (writing in the *Africana Bible*) recognize that in the early Exodus narratives Moses is saved by women long before he becomes the savior (an insight also mined by Jacqueline Lapsley), but only Fentress-Williams recognizes the varied ethnicity and class status of those female saviors, an observation pertinent to the question of inclusion and exclusion in narratives of Israelite identity.[6]

What practitioners of critical methods discern in the text is, to some degree, within the reader. Otherwise, how might we explain the diverse ways in which close readers of biblical texts discern the structure of biblical books? Within the book of Genesis, for example, is the covenant with Abraham *the* divine solution to the problem of human disobedience, as a string of Christian interpreters has argued?[7] Or, as Theodore Hiebert contends, is it *one of a series* of covenants that follows the divine re-creation of the world in the covenant with Noah and precedes the covenant with Moses?[8] The theology of Genesis shifts depending on whether one focuses on the singularity of Abraham or on the sequential nature of the covenants that the divine one makes with humanity.

I am not suggesting that all interpreters are intentionally biased; indeed, unconscious biases are perhaps the most formative and require the most distance and critique of others to notice. I can see the Eurocentric orientation of my own previous work only in retrospect, largely because of my engagement with scholars and students of color over the past decade.[9]

---

6. Jacqueline Lapsley, *Whispering the Word: Hearing Women's Stories in the Old Testament* (Louisville: Westminster John Knox, 2005); Judy Fentress-Williams, "Exodus," in *Africana Bible: Reading Israel's Scriptures from Africa and the African Diaspora*, ed. Hugh R. Page Jr. et al. (Minneapolis: Fortress, 2010); Dennis T. Olson, "Exodus," in *Theological Bible Commentary*, ed. Gail R. O'Day and David L. Petersen (Louisville: Westminster John Knox, 2009), 27–40.

7. For example, Bill Arnold, *Genesis*, NCBC (Cambridge: Cambridge University Press, 2009).

8. Theodore Hiebert, "Genesis," in O'Day and Petersen, *Theological Bible Commentary*, 3–25.

9. My 2008 book *Challenging Prophetic Metaphor* addresses gender ideology in

To see what one does not naturally see requires ongoing conversations with others—those different from the interpreter in race, class, gender, ability, and immigrant status. Clearly, all those who attempt biblical theology must discern and name the role of their own assumptions in their constructions of meaning, both via self-reflection and in conversation with readers from different social locations.

2. The (Historical) Context of Texts

While vitally concerned with the context of the reader, I also advocate for careful study of the history of the text's *production*. Historical work can function in much the same way that the juxtaposition of socially located readings does: demonstrating that texts do not have one single inherent meaning or theology. Acknowledging the distance between the world of the reader and the world of the text's production, like acknowledging the distance between the worlds of different modern readers, can demonstrate that texts do not necessarily speak our language—literally and figuratively.

My conviction that historical criticism is essential to biblical theology places me at odds with secular postmodernist manifestos that insist on the theoretical bankruptcy of historical-critical assumptions, even of biblical scholarship itself.[10] More importantly, it sharply distinguishes me from those practicing what has been deemed *theological exegesis* by an influential group of Christian biblical scholars, the most well known of whom is Richard B. Hays.

In his 2007 article on how to do theological exegesis, Hays insists that secular study of the Bible (within which he includes historical criticism) is at a dead-end. Since, he claims, there is no reason to read the Bible apart from the faith communities that fashioned it, exegesis instead should be

---

the Prophets but pays scant attention to the ideologies of class and race. My chapter on the history of interpretation is limited to German, American, and British scholars and does not consider the traditions of reading the prophets within Christian Pentecostalism, millenialist movements, or the developing world.

10. On historical critical assumptions, see George Aichele, Peter D. Miscall, and Richard Walsh, "An Elephant in the Room: Historical-Critical and Postmodern Interpretations of the Bible," *JBL* 128 (2009): 383–404. On biblical scholarship itself, see Hector Avalos, "The Ideology of the Society of Biblical Literature and the Demise of an Academic Profession," *SBL Forum*, n.p. (April 2006).

explicitly confessional: it is a "practice of and for the church."[11] Among his twelve identifying marks of theological exegesis, Hays includes three claims relevant to this study:

1. "Theological exegesis can never be content only to describe the theological perspectives of the individual biblical authors; instead, it always presses forward to the synthetic question of canonical coherence."
2. "Theological exegesis thereby is committed to the discovery and exposition of multiple senses in biblical texts. Old Testament texts, when read in conjunction with the story of Jesus, take on new and unexpected resonances as they prefigure events far beyond the historical horizon of their authors and original readers."
3. "Learning to read the text with eyes of faith is a skill for which we are trained by the Christian tradition.... Consequently, theological exegesis will find hermeneutical aid, not hindrance, in the church's doctrinal traditions."[12]

In his later work, Hays also has been a proponent of cultivating the "scriptural imagination"; he not only traces the contours of the scriptural imagination of the apostle Paul but also calls for modern believers to think of themselves in biblical language.[13]

Hays is not alone in his confessional challenge to the exegetical dominance of historical criticism. A host of scholars have taken up his call to explore the echoes of the Old Testament in the New Testament, and several commentary series have been launched to retrieve ancient Christian practices of biblical interpretation.[14] Stephen E. Fowl's *Engaging Scripture*

---

11. Richard B. Hays, "Reading the Bible with Eyes of Faith: The Practice of Theological Exegesis," *JTI* 1 (2007): 10–11.

12. Hays, "Reading the Bible with Eyes of Faith," 13–14.

13. On Paul's scriptural imagination, see Richard B. Hays, *The Conversion of the Imagination: Paul as Interpreter of Israel's Scripture* (Grand Rapids: Eerdmans, 2005). Hays and others discuss the scriptural imagination in an issue of the Duke Divinity School magazine: Richard B. Hays, Ellen Davis, and Stanley Hauerwas, "The Formation of the Scriptural Imagination and the Renewal of the Church," *Divinity* 12 (2013): 28–31.

14. On echoes, see, e.g., Christopher A. Beetham, *Echoes of Scripture in the Letter of Paul to the Colossians* (Leiden: Brill, 2008); Kenneth D. Litwak, *Echoes of Scripture in*

strongly argues that Christian readers must move away from historical criticism to embrace an explicitly theological hermeneutic that draws from the best of the Christian tradition.[15] Dale B. Martin extends the logic of this approach to argue that Christian clergy should be trained first in theology and only subsequently in the methods of biblical study.[16]

I find theological exegesis as articulated by Hays, Fowl, and others flawed both in theory and in practice. In theory, it anachronistically assumes a commonality between those who produced the text and those who continue to read it. Although Hays claims to value historical study, the dominant imperative of his approach is to downplay the historical contingencies in which biblical texts were produced: "If we read the texts as testimony, we will find ourselves constantly reminded that the Bible is chiefly about God, not about human religious aspirations and power struggles."[17]

Counter to theological exegesis, I find maintaining the distance between past and present to be vitally important—exegetically and ethically. Entertaining the question of what a text might have meant within its ancient social, economic, and ideological contexts challenges readers to acknowledge that texts rarely share our own assumptions.

The importance of engaging the historical contexts of biblical texts can be seen, for example, in debates within religious communities and even secular societies regarding biblical theologies of marriage. I intentionally say theologies of marriage because in various contexts marriage is being discussed not primarily as a social institution but as a means by which humans participate in divine activity and divine intentionality. To call heterosexual monogamous marriage the "creation order" and the primary model for God's relationship with a community is to claim that it is not an ancillary sociological matter but a profoundly theological one.

Historically speaking, however, equating modern notions of heterosexuality with creation order is a misguided theological claim. When Gen 1 is read within the historical context of its likely production, which I identify

---

Luke-Acts: Telling the History of God's People Intertextually, JSNTSup 282 (New York: Clark, 2005). On ancient Christian interpretive practices, see, e.g., the series Ancient Christian Commentary on Scripture (Downers Grove, IL: InterVarsity Press, 1998–).

15. Stephen E. Fowl, *Engaging Scripture: A Model for Theological Interpretation* (Oxford: Blackwell, 1999).

16. Dale B. Martin, *Pedagogy of the Bible: An Analysis and Proposal* (Louisville: Westminster John Knox, 2008).

17. Hays, "Reading the Bible with Eyes of Faith," 12, quote at 13.

as the Persian period, it underscores not relationship or mutual covenant making but procreation and dominion. It reflects the same concerns as Ezra and Nehemiah: repopulating the land with returning exiles and regulating the extended household within a foreign tributary mode of production; its similarity with the sexual ideology of the Holiness Code reflects not only a shared source but also a shared focus on procreation and identity formation through sexual selection.[18] Modern assumptions that sexuality is an aspect of human living, that marriage involves the mutual exchange of vows, that sexual acts are primarily expressions of affection and/or one's orientation, and that gender is biologically determined are distinctively modern, as historians and sociologists have well documented.[19] Moreover, as Ken Stone demonstrates, identifying the sexual dimensions of the creation stories as their primary teaching also is a relatively modern move. In early Christian interpretation, Gen 1–3 was understood as primarily about food; in the early centuries of Christianity, it was used to argue for the eradication of sexual desire, especially within marriage.[20] Engaging in historically informed gender-critical work helps explain the nontextual origins of contemporary assumptions, as demonstrated throughout the *Oxford Encyclopedia of the Bible and Gender Studies*, which intersperses entries on contemporary theory with entries by scholars of the ancient Near East, Bible, and classics exploring ancient understandings of sex and gender.[21] Clearly, what sex acts signified to the writers of Genesis is not the same as what they signify to contemporary readers, an anachronism for which Hays has been roundly critiqued by Martin.[22]

My example of marriage might be seen as one not of biblical theology per se but of a social form in which biblical theology is expressed.

---

18. See, for example, Cynthia Shafer-Elliott, "Economics, Subentry Hebrew Bible," in *The Oxford Encyclopedia of the Bible and Gender Studies*, ed. Julia M. O'Brien, 2 vols. (Oxford University Press, 2014), 2:119–25. Also, E. Theodore Mullen Jr., *Ethnic Myths and Pentateuchal Foundations: A New Approach to the Formation of the Pentateuch* (Atlanta: Scholars Press, 1997).

19. For example, see Hanne Blank, *Straight: The Surprisingly Short History of Heterosexuality* (Boston: Beacon, 2012).

20. Ken Stone, *Practicing Safer Texts: Food, Sex and Bible in Queer Perspective*, QTS (London: T&T Clark International, 2005).

21. O'Brien, *Oxford Encyclopedia of the Bible and Gender Studies*.

22. Dale B. Martin, *Sex and the Single Savior: Gender and Sexuality in Biblical Interpretation* (Louisville: Westminster John Knox, 2006); Martin, "Heterosexism and the Interpretation of Romans 1:18–32," *BibInt* 3 (1995): 332–55.

Our field has a long history of distinguishing between the temporal social forms in which biblical theology is actualized and the principles or themes that transcend those social structures. I contend that the two are inseparable. Israelite testimony to the fatherhood or husbandhood of God depends fully on ancient concepts of family; understanding the import of biblical metaphors for the divine and the human requires understanding the conceptual domains in which Israel's theology was *formed* and not simply *expressed*. As metaphor theory insists, the conceptual frameworks of metaphors shape thinking.[23]

Other examples of the difference that historical analysis makes in determining a text's theology could be explored. For example, while Christianity has long vilified the ideology of the Ezra-Nehemiah reforms as xenophobic, exclusivist, even racist, contemporary historical analysis informed by postcolonial analysis stresses the role of fifth-century Persian imperial policy in determining the boundaries of tribute states and the crises of identity and community cohesion experienced by the colonized.[24] The reforms of Ezra and Nehemiah may not reflect the "weaknesses of Judaism," as several editions of Bernhard W. Anderson's *Understanding the Old Testament* have claimed, but, according to Samuel Adams, a community's use of endogamous marriage to "consolidat[e] wealth, resources, and social identity into one identifiable subset of persons" as a survival strategy.[25]

In practice, theological exegesis values only certain voices within the Christian interpretive tradition and only certain trajectories of reading of New Testament texts. By "always press[ing] forward to *the synthetic question of canonical coherence*," it assumes that coherence is in the text waiting to be discovered rather than in the perception of readers and their interpretative communities.[26] Not surprisingly, the principle of coherence

---

23. George Lakoff, "The Contemporary Theory of Metaphor," in *Metaphor and Thought*, ed. Andrew Ortony (Cambridge: Cambridge University Press, 1992); George Lakoff and Mark Johnson, *Metaphors We Live By* (Chicago: University of Chicago Press, 1980); Julia M. O'Brien, "Imagery, Gendered: Prophetic Literature," in O'Brien, *Oxford Encyclopedia of the Bible and Gender Studies*, 1:355–60.

24. See for example Daniel L. Smith-Christopher, "Ezra and Nehemiah," in O'Day and Petersen, *Theological Bible Commentary*, 155–64.

25. Bernhard W. Anderson, *Understanding the Old Testament*, 4th ed. (Englewood Cliffs, NJ: Prentice-Hall, 1986), 538; Samuel Adams, *Social and Economic Life in Second Temple Judea* (Louisville: Westminster John Knox, 2014), 23.

26. Hays, "Reading the Bible with Eyes of Faith," 13.

discerned in the text always matches the interpreter's own theology. One might well argue that the most prevalent and overarching theme of both Christian Testaments is patriarchy (indeed, Erhard S. Gerstenberger has done so), but theological exegesis rarely identifies patriarchy as the hallmark of canonical coherence.[27]

Practitioners of theological exegesis also rarely address the clear supersessionist implications of insisting that the Christian New Testament determines what the Christian Old Testament can mean. Since the 1970s, most Christians trained within academic Hebrew Bible scholarship have been taught that a hermeneutic that judges the Old Testament by the standards of the New is methodologically passé and irredeemably anti-Jewish. Many Christian institutions now refer to the *Hebrew Bible* or use the hybrid term *Hebrew Bible/Old Testament*.[28] Jewish scholars now sit on divinity school faculties and/or teach in joint divinity/Jewish Studies programs.[29] Textbooks in the field, especially those with a theological orientation, explicitly challenge Christian supersessionism in their introductory pages and insist that the text should be interpreted on its own terms and alongside Jewish readers.[30]

Trained within distinctively post-Holocaust biblical scholarship, my own sensibilities have been molded not only by Jewish professors and institutions but also, more fundamentally, by Christian professors, textbooks, and theologians working within a post-Holocaust framework. One of my primary goals in teaching, writing, and speaking is to challenge supersessionist, anti-Jewish readings of the Bible. In teaching, I insist that we read the Hebrew Bible apart from—and usually in distinction to—traditional or even modern Christian claims and apart from the New Testament. I resist making Christian traditions of reading the Hebrew Bible determinative of their present meaning. In sum, I have much more energy for

---

27. Erhard S. Gerstenberger and Frederick J. Gaiser, *Yahweh the Patriarch: Ancient Images of God and Feminist Theology* (Minneapolis: Augsburg Fortress, 1996).

28. For the former, see Wesley Theological Seminary, Chicago Theological Seminary, Harvard Divinity School, Vanderbilt Divinity School, and Claremont School of Theology; for the latter, see Yale Divinity School, Louisville Presbyterian Seminary, and Lancaster Theological Seminary.

29. For example, Vanderbilt Divinity School, Harvard Divinity School, Duke Divinity School, and Brite Divinity School.

30. For example, see Johanna van Wijk-Bos, *Making Wise the Simple: The Torah in Christian Faith and Practice* (Grand Rapids: Eerdmans, 2005).

challenging Christian traditions of reading its Old Testament than for per-
petuating them.

For this reason, I also resist the practice of canonical criticism as
advanced by Childs and his students.[31] I suggest instead that the confessional *usage* of books, rather than the *shape of the canon itself*, influences
meaning. For example, looking at the structure of the Tanak apart from
the traditions of its interpretation might lead one to assume that the Writings are more important than the Torah, since they get the last word, or
that in the New Testament Philemon is more important than Matthew.
Should one assume that first is best, then Christians might place more
weight on Genesis than John. The *shape of the canon* does not rule out
these valuations; *traditions of reading* do. I also notice that while canonical
critics often stress the importance of the dialogical nature of canon, they
fail to notice that the shape of the canon does not explain the principles
by which a reader is supposed to process this dialogue. Do all canonical
voices have the same weight? Do the most prominent ones or the most
unusual ones get the most attention? In my observation, canonical critics
often control potential meanings of texts by invoking *canonical intentionality*, which somehow always mirrors the theologian's own beliefs.

The scriptural imagination that Hays seeks to cultivate can prove
problematic as well. While I do find the formative function of narratives
powerful, I share with Carolyn J. Sharp the concern that in seeking to find
the relevance of biblical texts we often ignore the realities of other people's
lives. For example, existentializing the term *exile*, equating it with all forms
of alienation or dislocation, denies the particularity of the Neo-Babylonian deportation and what it meant to the people who experienced it.[32]
Thinking of ourselves as exiles might help us relate and feel connection
to the past, but it does so at the expense of colonializing the realities of
other people. I believe that acknowledging the differences between past
and present is an essential step not only in being honest about what is
and is not in a biblical text but also in taking accountability for our own
appropriation of texts.

The writings of ancient Israel now preserved in the canons of contemporary religious communities are themselves the products of contextual

---

31. Brevard S. Childs, *Introduction to the Old Testament as Scripture* (Philadelphia: Fortress, 1979).

32. Carolyn J. Sharp, "The Trope of 'Exile' and the Displacement of Old Testament
Theology," *PRSt* 31 (2004) 153–69.

theologizing. Just as the contexts of modern theologizing must be named, so also the contexts of ancient theologizing must be imagined, especially in contexts in which "what the Bible really says" is given authority.

3. For the Sake of the World

I applaud the increased attention that academic biblical scholars are paying to the ethical import of their work. Historically oriented texts regularly raise questions about violence, the treatment of women, and xenophobia, and dedicated volumes address the questions of the ethics of the texts we study.[33] I am dismayed, however, that ethics is usually invoked as a self-evident category, without any discussion of *whose* ethics provide the criterion of judgment. Marvin A. Sweeney, for example, argues that support for the state of Israel is essential to all post-Shoah biblical theology, while for Palestinian Christian theologians attitudes that do not resist occupation cannot truly be ethical.[34] No ethical engagement can truly be *critical* in the Enlightenment sense of the term; it is a claim of value that requires explication.

The engagement of modern readers with ancient texts is messy, complicated, and epistemologically confusing. When we value particular texts, are we valuing our own constructions of it? When we resist them, are we resisting our own projections?

When I am discouraged by the messiness, I find it important to remember why ancient people and modern people bother with the enterprise. They are trying to understand their worlds, their communities, and the divine. They believe—or at least want to believe or have been taught to believe—that the texts of the Bible can provide guidance.

I, too, believe such guidance is available, though not in a simple, direct way. Biblical texts provide us testimony of people doing theology in their own contexts. As we encounter the writings of these communities struggling with issues of justice and fairness, trauma and identity, I believe we

---

33. John J. Collins, *Introduction to the Hebrew Bible* (Minneapolis: Fortress, 2004); Eryl Davies, *The Immoral Bible: Approaches to Biblical Ethics* (London: T&T Clark, 2010).

34. For the former, see Marvin A. Sweeney, "Reconceiving the Paradigms of Old Testament Theology in the Post-Shoah Period," *BibInt* 6 (1998): 161. For the latter, see Mitri Raheb, *The Biblical Text in the Context of Occupation: Towards a New Hermeneutics of Liberation*, CTS (Bethlehem: Diyar, 2012).

can learn from their successes as well as their failures, even as their testimony encourages us to recognize the blind spots of our own.

Bibliography

Adams, Samuel. *Social and Economic Life in Second Temple Judea.* Louisville: Westminster John Knox, 2014.

Aichele, George, Peter D. Miscall, and Richard Walsh. "An Elephant in the Room: Historical-Critical and Postmodern Interpretations of the Bible." *JBL* 128 (2009): 383–404.

Anderson, Bernhard W. *Undestanding the Old Testament.* 4th ed. Englewood Cliffs, NJ: Prentice-Hall, 1986.

Arnold, Bill. *Genesis.* NCBC. Cambridge: Cambridge University Press, 2009.

Avalos, Hector. "The Ideology of the Society of Biblical Literature and the Demise of an Academic Profession." *SBL Forum*, n.p. (April 2006).

Banks, Diane. *Writing the History of Israel.* LHBOTS New York: T&T Clark, 2006.

Barr, James. *The Concept of Old Testament Theology: An Old Testament Perspective.* Minneapolis: Fortress, 1999.

Beetham, Christopher A. *Echoes of Scripture in the Letter of Paul to the Colossians.* Leiden: Brill, 2008.

Blank, Hanne. *Straight: The Surprisingly Short History of Heterosexuality.* Boston: Beacon, 2012.

Childs, Brevard S. *Introduction to the Old Testament as Scripture.* Philadelphia: Fortress, 1979.

Collins, John J. *Introduction to the Hebrew Bible.* Minneapolis: Fortress, 2004.

Davies, Eryl. *The Immoral Bible: Approaches to Biblical Ethics.* London: T&T Clark, 2010.

Fentress-Williams, Judy. "Exodus." Pages 27–40 in *Africana Bible: Reading Israel's Scriptures from Africa and the African Diaspora.* Edited by Hugh R. Page Jr. et al. Minneapolis: Fortress, 2010.

Fowl, Stephen E. *Engaging Scripture: A Model for Theological Interpretation.* Oxford: Blackwell, 1999.

Gerstenberger, Erhard S., and Frederick J. Gaiser. *Yahweh the Patriarch: Ancient Images of God and Feminist Theology.* Minneapolis: Augsburg Fortress, 1996.

Hays, Richard B. *The Conversion of the Imagination: Paul as Interpreter of Israel's Scripture*. Grand Rapids: Eerdmans, 2005.

———. "Reading the Bible with Eyes of Faith: The Practice of Theological Exegesis." *JTI* 1 (2007): 5–21.

Hays, Richard B., Ellen Davis, and Stanley Hauerwas. "The Formation of the Scriptural Imagination and the Renewal of the Church." *Divinity* 12 (2013): 28–31.

Hiebert, Theodore. "Genesis." Pages 3–25 in *Theological Bible Commentary*. Edited by Gail R. O'Day and David L. Petersen. Louisville: Westminster John Knox, 2009.

Lakoff, George. "The Contemporary Theory of Metaphor." Pages 202–51 in *Metaphor and Thought*. Edited by Andrew Ortony. Cambridge: Cambridge University Press, 1992.

Lakoff, George, and Mark Johnson. *Metaphors We Live By*. Chicago: University of Chicago Press, 1980.

Lapsley, Jacqueline. *Whispering the Word: Hearing Women's Stories in the Old Testament*. Louisville: Westminster John Knox, 2005.

Litwak, Kenneth D. *Echoes of Scripture in Luke-Acts: Telling the History of God's People Intertextually*. JSNTSup 282. New York: T&T Clark, 2005.

Long, Burke O. *Planting and Reaping Albright: Politics, Ideology, and Interpreting the Bible*. University Park: Pennsylvania State University Press, 1997.

Martin, Dale B. "Heterosexism and the Interpretation of Romans 1:18–32." *BibInt* 3 (1995): 332–55.

———. *Pedagogy of the Bible: An Analysis and Proposal*. Louisville: Westminster John Knox, 2008.

———. *Sex and the Single Savior: Gender and Sexuality in Biblical Interpretation*. Louisville: Westminster John Knox, 2006.

Mullen, E. Theodore, Jr. *Ethnic Myths and Pentateuchal Foundations: A New Approach to the Formation of the Pentateuch*. Atlanta: Scholars Press, 1997.

O'Brien, Julia M. *Challenging Prophetic Metaphor: Ideology and Theology in the Prophets*. Louisville: Westminster John Knox, 2008.

———. "Imagery, Gendered: Prophetic Literature." Pages 1:355–60 in *The Oxford Encyclopedia of the Bible and Gender Studies*, edited by Julia M. O'Brien. 2 vols. New York: Oxford University Press, 2014.

———, ed. *The Oxford Encyclopedia of the Bible and Gender Studies*. 2 vols. New York: Oxford University Press, 2014.

Olson, Dennis T. "Exodus." Pages 27–40 in *Theological Bible Commentary.* Edited by Gail R. O'Day and David L. Petersen. Louisville: Westminster John Knox, 2009.

Raheb, Mitri. *The Biblical Text in the Context of Occupation: Towards a New Hermeneutics of Liberation.* CTS. Bethlehem: Diyar, 2012.

Shafer-Elliott, Cynthia. "Economics, Subentry Hebrew Bible." Pages 2:119–25 in *The Oxford Encyclopedia of the Bible and Gender Studies.* Edited by Julia M. O'Brien. 2 vols. Oxford University Press, 2014.

Sharp, Carolyn J. "The Trope of 'Exile' and the Displacement of Old Testament Theology." *PRSt* 31 (2004) 153–69.

Smith-Christopher, Daniel L. "Ezra and Nehemiah." Pages 155–64 in *Theological Bible Commentary.* Edited by Gail R. O'Day and David L. Petersen. Louisville: Westminster John Knox, 2009.

Stone, Ken. *Practicing Safer Texts: Food, Sex and Bible in Queer Perspective.* QTS. London: T&T Clark International, 2005.

Sweeney, Marvin A. "Reconceiving the Paradigms of Old Testament Theology in the Post-Shoah Period." *BibInt* 6 (1998): 141–61.

Washington, Harold C. "Violence and the Construction of Gender in the Hebrew Bible: A New Historicist Approach." *BibInt* 5 (1997): 324–63.

Wijk-Bos, Johanna van. *Making Wise the Simple: The Torah in Christian Faith and Practice.* Grand Rapids: Eerdmans, 2005.

Hebrew Bible Theology:
A Jewish Descriptive Approach

Dalit Rom-Shiloni

1. Introduction

The topic of this paper seems to require at the outset some words on the contexts, personal and academic, in which I am situating my study of Hebrew Bible theology. To begin, I am a Jewish, Israeli, nonreligious Hebrew Bible scholar. I would define my critical work in two ways. To state what I am not: I am not a theologian (nor a rabbi) but an intrigued scholar, fascinated by the religious thought world of Hebrew Bible authors. My main interest in Hebrew Bible studies is in conceptions of God in times of national(-collective) crisis, when fundamental, shared ideas collapse and need to be challenged. I have dealt with different aspects of this topic in my 2009 study (in Hebrew), *God in Times of Destruction and Exiles.*[1] In the course of that previous project and constantly since, I have become more cognizant of and also frustrated by, as a Jewish scholar, the seeming inadequacy of the terminology and categories that are the traditional organizational tools of biblical theology. This has led me toward my present

This paper was published under the same title in *JR* 96 (2016): 165–84, and it is republished here with permission. It was originally written for the Society of Biblical Literature Annual Meeting, San Diego, November 2014, Theology of the Hebrew Scriptures section panel: Biblical Theology in Context: Jewish, Christian, and Critical Approaches to the Theology of the Hebrew Bible. The panel was chaired by Marvin A. Sweeney, and the participants were Julia O'Brien, Jacqueline Lapsley, David Frankel, and Peter Pettit served as respondent. I thank my colleagues and the respondent for a stimulating discussion, I thank the anonymous reviewers for their support and critical comments, and I am indebted to Dr. Ruth Clements for her comments and insights.

1. Dalit Rom-Shiloni, *God in Times of Destruction and Exiles: Tanak (Hebrew Bible) Theology* [Hebrew] (Jerusalem: Magnes, 2009).

(and nearly completed) study (in English), *Theodical Discourse: Justification, Doubt, and Protest in Face of Destruction*, and to the questions raised in this paper. Within this trajectory of inquiry, it has seemed both natural and appropriate to the material to conceive of Hebrew Bible theology as a descriptive study of the talk to and about God in the various documents that make up the Hebrew Bible, asking simply: What did *they* (i.e., ancient authors and the others they quoted) say about *their* God.

My goal in this paper is to elucidate two issues with which I found myself struggling while searching out my own methodological approach in this highly complicated field of research. The first issue is that of the proper borders of the corpus that should be the basis for Hebrew Bible theology, an issue that impinges directly on the question of the ultimate goals of Hebrew Bible theology. The second issue is that of the origins and appropriateness of the terminology commonly used in Hebrew Bible theology research. The first topic addresses disagreements among Jewish scholars of Hebrew Bible theology; the second poses a challenge to both Christian and Jewish scholars. Both issues boil down to the same basic question: Is Hebrew Bible theology different from any other field of critical Hebrew Bible research, and, if so, in what ways?

2. The Corpus for (a Descriptive) Hebrew Bible Theology, and the Question of Dialogical Model

In a series of studies, Marvin A. Sweeney has elaborated on the fundamental differences between the Old Testament corpus and the Tanak, differences that go much beyond the questions of the distinct order of the books, or the larger number of writings in the Old Testament.[2] Rather,

---

2. Marvin A. Sweeney, "Tanakh versus Old Testament: Concerning the Foundation for a Jewish Theology of the Bible," in *Problems in Biblical Theology: Essays in Honor of Rolf Knierim*, ed. Henry T. C. Sun and Keith L. Eades (Grand Rapids: Eerdmans, 1997), 353–72; Sweeney, "Why Jews Should be Interested in Biblical Theology," *CCAR* 44 (1997): 67–75; Sweeney, *Tanak: A Theological and Critical Introduction to the Jewish Bible* (Minneapolis: Fortress, 2012), 3–41. For the "biblical corpus" in Christian biblical theology, see Walther Eichrodt, *Theology of the Old Testament*, vol. 1, trans. J. A. Baker, OTL (Philadelphia: Westminster; London: SCM, 1961), 1:26–27 (German editions: 1933, 1957, 1964); Gerhard von Rad, *Old Testament Theology*, trans. David M. G. Stalker (New York: Harper & Row, 1962), 2:309–429, especially the concluding words in 428–29 (German edition: 1957). This approach continues to characterize scholars following von Rad, such as Gerhard F. Hasel, *Old Testament Theology: Basic*

to Sweeney, these differences constitute the distinction between the conceptions of canon inherent in each corpus: the Christian conception of Old Testament/New Testament operates by "a linear principle," in that it builds toward "the revelation of Christ as the culmination of human history"; in comparison, "a cyclical pattern" characterizes the Tanak, which in Sweeney's view is structured according to "the ideal Jewish life, the disruption of Jewish life, and the restoration of that ideal."[3] Without entering here upon the content of this cyclical pattern, the essential point is that Sweeney, like many other scholars (Jewish and Christian), feels that the Hebrew Bible is self-contained and closed in on itself, whereas the Christian Old Testament canon requires the notion of linear progression toward the New Testament.[4]

Issues in the Current Debate (Grand Rapids: Eerdmans, 1972), 89–91. It is a common thread in the collection edited by John Reumann, *The Promise and Practice of Biblical Theology* (Minneapolis: Fortress, 1991); see his introductory remarks on pp. 1–2 under the title: "Introduction: Whither Biblical Theology?," 1–31. Jon D. Levenson explained that the primary difference between Jewish and Christian approaches to the corpus stems from the different understanding of *Scripture* in each tradition. He contrasted the Christian, and especially Protestant, emphasis upon *sola scriptura* to the traditional Jewish conception of the Bible as תורה שבכתב (Written Torah) and תורה שבעל פה (Oral Torah, i.e., the rabbinic corpus). See Levenson, "Why Jews Are Not Interested in Biblical Theology," in *The Hebrew Bible, the Old Testament, and Historical Criticism: Jews and Christians in Biblical Studies* (Louisville: Westminster John Knox, 1993), 33–61, esp. 45–51. While according to the rabbinic (mainstream Judaism) perspective the written and the oral Torah indeed coalesce in disputation with the Karaites, I would claim that in academic discussion the two should be kept apart; see below.

3. Sweeney, *Tanak*, 24.

4. See von Rad, *Old Testament Theology*, 2:309–429, immediately at the opening sentences, 309, or in 321: "The way in which the Old Testament is absorbed in the New as the logical end of a process initiated by the Old Testament itself"; see Manfred Oeming, *Gesamt biblische Theologien der Gegenwart: Das Verhältnis von AT und New Testament in der hermeneutischen Diskussion seit Gerhard von Rad*, 2nd ed. (Stuttgart: Kohlammer, 1987), 20–33 and 77–80; James Barr, *The Concept of Biblical Theology: An Old Testament Perspective* (Minneapolis: Fortress, 1999), 497–505. As has happened in other fields of the critical study of the Hebrew Bible, the borders of the corpus for biblical theology have generally been set according to the Christian canon. Rolf Rendtorff bravely pointed out, concerning the history of scholarship, that this definition of the Christian corpus framed the task in such a way that the work of Jewish scholars on the Hebrew Bible always appeared to be only partial; see Rolf Rendtorff, "A Christian Approach to the Theology of Hebrew Scriptures," in *Jews, Christians, and the Theology of the Hebrew Scriptures*, ed. Alice Ogden Bellis and Joel S. Kaminsky (Atlanta:

Keeping in mind this "linear principle" of the Old Testament/New Testament over against the self-contained "cyclical pattern" of the Tanak, I would like to focus on another aspect of this same issue of corpus and canon and ask: Should Christian *and* Jewish literary traditions that fall outside the Hebrew Bible canon still be considered within the borders of discussion for a Hebrew Bible theology?[5]

Jewish scholars seem to take one of three paths in articulating the relevance of rabbinic and other later Jewish traditions for the particular study of Hebrew Bible theology.[6] All Jewish Hebrew Bible scholars mentioned below are masters of Hebrew Bible critical (modern and postmodern) scholarship and, as a matter of course, are aware of diachronic issues and literary layers within the Hebrew Bible, yet some of them are more

---

Society of Biblical Literature, 2000), 137–51, esp. 139–40. In response, Jewish scholars, and subsequently Christian scholars and theologians such as Rendtorff himself, advanced the Hebrew Bible, the Tanak, as the independent corpus for their research. The Hebrew Bible is taken as an independent corpus for study also by Collins, Hasel, Knierim. Along similar lines, the Society of Biblical Literature section "Theology of the Hebrew Scriptures" is "corpus-sensitive," so to speak, and sets the limits of the corpus as the Tanak/Old Testament.

5. There is a profound disagreement among Jewish scholars about what is included in the "postbiblical" corpus, where it starts and what it includes. The range of answers could be from Second Temple literature of the Hellenistic and Roman periods, to rabbinic Oral Torah, and even up to modern Jewish thought. The conception of canon and the process of canonization have been appreciated quite differently by Jewish and Christian scholars. I follow Menahem Haran in his important distinctions between the two religious traditions on this matter (*The Biblical Collection: Its Consolidation to the End of the Second Temple Times and Changes of Form to the End of the Middle Ages* [Hebrew] [Jerusalem: Bialik and Magnes, 1996], 23–78). According to Haran, the Jewish conception of canonization suggests an internal growing and ongoing process of collecting and gradually sanctifying traditions and full compositions already within the Hebrew Bible literature. The bulk of this long process closes by the end of the early Hellenistic period, with minor additions up to the second century CE. This indeed explains the lack of clear cut chronological distinctions between biblical and non-biblical compositions.

6. While Christian theologians are oftentimes committed to the New Testament (and to subsequent Christian literature), as is the case with the theologies of Eichrodt, von Rad, and many others, several Christian scholars have cut this tie. See Barr, *Concept of Biblical Theology*, 4–5; Rolf Rendtorff, *Canon and Theology*, trans. and ed. Margaret Kohl, OOTT (Minneapolis: Fortress, 1993), 13–16, 34–36, 40; Wolfhart Pannenberg, "Problems in a Theology of (Only) the Old Testament," in Sun and Eades, *Problems in Biblical Theology*, 275–80, esp. 276.

ready than others to cross the barriers of time and trace lines of continuity between the Hebrew Bible and later Jewish traditions (from the Hellenistic period on). The approaches taken are clearly connected to a scholar's denominational/confessional and/or academic commitments (at times even explicitly proclaimed). While some of the differences between these approaches might seem quite mild, at most a matter of nuance, they do lead to very different results in the theological discussion itself.[7]

The first approach is synchronic, in that it sees an organic continuity between Hebrew Bible theology and the theology of later traditions, such that it requires dialogical relationships between the Hebrew Bible and later Jewish traditions. Benjamin D. Sommer defined the scope and the goals of this dialogical study as follows:[8]

> Dialogical biblical theology would attempt to construct a discussion between biblical texts and a particular postbiblical theological tradition. Such a theology would bring biblical texts to bear on postbiblical theological concerns—specifically, on modern Jewish and Protestant or Catholic or Orthodox or post-Christian theological concerns. A work of this field would belong to the fields of both biblical scholarship and either Jewish thought or constructive Christian theology; indeed, it ought to draw on and contribute to all these fields.

This seemingly necessary organic connection raises the challenge of whether a self-contained Hebrew Bible theology can at all be achieved. This position is represented by the work of Jon D. Levenson and Benjamin D. Sommer.[9]

---

7. The limited list of Hebrew Bible scholars mentioned below in reference to each of the three approaches contains scholars who have focused their writings on theology and its study. If literary and diverse thematic interests were in consideration, many other scholars might have been mentioned in reference to each of these approaches; however, I have restricted my perspective here to theology.

8. See Benjamin D. Sommer, "Dialogical Biblical Theology: A Jewish Approach to Reading Scripture Theologically," in *Biblical Theology: Introducing the Conversation*, ed. Leo G. Perdue, Robert Morgan, and Benjamin D. Sommer (Nashville: Abingdon, 2009), 1–53, quotation from 21. Sommer embraced this dialogical approach from Oeming (*Gesamt biblische Theologien der Gegenwart*, 20–33) in reference to Christian biblical theology.

9. Jon D. Levenson designated the Jewish traditions as "evolutionary" in reference to the Hebrew Bible, whereas the New Testament is "revolutionary" in its claim for a new Israel, a new covenant, etc. (*Sinai and Zion: An Entry into the Jewish Bible*

The second approach perceives the Hebrew Bible and Jewish traditions as distinct but still sees the latter as in dialogue with the former. This approach is often also concerned with the constructive relevance of the Hebrew Bible message to the contemporary Jewish (Israeli) world.[10] But such scholars begin with a focus on Hebrew Bible texts, before going on to describe the literary dependence of the later Jewish traditions on the Hebrew Bible, defining these relationships as exegetical by nature. Hence, *dialogue* in this framework is more of a one-way engagement of later Jewish traditions with the foundational corpus of the Hebrew Bible. This position is currently represented by Marvin A. Sweeney, Marc Z. Brettler, and David Frankel.[11]

The third approach *accentuates* the diachronic differences between the Hebrew Bible and later Jewish traditions and argues for a clear independence

---

[Minneapolis: Winston, 1985], 3–5, esp. 4). Levenson's view drew valid criticism from Barr (*Concept of Biblical Theology*, 286–311, esp. 294–302). Sommer, "Dialogical Biblical Theology."

10. See David Frankel, *The Land of Canaan and the Destiny of Israel: Theologies of Territory in the Hebrew Bible*, Siphrut 4 (Winona Lake, IN: Eisenbrauns, 2011), viii: "Only after the biblical conceptions are accurately identified, analyzed, and categorized can one begin the process of discussing the possible relevance of these conceptions for the contemporary situation" (and see 382–400).

11. Sweeney, *Tanak*, 3–41; Marc Z. Brettler, "Biblical History and Jewish Biblical Theology," *JR* 77 (1997): 563–83; Brettler, "Psalms and Jewish Biblical Theology," in *Jewish Bible Theology: Perspectives and Case Studies*, ed. Isaac Kalimi (Winona Lake: Eisenbrauns, 2012), 187–98; Frankel, *Land of Canaan*, viii, 382–400. This was also the approach held by Moshe Greenberg, *On the Bible and Judaism: A Collection of Writings* (Tel Aviv: Am Oved, 1984). See Sweeney, *Tanak*, 3–4: "With regard to the Tanak and the rest of Jewish tradition, it is not clear that the Tanak was composed to be in intentional dialogue with the later works, but it is clear that most of the later writings were intentionally composed to be in dialogue with the Torah and the rest of the Tanak to some degree. In order to understand that dialogue fully, it is essential to understand the literature of the Torah and the rest of the Tanak in and of itself, recognizing that the Tanak cannot function as a complete and self-contained revelation analogous to the manner in which the Old and New Testaments are read in much of Protestant Christianity." Yet, Sweeney himself did not give up on a dialogical approach and explained that in distinction to the Old Testament/New Testament relationship, the relationship of the Tanak to the Jewish tradition is that of an "organic and integrated process of development" (25). His following observation is of a *constructive* nature: "The Torah and the rest of the Tanak are the foundation of Jewish tradition, but the Tanak cannot be viewed as complete in Judaism without ongoing dialogue with the rest of the tradition that constitutes Judaism throughout its history and into the future" (4).

of the two, leaving the theological discussion confined within the Tanak. This approach has guided the programmatic papers of Matitiahu Tsevat, Moshe Goshen-Gottstein, and Isaac Kalimi (and possibly also Ziony Zevit).[12]

For the purpose of the present discussion, I want to address briefly the quite recent suggestion of Sommer, who seems to have taken the first approach to Hebrew Bible theology to an extreme. As a Hebrew Bible scholar who educates rabbinical students at the Jewish Theological Seminary, Sommer has defined his role as that of "a dialogical biblical theologian" whose primary task is to bring the Hebrew Bible "to participate in contemporary Jewish or Christian religious thought" by looking into the two religious traditions' long history of exegesis.[13] In the opening sentences of his "Dialogical Biblical Theology" (2009), Sommer offered a provocative proposition:

> Strictly speaking, there can be no such thing as Jewish biblical theology. While many definitions of the term "biblical theology" exist, they all accord some privileged place to the Bible. *All forms of Jewish theology, however, must base themselves on Judaism's rich post-biblical tradition at least as much as on scripture, and hence a Jewish theology cannot be chiefly biblical.*[14]

Sommer defined "Dialogical Jewish Theology" as a type of "intellectual history." Given its scope, this history should start with "a structural phenomenology" of the Hebrew Bible (as suggested by Goshen-Gottstein), yet the dialogical theologian does not stop there, and at times it does not even begin with a biblical issue but is free to draw on the storehouse of Jewish tradition from postbiblical to modern times in a manner understood

---

12. See Moshe Goshen-Gottstein, "Tanakh Theology: The Religion of the Old Testament and the Place of Jewish Biblical Theology," in *Ancient Israelite Religion: Essays in Honor of F. M. Cross*, ed. Patrick D. Miller, Paul D. Hanson, S. Dean McBride (Philadelphia: Fortress, 1987), 617–44; Matitiahu Tsevat, "Theology of the Old Testament: A Jewish View," *HBT* 8 (1986): 33–50; Isaac Kalimi, "History of Israelite Religion or Hebrew Bible/Old Testament Theology? Jewish Interest in Biblical Theology," *JSOT* 11 (1997): 100–123; Kalimi, *Early Jewish Exegesis and Theological Controversy: Studies in Scriptures in the Shadow of Internal and External Controversies*, JCHS 2 (Assen: Royal van Gorcum, 2002). Ziony Zevit, in his words of praise to Kalimi's approach, seems to support this path as well ("Jewish Biblical Theology: Whence? Why? Whither?," *HUCA* 76 [2005]: 289–340, esp. 314–17, and see 337).

13. Sommer, "Dialogical Biblical Theology," 51.

14. Sommer, "Dialogical Biblical Theology," 1, emphasis added.

as "*synthetic* in the Kantian sense."[15] Sommer enthusiastically accepted Manfred Oeming's suggestion (from a Christian perspective) that biblical theology should be understood as "value-related exegesis," that is, from the Christian point of departure, an exegesis that initiates a dialogical relationship between the Old Testament and the New Testament, enriching the understanding of both.[16] Another important principle that Oeming suggested, and that Sommer was happy to embrace, was the openness of this model of Old Testament theology to Jewish as well as Christian exegesis and to all stages of their religious traditions.[17] Sommer thus suggested that a "Jewish biblical theology" might be constructed using Oeming's approach to "individual texts and issues." He found Oeming's approach to be close to that of Jewish biblical scholars, with whom Sommer suggested Oeming shares "an openness to—indeed, a love of—the Bible's (proto-rabbinic) multi-vocality; and an awareness of what I have called the synthetic rather than analytic nature of Christian measures of value applied to biblical texts."[18] Applying these principles to conducting "Jewish Dialogical Biblical Theology," Sommer illustrated his approach through two examples by which he sharpened his arguments. At the conclusion of his first example, "The Primary Religious Value according to the Psalter and Later Judaism," he said:

> A Jewish biblical theology *need not—in fact, should not—see for itself the goal of definitively stating what the Bible says; rather, it should look for what the Bible invites us to attend to,* and it should examine how rabbinic and later Jewish literatures pick up that invitation. It is by attending to the same issues, and by turning them over and turning them over again,

---

15. Sommer, "Dialogical Biblical Theology," 22–23. The synthesis that Sommer suggested (23) is posed in opposition to what he (following Oeming) defined as an *analytic* approach; that is, one that preserves historical, diachronic distinctions between layers of traditions. See Sommer's exemplary discussion (29–43), where he traced a biblical conflict through rabbinic and medieval midrash, and even in the Hasidic/Mitnagdic conflict of the eighteenth century.

16. Oeming, *Gesamt biblische Theologien der Gegenwart*, 11–19. Oeming advocated a "biblischen Thelogie als wertbeziehen der Exegese" (226–41).

17. Oeming, *Gesamt biblische Theologien*, 237–41.

18. Sommer, "Dialogical Biblical Theology," 24. Sommer completed his evaluation of Oeming's approach with the remarkable note that "not one of the reasons Levenson gives for Jews' lack of interest in biblical theology would apply to a Christian biblical theology that follows Oeming's proposal" (24).

that Jewish biblical theology can become part of the all-encompassing discussion that is Torah.[19]

Here we can see how the boundaries of the corpus are determined by the goals of the individual scholar. As a Hebrew Bible scholar, Sommer structures his theological framework as a "three-way discussion" that incorporates (1) ancient Near Eastern texts and the Hebrew Bible, (2) rabbinic literature, and (3) modern Jewish communities of readers. However, his major goal extends far beyond the limits of the study of the Hebrew Bible to include facilitating a discussion that is "an unambiguously confessional enterprise" among "confessional traditions," with the aim to "renew the Hebrew Bible's status as a Jewish book and as a Christian book," highlighting the shared and distinctive traditions of each faith community.[20]

Sommer's thoughtful paradigm clearly constitutes an important contribution to the current discussion around constructing *contemporary* Jewish theology. But considered in relation to the more limited boundaries of a critical academic study of *Hebrew Bible* theology, I find two basic limits to his methodology. The first touches on the issue of the corpus. The linear connection and the dialogical relationship between the Old Testament and the New Testament, suggested by Oeming, is less relevant to the Tanak as a self-contained corpus and subject of critical study. The *synthetic* approach Sommer advances is highly interesting and certainly has an educational-theological role in confessional contexts, but it does not assist the critical discussion of the Hebrew Bible.[21] The second limitation concerns the dialogical jumps between late and early sources, from Hasidism to the Psalms and back, enabled by Sommer's model. Sommer's examples are clear illustrations of the reading of postbiblical issues and perspectives back into the Hebrew Bible, which raises the problematic possibility of mistaking externally imposed meanings for the contextually determined meaning of the biblical text. This retrojection (in my eyes; Sommer would probably consider it a continuation of organic theology) seems to me one

---

19. Sommer, "Dialogical Biblical Theology," 43, emphasis added.

20. Sommer, "Dialogical Biblical Theology," 51, 53.

21. This is not to devaluate the need or the achievements of such confessionally based reflections. Like Sommer, Oeming had indeed argued for the necessity of developing panbiblical theological methods, to capture a middle place combining the insights of the historical and doctrinal disciplines (*Gesamt biblische Theologien der Gegenwart*, 215–25).

of the most problematic aspects of Christian biblical theology. Sommer's theological model, I fear, has now recast this problem of corpus in a Jewish context.

From my different point of departure as a secular Hebrew Bible scholar and with the different goal of developing a critical and descriptive model for Hebrew Bible theology, I take the third approach to Hebrew Bible theology mentioned above.[22] I recognize a diachronic distinction between the Hebrew Bible corpus and later traditions; while later Jewish traditions do rely on the Hebrew Bible as their foundational corpus, they are linked by a one-way relationship of exegesis that does not compromise the essential distinctiveness of the Hebrew Bible corpus in itself. I thus subscribe to James Barr's clear and delimited definition of biblical theology:

> The term "biblical theology" has clarity only when it is understood to mean theology as it existed or was thought or believed within the time, languages and cultures of the Bible itself. Only so can its difference from doctrinal theology, from later interpretation, and from later views about the Bible be maintained.... What we are looking for is a "theology" that existed back there and then.[23]

Barr included within the framework of "biblical times and cultures" the time of the events, the time of the original writing of the texts, and the time of their finalization. While as a Christian scholar he often treated the Bible synthetically as encompassing both the Old Testament and the New Testament, he argued that the Old Testament and the New Testament represent two different sets of times and cultures.

From the point of view of the corpus, Jewish *or* Christian literary corpora and interpretive traditions share the basic feature: they are both *beyond* the Hebrew Bible with regard to their respective literatures and theologies. In order to construct a descriptive literary-philological-historical Hebrew Bible theology on the model of Barr, it is necessary to recognize the Hebrew Bible as a self-contained corpus independent of both its Christian *and* its Jewish contingent interpretive corpora.[24]

---

22. While secularity or religiosity do not necessarily affect such approaches in other disciplines within Hebrew Bible studies, when theological perspectives are at stake, awareness to this dimension in the scholar's point of departure seems in place.

23. Barr, *Concept of Biblical Theology*, 4.

24. See the important definition laid by Tsevat "[The theology of the Old Testament] ... it is part of that branch of the study of literature which has the Old Testa-

I must admit that my Jewish (Israeli) but nonreligious, delimited, and descriptive critical approach to the theology of the Hebrew Bible corpus would probably have earned me the label "Neo-Karaite" from more than one of my respected Jewish scholarly colleagues in the discipline.[25] How-

---

ment for its subject; it is philology of the Old Testament. It is objective (the word has already been used) in the sense and to the extent that the humanities, especially those whose primary task is understanding, are assured of the objectivity of their statements. Within the total philology of the Old Testament, theology is concerned with the understanding of its ideas, particularly, if not exclusively, the religious and, more precisely, the God-related ideas.… Theology so conceived is indispensable to the Old Testament research" ("Theology of the Old Testament," 48–49). Tsevat considered this "objective" research to be distinct from Jewish theology, in which biblical insights are seen through on the Talmud and Midrash.

25. Jon D. Levenson, for example, objected to what he labeled as Neo-Karaite, Reform Jewish, or secular Zionist approaches, on the grounds that they all adopt "protestant" stances of advocating *sola scriptura*. See Levenson, "Why Jews Are Not Interested," 33–61, esp. 45–51. My approach stands in further contrast to that of my late teacher of Ancient Semitic Languages, Professor Moshe Goshen-Gottstein ("Tanakh Theology," 617–44), who argued that a Tanak theology requires the personal commitment of "a practicing member of the community of faith" (629); see similarly his earlier paper in Hebrew ("Jewish Biblical Theology and the Study of Biblical Religion," Tarbiz 50 [1980]: 47–48 n. 22), where he considered Reform perspectives as raising the danger of Neo-Karaitism by applying Hebrew Bible theology to practical issues in contemporary Judaism. I profoundly disagree with Goshen-Gottstein on this point. This "Neo-Karaite" label is in itself an improper, even misleading analogy, and, mostly, its denigratory value is unfortunate, as it retains the lines of rivalry. It is based on the Karaites' disconnect of the oral from the written Torah, as "revealed" traditions. For the Islamic-Arabic context of literacy behind the Karaite conceptions of the authority of the written Scriptures over oral ones (the Mishnah and Talmud), see Meirah Polliak, "The Karaite Inversion of 'Written' and 'Oral' Torah in Relation to the Islamic Arch-Models of Qur'an and Hadith," *JSQ* 22 (2015): 243–302, esp. 243–56 (and see the use of "validation" and "invalidation" terms respectively, 268). Nevertheless, in many respects (language, interpretation, literary conceptions, theology, etc.), Karaite exegesis is well informed in, and in explicit and implicit negotiation with, rabbinic language and interpretive traditions, upon which it has established its own traits and points of interest; as for instance in the formation of the text (see 258–61), and in utilizing the rhetorical technique of inversion confronting both the external-Islamic front and the internal-rabbinite front (275–79, 280–86); and see Daniel Frank, "The Limits of Karaite Scripturalism: Problems in Narrative Exegesis," in *A Word Fitly Spoken: Studies in Medieval Exegesis of the Hebrew Bible and the Qur'an Presented to Haggai Ben-Shammai*, ed. Meir M. Bar-Asher et al. (Jerusalem: The Ben Zvi Institute, 2007), *41–82.

ever, as a secular Zionist I am engaged in the study of this foundational corpus, and in what follows I will advocate for the importance of a descriptive (and nonconfessionally contingent) model for the study of Hebrew Bible theology.

One of the major reasons for the need of this corpus distinction is the danger of retrojecting theological conceptions and terminologies of later origins back into the critical interpretation of the Hebrew Bible text, and this is addressed in the next section of this paper.

3. Looking for Non-Christian Terminology

The presence of Christian supersessionism in nineteenth- and twentieth-century theological studies of the Hebrew Bible has become widely recognized in the last few decades by both Christian and Jewish scholars. From a post-Shoah perspective on Hebrew Bible theology, supersessionism has become an unacceptable stance for the academic study of the Hebrew Bible. I would like to touch here on a related topic: the superimposition of certain Christian religious thought on Hebrew Bible theology in a more subtle form, that is, the influence of Christian theological categories on scholarly terminology that commonly, consciously or unconsciously, continues to be used for Hebrew Bible theology. I will look briefly here at conceptions of anthropomorphism, spirituality, immanence, and transcendence as they make their appearance in critical study of the Hebrew Bible.

These four terms were brought together in relation to Hebrew Bible theology by Walther Eichrodt. In his *Theology of the Old Testament*, his chapter on "The Nature of the Covenant God" features a section titled "Affirmations about the Divine Being" with three subsections: "(1) God as personal; (2) God as spiritual; and (3) God as one."[26]

Eichrodt's discussion deserves careful attention; I will limit myself here to three points: First, Eichrodt located the personal quality of God in God's name. God's choice to reveal his name to humankind expresses his presence, his closeness, and his help. For instance, Eichrodt saw in Exod 20:24 ("In every place where I cause my name to be mentioned I will come to you and bless you") an illustration of God's openness and accessibility to human beings. Even when the text uses general names (e.g., El, Elohim),

---

26. Eichrodt, *Theology of the Old Testament*, 1:104–6, 206–27.

Eichrodt insisted that those names reveal God's personal character.[27] In reading this section, I could not but feel the undercurrents of a Christian theology of "persona" conceptions (accentuating the divine name as a quality of personhood), as well as a Christian elitist perspective of monotheism over against "primitive peoples" who hold to polytheistic anonymous and mystical natural forces.[28] His closing passage is a remarkable example of much that needs to be changed in the writing of Hebrew Bible theology:

> Even, however, where this sense of the immediate reality of the divine presence is weakened, the overriding certainty of God's all-ruling will still make itself felt in another way. For the existence of God is quite independently retained as the basic assumption of all thinking, as the unshakable cornerstone of man's whole attempt to construct a picture of life and the world. In the thick of the gravest fightings and fears on the subject of God's behaviour, as for instance in Job or Ecclesiastes, his existence remains at all times unquestioned. It is simply beyond dispute.[29]

This passage is a good example of the way Eichrodt, in his pietistic Christian approach, seems to be closing the door on a polemical, intra-Hebrew Bible discussion concerning divine presence and the extent of its involvement in human life (on the individual or collective levels), a theological discussion waged far beyond the borders of Job and Ecclesiastes, with multiple and polar expressions in Hebrew Bible literature (see, e.g., Ezek 8:12; 9:9; Jer 5:2).

Second, Eichrodt's subheading "God as Spiritual" is rather misleading, since most of this section actually deals with the issue of the anthropomorphic representation of God. Eichrodt did get to the "spiri-

---

27. Eichrodt, *Theology of the Old Testament*, 1:206, 209.

28. See for instance Ralph L. Smith (*Old Testament Theology: Its History, Method, and Message* [Nashville: Broadman & Holman: 1993], 94–121), who opened his study with a discussion of revelation that developed to a discussion of the revelation of God's name. Smith (120–21) agreed with Eichrodt that the name of God is a personal name, not an abstract noun, and thus that the revelation of the name in the Hebrew Bible stands against intellectual and mystical notions of "an abstract concept of deity and a nameless 'ground of being'" (120). All these create a connection between name and essence (116), name and presence (120), and the revelation of the personal name and the personal connection, thus immanence of God within the human arena. See Barr (*Concept of Biblical Theology*, 62–67) for an evaluation of such inconsistencies in Eichrodt's *Theology* that push his discussion toward dogmatic or normative theology.

29. Eichrodt, *Theology of the Old Testament*, 1:210.

tual" aspect near the end of this discussion, where he claimed that the "doctrine" of God as spirit is not in the Hebrew Bible but is introduced for the first time in the New Testament (in John 4:24). Giving this section the title "God Is Spiritual" points up the "inadequacy" of the Hebrew Bible (and Judaism) in this regard and is yet another example of an explicitly supersessionist approach.

Third, Eichrodt's discussion of anthropomorphism is of special interest. It is not easy to follow, mainly because of the mixture of terms interwoven together. I will try to summarize his argument as briefly and as accurately as possible. Eichrodt identified what he considered a real theological danger in the Hebrew Bible's use of anthropomorphic expressions for conceptions of the divine. According to Eichrodt, anthropomorphic language demonstrates the "personhood" of God, which he understood as designating God's closeness to his creation and to his people, thus reflecting an immanent conception of the divine.[30] In the presumed evolution of religious feelings over time, relationships between God and human beings came to be conceived of in terms of personal relationship; thus the danger increased that "the immanence of God threatened to overshadow his transcendence."[31] The greatest theological-conceptual threat to a conception of God's transcendence, according to Eichrodt, came from those anthropomorphic and anthropopathic expressions that so often throughout the Hebrew Bible refer to God's limbs, physical actions, talk, emotions, thoughts, and the like.[32]

---

30. Eichrodt, *Theology of the Old Testament*, 1:210–11, 216–17; Eichrodt further argued that God's portrayals transform into distant and transcendent ones only within Priestly and Persian-period writings (217–18). For a discussion of "persona" in Christian theology, see Hugh S. Pyper, "Person," in *The Oxford Companion to Christian Thought: Intellectual, Spiritual, and Moral Horizons of Christianity*, ed. Adrian Hastings, Alistair Mason, and Hugh Pyper (Oxford: Oxford University Press, 2000), 532–33. Pyper said, "We are steeped in an intellectual heritage which, from the rise of humanism, has agreed with Aquinas in according supreme value to personhood, but accounts for this in terms of self-consciousness and the capacity for relationship rather than metaphysical status" (533).

31. Eichrodt, *Theology of the Old Testament*, 1:211.

32. Eichrodt went on to further discuss the extensive and persistent usage of anthropomorphisms in the Hebrew Bible (*Theology of the Old Testament*, 1:210–17). He argued that it signifies neither naïve childish talk nor a poetic disguise of a religious experience but rather a social distinction among the hearers of the prophetic proclamations (1:211): "the great mass of the people" took these expressions literally,

Thus here is the problem: anthropomorphism designates a perception of God's personhood that means closeness; closeness means an immanent conception of the divine (though of "a *superhuman* personality").[33] If God is presented in anthropomorphic terms, thus in the language of immanence, how can he continue to be conceptualized as transcendent?[34] In other words, it seems that for Eichrodt conceptions of immanence and transcendence are mutually exclusive for the Hebrew Bible; they cannot exist in dialectical tension. I will argue below that this grave theological problem for Eichrodt is alien to the collected Hebrew Bible documents and that by presenting it so this distinguished scholar superimposed his own Christian perceptions on the Hebrew Bible.

The study of anthropomorphism among Hebrew Bible scholars has made significant steps since Eichrodt's discussion. The major step, to my mind, has been that of reconceiving anthropomorphism as a matter of metaphor, as one expression of the image of God, the formal representation of him in languages of personification.[35]

---

whereas the spiritual leadership adopted their usage to advance piety, because they did not feel such literal conceptions as a threat. So he gathered from the plenty of anthropomorphisms in the prophets (1:216–17). But, of course, neither later Judaism nor Alexandrian philosophy could accept such descriptions as literally intended and dealt with them by means of allegoric explanations. I would challenge Eichrodt's basic premise that prophets utilized anthropomorphism only to enhance piety (1:217) and argue that they used it extensively and intentionally as a metaphorical tool to portray God in his various roles and actions with his people and the world.

33. Eichrodt, *Theology of the Old Testament*, 213.

34. For a definition of these biblical terms that draws on Christian categories, see Charles Hartshorne, "Transcendence and Immanence," *Encyclopedia of Religion* 15 (1985): 16–21.

35. On anthropomorphic language as metaphor, see Tryggve N. D. Mettinger, "The Study of the Gottesbild—Problems and Suggestions," *SEÅ* 54 (1989): 135–45, esp. 135. Mettinger followed Tord Olsson, "Gudsbild, talsituation och literature genre," *AFLR* 16 (1983): 91–109; Olsson, "Gudsbildens gestaltning: literäre kategorier och religiös tro," *SRA* 1 (1985): 42–63. See some challenges raised to both by Hanne Løland, *Silent or Salient Gender? The Interpretation of Gendered God-Language in the Hebrew Bible, Exemplified in Isaiah 42, 46, and 49* (Göttingen: Mohr Siebeck, 2009), 27–29. Note also Marc Z. Brettler, *God Is King: Understanding an Israelite Metaphor*, JSOTSup 76 (Sheffield: Sheffield Academic, 1989), 17–28; Brettler, "The Metaphorical Mapping of God in the Hebrew Bible," in *Metaphor, Canon, and Community: Jewish, Christian, and Islamic Approaches*, ed. Ralph Bisschops and James Francis (Bern: Lang, 1999), 219–32; Esther J. Hamori, "Varieties of Anthropomorphism," in *"When Gods*

The grave problems of terminology and definition posed here seem clear. If we investigate a range of Hebrew Bible (and ancient Near Eastern) texts, we see a significantly different notion of anthropomorphism from that presented by Eichrodt. (1) Hebrew Bible anthropomorphism is clearly not determinative of nor limited to the personhood of God in its Christian formulation, nor does it necessarily designate God's closeness (see, e.g., Jer 23:24–25).[36] (2) Anthropomorphism is not confined to immanent conceptions of the divine. Rather, as has been argued time and again, anthropomorphism occurs also in portrayals of God as transcendent, in heaven (e.g., 1 Kgs 22:19–23; Isa 6; Ezek 1; Ps 33:13–15).[37] Therefore, (3) anthropomorphism cannot threaten the transcendence of God, mainly because, as a metaphoric device, anthropomorphic imagery may be and is used to construct both conceptions: that of divine immanence and that of divine transcendence (and other conceptions of God as well).[38]

Anthropomorphic language used in eighth- and sixth-century BCE literature does not square with the paradigm set in Eichrodt's discussion (or in many similar scholarly studies), that is, with the notion of a linear development in the conceptualization of God, from concrete to abstract, from a close God to a distant and remote one, from a conception of imma-

---

Were Men": The Embodied God in Biblical and Near Eastern Literature, BZAW 384 (Berlin: de Gruyter, 2008), 26–64.

36. See Eilert Herms's discussion of "Person" in *Religion Past and Present*, ed. Hans Dieter Betz et al., 14 vols. (Leiden: Brill, 2012), 9:730–35, esp. 734–35; and Ulrich H. J. Körtner, "Anthropomorphism: VI. Dogmatics," in Betz et al., *Religion Past and Present*, 1:262; and the discussions of "transcendence and immanence" by various authors (Niels H. Gregersen, Johann Figl, Michael Steinmann, Christian Danz, Birgit Recki), who all articulated their positions in opposition to Kant and his philosophy, of the eighteenth century (12:62–68).

37. Hamori established separate categories of "immanent anthropomorphism" and "transcendent anthropomorphism" ("Varieties of Anthropomorphism," 26–32). Typologically, however, I would argue that there is no difference between these anthropomorphic descriptions; that is, God may be represented as both immanent and transcendent by anthropomorphic metaphors. It seems that this distinction is only relevant in relation to counter *scholarly* presuppositions (and very Christian ones), such as those of Eichrodt's discussed here (*Theology*, 1:206–27, see esp. 206–10, and 212–14).

38. The *Gottesbild* and its implications for the *Gottesvorstellung* in Mesopotamia, Ugarit, and Israel were discussed by Manfried Dietrich and Oswald Loretz in *"Jahwe und seine Aschera": Anthropomorphes Kultbild in Mesopotamien, Ugarit, und Israel, Das biblische Bilderverbort*, UBL 9 (Darmstadt: Ugarit, 1992), 1–6, 183–88.

nence to one of transcendence. In fact, spirituality in Eichrodt's sense of abstraction is not a Hebrew Bible concept.

Alternatively, I would say that the Hebrew Bible literature of the eighth to sixth centuries, however, demonstrates the alertness of different authors (at times relatively synchronic) to diverse literary options for describing God in ways that almost touch upon pictorial-iconic anthropomorphism (see, e.g., Isa 6:1–3; Ezek 1:24–26, in contrast to Jer 1:4–10), but these authors differ in their perceptions of the limits and restrictions that may be applied to the literary portrayal of God.[39]

To illustrate my point, I will focus on a well-known set of examples: God's revelation by a vision or by voice in three prophets' commission prophecies (Isa 6; Ezek 1; Jer 1:4–10). The use of anthropomorphisms in the Hebrew Bible in general, and in prophetic literature in particular, is not unified or one-dimensional; the opposite is closer to the truth. Isaiah son of Amoz saw God sitting on his throne in the temple; the skirts of his robe filled the temple (is it a heavenly temple or the earthly one?), and he was surrounded by seraphs who covered him (or themselves? Isa 6:2) and proclaimed God's universal majesty (Isa 6:3).[40] It is intriguing that even

---

39. From a different angle altogether, Kirsten Nielsen argues that the mixture of personal and impersonal metaphors for God in one context is the best proclamation of his transcendence of the human personalization represented by anthropomorphism ("Metaphors and Biblical Theology," in *Metaphor in the Hebrew Bible*, ed. Pierre van Hecke, BETL 187 [Leuven: Leuven University Press and Peeters, 2005], 263–73). While Nielsen, of course, admits that the root metaphors are those she categorizes as "personal metaphors," the metaphors of God as king, father, shepherd, etc., the variety of metaphors for God in themselves make a theological statement. In Nielsen's formulation, "God is more and God is different," a fact that comes to the fore in the variety of metaphors needed to portray the different aspects of God's activity. While the personal metaphors bear the task of representing the relationship between God and human beings, the impersonal metaphors, according to Nielsen, perform the special function of "reminding us that there is more to be said about God than just saying that God is like a human. God transcends the boundaries of human life" (264, and see 265, 268.) For Nielsen, the challenge of biblical theology is to find the combination of (or the balance between) both, to assure that the result does not imply any identification of God with "anything else" following Exod 20:4.

40. Samuel D. Luzzatto, aligned with traditional interpretation and in analogy with Ezek 1:11, argued that the seraphs covered themselves in awe of God (see also Rashi, Qimhi, Ibn Ezra, and others); yet Luzzatto did recognize that "if it had not been for Ezekiel, it might have been interpreted as the Seraphs that cover God's face and feet with their wings," so that the divine would not be seen" (*Isaiah*, repr. ed. [Tel

in this most anthropomorphic presentation, there is no real description
of God that can be translated into a pictorial presentation, and I consider this syntactical vagueness concerning the details to be intentional.[41]
Ezekiel 1:26–28 puts forth a different presentation of God's theophany.
It portrays God in both human terms, דמות כמראה אדם ("There was the
semblance of a human form," 1:26), and as remote, above the expanse
of the heavens. Of even more significance is that, although two human
body parts are mentioned in the description, no further specific physical details are given; on the contrary, those two parts are characterized
as כמראה אש ("what looked like a fire," 1:27a and b), surrounded by
radiance (ונגה לו סביב, 1:27).[42] Finally, Jeremiah's call (1:4–10) was of

---

Aviv: Dvir, 1970], 62–64). Brevard S. Childs referred to this anthropomorphic scenery
that transforms the Jerusalem temple into a heavenly one and argued that the seraphs
cover themselves to keep themselves from seeing God so that they can serve God
properly in "worship and praise" (*Isaiah*, OTL [Louisville: Westminster John Knox,
2001], 55). John D. W. Watts (*Isaiah 1–33*, WBC 24 [Waco, TX: Word, 1985], 73–74)
and Christopher S. Seitz (*Isaiah 1–39*, IBC [Louisville: John Knox, 1993], 54) had earlier argued along similar lines. Hamori referred to this scene as transcendent anthropomorphism ("Varieties of Anthropomorphism," 26–32).

41. Vagueness in the description of the scene characterizes the Aramaic Targum
and the Masoretic accentuations to Isa 6:2–3. This is followed by medieval Jewish commentators; see Luzatto, *Isaiah*, 62–63; Otto Kaiser, *Isaiah 1–12*, trans. R. A. Wilson,
OTL (Philadelphia: Westminster, 1972), 74–75. Kaiser notes that "the prophet does
not actually describe Yahweh himself" (74).

42. See Moshe Greenberg, *Ezekiel 1–20*, AB 22 (New York: Doubleday, 1983),
50–51. Greenberg further argues that the meaning of "like the appearance of" designates exactness (the *opposite* of vagueness), which "does not signify a reservation with
respect to looks but with respect to substance" (52–53). He bases his argument on Judg
13:6 and claims that this accurate anthropomorphism was allowed in a vision. The
combination of the diverse modes in describing the divine appearance symbolizes,
according to Greenberg, "powerfully, and in concentrated form, God's support of and
intimate presence with the prophet" (54, and see 80–81). Compare to Walther Eichrodt, *Ezekiel*, trans. Cosslett Quin, OTL (Philadelphia: Westminster, 1970), 58–59.
Eichrodt quite briefly mentions that "of the figure to be perceived upon the throne we
get only a vague outline. Isaiah, too, shows a similar restraint in his description" (58).
In reference to Ezekiel 8–11, Eichrodt argues that "the imagery of the vision in Ezek.
I made it possible to regard the object standing in the holy of holies as a mere out-
ward shadow of a transcendental reality, the doxa of which was not touched by earthly
catastrophes, but could, when the temple was destroyed, be taken up into the heavenly
sphere" (116–17). Joseph Blenkinsopp presents a pious Christian perspective on God
"in humanity's image" (*Ezekiel*, IBC [Louisville: John Knox, 1990], 22–23).

an audial character (1:4). But could that still be considered a sign of an abstraction, when at the crucial moment the hand of God touches the prophet's lips (1:9)?[43]

Furthermore, these three texts call for another comment on the divine personhood and closeness that each of the three prophets feels upon his commission, although they portray God as transcendent and/or imminent. The intimacy of God's relationship with Jeremiah may be seen in the dialogue between them (1:4–10) and in the image of God's hand putting the divine words into the prophet's mouth (1:9). Isaiah son of Amoz and Ezekiel each use anthropomorphic language related to the metaphor of God as king (Isa 6:2–3; Ezek 1:26–28), and each in his own way emphasizes his intimate closeness to that transcendent yet immanent God, of whom they become the messengers (Isa 6:5–13; Ezek 1:28; 8). In his "visions of God" in Jerusalem (Ezek 8–11), Ezekiel first portrays God as immanent in his house, but then God leaves the temple to stand on the eastern mountain (Ezek 10; 11:23). Throughout the passage God is dynamic in his presence: he can be both in Babylon and instantly thereafter in Jerusalem, riding in his cosmic chariot (8:1–4; 11:22–24). But this is also the God who takes the prophet and shows him the abominations of Jerusalem through the closest and most personal contact (8:5–17).

The point I am trying to make is that each of these three prophetic books (the prophets and/or their followers) seems to be negotiating the "proper" way to describe God in anthropomorphic terms. Each searches and finds its own way of doing it, but when carefully read, they all hide more than they reveal. Jeremiah is no less concrete, or no more abstract, in his usage of anthropomorphic languages than Ezekiel or any other of their contemporaries.[44]

---

43. The question of anthropomorphism is rarely referred to in reference to Jer 1:9, while scholars do address the more general question of whether it was an audial or a visual theophany. See William McKane, *Jeremiah I–XXV*, ICC (Edinburgh: T&T Clark, 1986), 9–10; Jack R. Lundbom, *Jeremiah 1–20*, AB 21A (New York: Doubleday, 1999), 234, 236–37; compare to Isa 6:7 and see Ezek 2:8–9. For a broader discussion, see Walther Zimmerli, "Visionary Experience in Jeremiah," in *Israel's Prophetic Tradition: Essays in Honour of Peter R. Ackroyd*, ed. R. Coggins, A. Phillips, and M. Knibb (Cambridge: Cambridge University Press, 1982), 95–118.

44. I would apply this observation to the entire collection of conceptions of God in Jeremiah, as I do not see signs of abstraction in any of them, counter to Moshe Weinfeld; see, for instance, Weinfeld, "Jeremiah and the Spiritual Metamorphosis in Israel," *ZAW* 88 (1976): 17–56. This is not to deny distinctions between Jeremiah and

The differences between the three prophets in reference to their portrayal of God may be defined along the iconic/anti-iconic spectrum in
their literary expression. Isaiah son of Amoz and Ezekiel portray only in
very general lines a picture that is close (but clearly not similar) to iconographic anthropomorphism. It may be plausibly surmised that, due to
the similarity of the anthropomorphic verbal description to a perceptible
image, this verbal description has been modified by each of the prophecies
so as to portray only very general, partial, or remote images; however, they
all describe God in anthropomorphic terms, even if behind a thick veil.
Jeremiah clearly refrains from describing God as appearing before him
as a full human image, and in this he differs from the prophets who pre-
ceded him: Amos (7:7; 9:1), Isaiah son of Amoz (6), Ezekiel (1; 8–11; 43),
and especially Moses (i.e., Exod 33:12–23), who in many respects served
as a model for Jeremiah.[45] The way Jeremiah chooses to portray God is
anti-iconic in that it suggests only a fragmentary description. But Jeremiah
does use both physical and mental anthropomorphisms and references to
different spheres of human activity (such as the hand of God in Jer 1:9).
Thus it would be more accurate to define Jeremiah's attitude as an example
of an anti-iconic tendency that restricts even literary descriptions. But Jeremiah's reservations concerning a fully anthropomorphic representation
of God (even in words) are not equivalent to a rejection of anthropomorphism altogether, to an abstract concept of God, or to a tendency toward
transcendence and away from immanence; rather, all these are better
understood as expressions of a rejection of iconism.

To recapitulate: the textual evidence of the Hebrew Bible allows us
to distinguish the *theological* conceptions of God's immanence and transcendence from the *literary* device of anthropomorphic metaphor used to
represent both. If we keep this distinction in view, the usage of anthropomorphism need not be seen as compromising either of the two theological
conceptions; rather, anthropomorphic language appears to function in the

---

Ezekiel in the other areas Weinfeld mentioned, but I would challenge the spirituality
dimension with which Weinfeld characterized Jeremiah.

45. See William L. Holladay, "Jeremiah and Moses: Further Observations," *JBL* 85
(1966): 17–27. The avoidance of an actual vision of God (contrast with Num 12:6–8)
might be due to the clear hierarchical distinction Jeremiah sets between Moses and
himself. Vision and visionaries are for Jeremiah among the denigrated traits of the
"peace prophets" (Jer 23:16); and so he himself treats dreamers (23:25, etc.). This of
course counters Num 12:6; and other prophetic legitimate activity.

work of different biblical authors as a way of capturing not only God's transcendence and immanence but also the qualities of his sovereignty, justice, and so on.[46]

The theological problem of anthropomorphism, in Eichrodt's framework, arises precisely because of its place in the *theological* conceptual construct, built from certain Christian conceptions of spirituality, personhood, transcendence, and immanence, through which Eichrodt read the Hebrew Bible texts. With the construct gone, the problem might be redefined and differently solved.

Let me phrase the problem more specifically. To call attention to a theological term that does not work in relation to Hebrew Bible texts, and is clearly Christian, is an important step, and it has been done in studies of anthropomorphism, iconism and aniconism, and metaphorical God-talk. But raising scholars' awareness does not automatically mean that these terms have either been expunged from the scholarly lexicon or modified in a way more suitable for the scholarly discussions of Hebrew Bible texts and their theological messages. Eichrodt, among other Christian biblical theologians, has established the framework for the discussion of Old Testament theology with his string of four terms. Although our senses have indeed been sharpened to sense supersessionist arguments and our understandings of anthropomorphism have been refined, the terminology that connects anthropomorphism with immanence over against transcendence (and perhaps sees them on a linear trajectory of evolution) is still very much alive in scholarship. The grave problem is that these terms oftentimes do not work with the Hebrew Bible texts and with their conceptual world.

To conclude this discussion, I would advance the question, or actually the great challenge, of critically reevaluating the terminology used in our Hebrew Bible theological studies. From my point of view, as a Hebrew Bible scholar who reads Christian theology as well, this problem of terminology is a troubling one. In fact, this problem is related to that of the undefined boundaries between the Hebrew Bible and subsequent Jewish and Christian literatures and traditions. I hope, though, that both Jewish and Christian scholars will at least begin to reevaluate the very basic ter-

---

46. As Eichrodt argued, abstract notions of God are not Hebrew Bible notions at all. The nonbiblical origin of abstract conceptions of God was discussed also by Yehezkel Kaufmann in *Toledot ha'emunah hayisra'elit* [Hebrew], 4 vols. (Jerusalem: Bialik: 1956), 1:221, 226, 229.

minological conventions we all use and ask to what extent these terms are relevant to and valid for a critical discussion of the Hebrew Bible texts.

4. Summary and Suggestions for a Jewish Hebrew Bible Theology

In light of this exploration of but two of the many problems that ought to be confronted in order to conduct Hebrew Bible theology, the question that arises is: Are there positive possibilities for conducting Hebrew Bible theology? My following comments may seem as no more than an idiosyncratic formulation of one approach to Hebrew Bible theology; I fully accept this categorization, realizing that all of us are still searching for the correct goal, methodology, and so on, but I hope that the benefits of this direction may be appreciated.[47]

As I define my own goals for a Tanak theology, I prefer to remain with the descriptive questions: What *did* it mean (to them)? Even more specifically: What did *they* (the ancient authors) say about *their* God? My critical interest in Hebrew Bible theology is with the ancient thought, restricted to the Tanak as my corpus, self-contained as it is, studied from a critical-descriptive point of view that utilizes philological tools to read the Hebrew Bible and comparative methodologies to tap its ancient Near Eastern counterparts, maintaining clear distinctions from later Jewish or Christian traditions.

I have not set my goal as that of writing a comprehensive theology of the Hebrew Bible in its entirety; on the contrary, in *Theodical Discourse*, I have chosen to focus on one fairly limited period of time and only on the sources that directly address the political crises of the Babylonian destruction of Judah. These dramatic events of destruction and dislocation during the Neo-Babylonian period, occurring primarily in the first half of the sixth century BCE, gave rise to a rich theological deliberation among different authors in Hebrew Bible literature, within the historiographical writings, the prophetical corpus, and the poetry (for example, 2 Kings, Jeremiah, Ezekiel, selected Psalms, and Lamentations).

Methodologically I am interested in describing phenomenologically these texts' theological world of thought—identifying the topics in each text and articulating the texts' different perspectives, including more subtly expressed ones. Hence, methodologically this study seeks a middle way

---

47. Tsevat, "Theology of the Old Testament," 33–34.

between history of religion and philosophy of religion. It may be structured over synchronic and diachronic courses (as for instance, reflecting the early sixth-century BCE theology within roughly contemporaneous polemics, on the one hand, and taking the entire sixth—and possibly the fifth—century with its literary and theological developments, on the other hand), but it tries to avoid superimposition of later postbiblical ideas.

The plurality of voices must be examined within the Hebrew Bible itself. As Rolf Knierim, Jon D. Levenson, Walter Brueggemann, and many others have argued, the Hebrew Bible in itself (even without the polydoxy of Judaism) reflects a great multivocal theological deliberation concerning God and his roles in relation to the individual, to the people Israel, to the nations, and to the entire created world.[48] There seems not to be a pan-biblical organizing system, but there is a clear organizing hierarchy of themes that I would incorporate into any general or partial study of Hebrew Bible theology. This hierarchy, I suggest, is based on the metaphoric-anthropomorphic portrayal of God as king, in his different roles.[49] In my own project on sixth-century BCE conceptions of God, I have located three distinct theological approaches to God and his actions—justification, doubt, and protest—and I use them as categories (of both form and theme) broad enough to encompass the entire theological picture of the talk to and about God, which becomes quite complicated. The use of these three categories facilitates the study as a study from within and reveals a lively, relatively contemporaneous theological discourse along the Neo-Babylonian period and the early Persian one.

---

48. See Rolf P. Knierim, *The Task of Old Testament Theology: Substance, Method, and Cases* (Grand Rapids: Eerdmans, 1995), 1–20, esp. 1–2, 5: "The Old Testament contains a plurality of theologies.… The theological problem of the Old Testament does not arise from the separate existence of its particular theologies. It arises from their coexistence. The coexistence of these theologies in the Old Testament demands the interpretation of their relationship or correspondence, a task that is more than and different from the interpretation of each of them in its own right, which is done in historical exegesis—if exegesis does its work." Walter Brueggemann has written extensively on this polyphony; see his major contribution in *Theology of the Old Testament: Testimony, Dispute, Advocacy* (Minneapolis: Fortress, 1997), esp. 713–20.

49. Compare to Goshen-Gottstein, who suggested that specific themes and concepts should be investigated in Tanak theology, such as land, Sabbath, the people of Israel, collective-national salvation, and Temple ("Tanakh Theology," 630); I prefer to initiate my own study by looking at the major characteristic of the theological discourse: the talk to and about God.

I employ Goshen-Gottstein's initial distinctions on Tanak theology, together with the different programmatic statements of Tsevat, Barr, and Collins on the task of Hebrew Bible(/Old Testament) theology and Knierim's practical suggestions on how to recognize the plurality and its internal organization.[50] Thus I have learned from both Jewish and Christian scholars, and I basically accept the clear point of departure Tsevat articulated: that this type of study of the theology of the Hebrew Bible (Old Testament, for Tsevat) is part and parcel of the literary-philological study of the Hebrew Bible.

In distinction from Tsevat, however, I designate my study as a Jewish Hebrew Bible theology, Jewish in the fact that it is not Christian in its presuppositions. Indeed, the *Jewish* component functions here primarily as a counterdefinition, adding if I may, a seventh "contrastive notion" to the six James Barr listed, when he argued that "'Biblical theology' is essentially a *contrastive* notion."[51] By this, Barr meant that the designation *biblical theology* "came to be used in contrast with various other modes of studying the Bible that already existed. Thus it does not have clear independent contours of its own: it depends for its existence upon that with which it is contrasted."

I therefore suggest that a descriptive Jewish Hebrew Bible theology, which in itself possesses some of the features that Barr attributed to biblical theology overall, should be constructed as a contrastive discipline to Christian biblical theology. This contrastive task is not at all easy to frame. The two discussions brought here (the borders of Hebrew Bible theology and the terminology) illustrate some of those struggles for identity that seem to require a contextualized Jewish Hebrew Bible theology. As I have conceived the issues, it is necessary first to contend with models such as Sommer's conception of Jewish dialogical biblical theology, that is, to clarify and maintain the distinction between *constructive* Jewish dialogical biblical theology and *descriptive* Hebrew Bible theology. It is perhaps even more important to deal with Christian Hebrew Bible interpreters and interpretations in relation to the problem of terminology. A

---

50. See Barr, *Concept of Biblical Theology*, 4, 74; John J. Collins, "Is a Critical Biblical Theology Possible?," in *The Hebrew Bible and Its Interpreters*, ed. William Henry Propp, Baruch Halpern, and David Noel Freedman (Winona Lake, IN: Eisenbrauns, 1990), 1–17, esp. 9; Knierim, *Task of Old Testament Theology*, 1–2, 5; Tsevat, "Theology of the Old Testament," 48–49.

51. See Barr, *Concept of Biblical Theology*, 5–6 and the full discussion through p. 17.

Jewish Hebrew Bible theology needs to address the basic terms and conceptions we use and to reformulate them by means of a sensitive reading of Hebrew Bible texts on their own terms, released from their long histories of theological interpretation in relation to later documents, be they Jewish or Christian.

In this respect, a descriptive Hebrew Bible theology should be an integral part of the modern academic critical study of the Hebrew Bible yet remain a unique branch of study within historical-critical research. More than in other spheres of study of the Hebrew Bible, this is the one domain where a clear divide exists (which, to my mind, should not be underestimated) between Christian and Jewish scholars and their respective scholarship.

Bibliography

Barr, James. *The Concept of Biblical Theology: An Old Testament Perspective*. Minneapolis: Fortress, 1999.

Blenkinsopp, Joseph. *Ezekiel*. IBC. Louisville: John Knox, 1990.

Brettler, Marc Z. "Biblical History and Jewish Biblical Theology." *JR* 77 (1997): 563–83.

———. *God Is King: Understanding an Israelite Metaphor*. JSOTSup 76. Sheffield: Sheffield Academic, 1989.

———. "The Metaphorical Mapping of God in the Hebrew Bible." Pages 219–32 in *Canon, and Community: Jewish, Christian, and Islamic Approaches*. Edited by Ralph Bisschops and James Francis. Bern: Lang, 1999.

———. "Psalms and Jewish Biblical Theology." Pages 187–98 in *Jewish Bible Theology: Perspectives and Case Studies*. Edited by Isaac Kalimi. Winona Lake, IN: Eisenbrauns, 2012.

Brueggemann, Walter. *Theology of the Old Testament: Testimony, Dispute, Advocacy*. Minneapolis: Fortress, 1997.

Childs, Brevard S. *Isaiah*. OTL. Louisville: Westminster John Knox, 2001.

Collins, John J. "Is a Critical Biblical Theology Possible?" Pages 1–17 in *The Hebrew Bible and Its Interpreters*. Edited by William Henry Propp, Baruch Halpern, and David Noel Freedman. Winona Lake, IN: Eisenbrauns, 1990.

Dietrich, Manfried, and Oswald Loretz. *"Jahwe und seine Aschera": Anthropomorphes Kultbild in Mesopotamien, Ugarit, und Israel, Das biblische Bilderverbort*. UBL 9. Darmstadt: Ugarit, 1992.

Eichrodt, Walther. *Ezekiel.* Translated by Cosslett Quin. OTL. Philadelphia: Westminster, 1970.

———. *Theology of the Old Testament.* Vol. 1. Translated by J. A. Baker. OTL. Philadelphia: Westminster; London: SCM, 1961.

Frank, Daniel. "The Limits of Karaite Scripturalism: Problems in Narrative Exegesis." Pages *41–82 in *A Word Fitly Spoken: Studies in Medieval Exegesis of the Hebrew Bible and the Qur'an Presented to Haggai Ben-Shammai.* Edited by Meir M. Bar-Asher, Simon Hopkins, Sarah Stroumsa, and Bruno Chiesa. Jerusalem: The Ben Zvi Institute, 2007.

Frankel, David. *The Land of Canaan and the Destiny of Israel: Theologies of Territory in the Hebrew Bible.* Siphrut 4. Winona Lake, IN: Eisenbrauns, 2011.

Goshen-Gottstein, Moshe. "Jewish Biblical Theology and the Study of Biblical Religion." *Tarbiz* 50 (1980): 37–64.

———. "Tanakh Theology: The Religion of the Old Testament and the Place of Jewish Biblical Theology." Pages 617–44 in *Ancient Israelite Religion: Essays in Honor of F. M. Cross.* Edited by Patrick D. Miller, Paul D. Hanson, S. Dean McBride. Philadelphia: Fortress, 1987.

Greenberg, Moshe. *Ezekiel 1–20.* AB 22. New York: Doubleday, 1983

———. *On the Bible and Judaism: A Collection of Writings.* Tel Aviv: Am Oved, 1984.

Hamori, Esther J. "Varieties of Anthropomorphism." Pages 26–64 in *"When Gods Were Men": The Embodied God in Biblical and Near Eastern Literature.* BZAW 384. Berlin: de Gruyter, 2008.

Haran, Menahem. *The Biblical Collection: Its Consolidation to the End of the Second Temple Times and Changes of Form to the End of the Middle Ages* [Hebrew]. Jerusalem: Bialik and Magnes, 1996.

Hartshorne, Charles. "Transcendence and Immanence." *Encyclopedia of Religion* 15 (1985): 16–21.

Hasel, Gerhard F. *Old Testament Theology: Basic Issues in the Current Debate.* Grand Rapids: Eerdmans, 1972.

Herms, Eilert. "Person." Pages 9:730–35 in *Religion Past & Present.* Edited by Hans Dieter Betz, Don S. Browning, Bernd Janowski, and Eberhard Jiingel. 14 vols. Leiden: Brill, 2012.

Holladay, William L. "Jeremiah and Moses: Further Observations." *JBL* 85 (1966): 17–27.

Kaiser, Otto. *Isaiah 1–12.* Translated by R. A. Wilson. OTL. Philadelphia: Westminster, 1972.

Kalimi, Isaac. *Early Jewish Exegesis and Theological Controversy: Studies in Scriptures in the Shadow of Internal and External Controversies.* JCHS 2. Assen: Royal van Gorcum, 2002.

———. "History of Israelite Religion or Hebrew Bible/Old Testament Theology? Jewish Interest in Biblical Theology." *JSOT* 11 (1997): 100–123.

Kaufmann, Yehezkel. *Toledot ha'emunah hayisra'elit* [Hebrew]. 4 vols. Jerusalem: Bialik: 1956.

Knierim, Rolf P. *The Task of Old Testament Theology: Substance, Method, and Cases.* Grand Rapids: Eerdmans, 1995.

Körtner, Ulrich H. J. "Anthropomorphism: VI. Dogmatics." Page 1:262 in *Religion Past & Present.* Edited by Hans Dieter Betz, Don S. Browning, Bernd Janowski, and Eberhard Jiingel. 14 vols. Leiden: Brill, 2012.

Levenson, Jon D. "Why Jews Are Not Interested in Biblical Theology." Pages 33–61 in *The Hebrew Bible, the Old Testament, and Historical Criticism: Jews and Christians in Biblical Studies.* Louisville: Westminster John Knox, 1993.

Løland, Hanne. *Silent or Salient Gender? The Interpretation of Gendered God-Language in the Hebrew Bible, Exemplified in Isaiah 42, 46, and 49.* Tübingen: Mohr Siebeck, 2009.

Lundbom, Jack R. *Jeremiah 1–20.* AB 21A. New York: Doubleday, 1999.

Luzzatto, Samuel D. *Isaiah.* Repr. ed. Tel Aviv: Dvir, 1970.

McKane, William. *Jeremiah I–XXV.* ICC. Edinburgh: T&T Clark, 1986.

Mettinger, Tryggve N. D. "The Study of the Gottesbild—Problems and Suggestions." *SEÅ* 54 (1989): 135–45.

Nielsen, Kirsten. "Metaphors and Biblical Theology." Pages 263–73 in *Metaphor in the Hebrew Bible.* Edited by Pierre van Hecke. BETL 187. Leuven: Leuven University Press and Peeters, 2005.

Oeming, Manfred. *Gesamt biblische Theologien der Gegenwart: Das Verhältnis von AT und New Testament in der hermeneutischen Diskussion seit Gerhard von Rad.* 2nd ed. Stuttgart: Kohlammer, 1987.

Olsson, Tord. "Gudsbild, talsituation och literature genre." *AFLR* 16 (1983): 91–109.

———. "Gudsbildens gestaltning: literäre kategorier och religiös tro." *SRA* 1 (1985): 42–63.

Pannenberg, Wolfhart. "Problems in a Theology of (Only) the Old Testament." Pages 275–80 in *Problems in Biblical Theology: Essays in Honor of Rolf Knierim.* Edited by Henry T. C. Sun and Keith L. Eades. Grand Rapids: Eerdmans, 1997.

Polliak, Meirah. "The Karaite Inversion of 'Written' and 'Oral' Torah in Relation to the Islamic Arch-Models of Qur'an and Hadith." *JSQ* 22 (2015): 243–302.

Pyper, Hugh S. "Person." Pages 532–33 in *The Oxford Companion to Christian Thought: Intellectual, Spiritual, and Moral Horizons of Christianity.* Edited by Adrian Hastings, Alistair Mason, and Hugh Pyper. Oxford: Oxford University Press, 2000.

Rad, Gerhard von. *Old Testament Theology.* Translated by David M. G. Stalker. Edinburgh: Harper Collins, 1962.

Rendtorff, Rolf. *Canon and Theology.* Translated and edited by Margaret Kohl. OOTT. Minneapolis: Fortress, 1993.

———. "A Christian Approach to the Theology of Hebrew Scriptures." Pages 137–51 in *Jews, Christians, and the Theology of the Hebrew Scriptures.* Edited by Alice Ogden Bellis and Joel S. Kaminsky. Atlanta: Society of Biblical Literature, 2000.

Reumann, John. "Introduction: Whither Biblical Theology?" Pages 1–31 in *The Promise and Practice of Biblical Theology.* Minneapolis: Fortress, 1991.

———. *The Promise and Practice of Biblical Theology.* Minneapolis: Fortress, 1991.

Rom-Shiloni, Dalit. *God in Times of Destruction and Exiles: Tanak (Hebrew Bible) Theology* [Hebrew]. Jerusalem: Magnes, 2009.

Seitz, Christopher S. *Isaiah 1–39.* IBC. Louisville: John Knox, 1993.

Smith, Ralph L. *Old Testament Theology: Its History, Method, and Message.* Nashville: Broadman & Holman: 1993.

Sommer, Benjamin D. "Dialogical Biblical Theology: A Jewish Approach to Reading Scripture Theologically." Pages 1–53 in *Biblical Theology: Introducing the Conversation.* Edited by Leo G. Perdue, Robert Morgan, and Benjamin D. Sommer. Nashville: Abingdon, 2009.

Sweeney, Marvin A. *Tanak: A Theological and Critical Introduction to the Jewish Bible.* Minneapolis: Fortress, 2012.

———. "Tanakh versus Old Testament: Concerning the Foundation for a Jewish Theology of the Bible." Pages 353–72 in *Problems in Biblical Theology: Essays in Honor of Rolf Knierim.* Edited by Henry T. C. Sun and Keith L. Eades. Grand Rapids: Eerdmans, 1997.

———. "Why Jews Should be Interested in Biblical Theology." *CCAR* 44 (1997): 67–75.

Tsevat, Matitiahu. "Theology of the Old Testament: A Jewish View." *HBT* 8 (1986): 33–50.

Watts, John D. W. *Isaiah 1–33*. WBC 24. Waco, TX: Word, 1985.

Weinfeld, Moshe. "Jeremiah and the Spiritual Metamorphosis in Israel." *ZAW* 88 (1976): 17–56.

Zevit, Ziony. "Jewish Biblical Theology: Whence? Why? Whither?" *HUCA* 76 (2005): 289–340.

Zimmerli, Walther. "Visionary Experience in Jeremiah." Pages 95–118 in *Israel's Prophetic Tradition: Essays in Honour of Peter R. Ackroyd*. Edited by Richard Coggins, Anthony Phillips, and Michael Knibb. Cambridge: Cambridge University Press, 1982.

Beyond Dialogue:
Toward a Dialectical Model of Theology of the Hebrew Scripture/Old Testament

Wonil Kim

Susan Niditch rightly observes that "the particular violence of the Hebrew Scriptures has inspired violence, has served as a model of and model for persecution, subjugation, and extermination for millennia beyond its own reality."[1] Michael Prior bemoans the fact that "the ethnocentric, xenophobic and militaristic character of the biblical narratives of Israelite origins is treated in conventional biblical scholarship as if it were above any questioning on moral grounds, *even by criteria derived from other parts of the Bible*" (emphasis added).[2] Niditch's and Prior's piercing and riveting observations challenge us to articulate a clear and responsible method for biblical theology.

A canon of the Hebrew Bible/Old Testament *functions* as a normative literature. It has so functioned for millennia. It should therefore not surprise us that, despite the persistent and influential trajectory of the descriptive school for the last two centuries, the voices of the constructive/

---

1. Quote from Susan Niditch, *War in the Hebrew Bible: A Study in the Ethics of Violence* (Oxford: Oxford University Press, 1993), 4. See also Michael Prior, "A Land Flowing with Milk, Honey, and People (the Lattey Lecture 1997)," *Spring Britain* 28 (1998): 11; John J. Collins, "The Zeal of Phinehas: The Bible and the Legitimation of Violence," *JBL* 122 (2003): 3–21. There has been a plethora of publications on the topic of violence in the Bible in recent years. Some of the representative works include: Brad Kelle and Frank Ames, eds., *Writing and Reading War: Rhetoric, Gender, and Ethics in Biblical and Modern Contexts* (Atlanta: Society of Biblical Literature, 2008); Jerome F. D. Creach, *Violence in Scripture: Resources for the Use of Scripture in the Church* (Louisville: Westminster John Knox Press, 2013); James Crenshaw, *Defending God: Biblical Responses to the Problem of Evil* (Oxford: Oxford University Press, 2005).

2. Prior, "Land Flowing with Milk, Honey, and People."

normative school have been equally unrelenting. Thus Walter Brueggemann tells us that "one reason for [writing his *Theology of the Old Testament*] is to consider whether we are in a cultural, epistemological circumstance that may permit a rearticulation of the grounds for facing the normative-descriptive issue."[3]

But as Brueggemann's book shows, like Rolf Knierim's work a few years before him, the normative question no longer revolves just around the positive influence of the Hebrew Bible/Old Testament.[4] Leo Perdue does not mince words as he insists that "to sit back in silence [as a pure descriptionist] is to countenance the demonic behavior of racists, sexist, homophobes, militarists, terrorists, and fascists to which an unchallenged Bible, theology, and worldview ultimately lead."[5] It now appears that that future agenda for the Hebrew Bible/Old Testament theology will have to take this phenomenon of negative norms fully into account.

Excursus: Any discussion of *canon* would be incomplete without addressing the difference between the Tanak and the Old Testament and the ramifications this difference entails, especially in view of the increased participation by the Jewish scholars in biblical interpretation in recent decades. Marvin A. Sweeney welcomes this development as "one of the most foundational examples" of "the major advances in biblical studies and theology" that is characterized by "the inclusion of a diversity of voices in the field."[6] Yet, as Sweeney observes, "recognition of the hermeneutical significance of a distinctive form of the Jewish Bible known as the Tanak is rarely taken into account, as most scholars are trained to think of biblical interpretation only in relation to single books, texts within a book, or segments of scripture. But rarely are modern scholars prompted to ask 'what is the meaning of the whole.' "[7]

---

3. Walter Brueggemann, *Theology of the Old Testament: Testimony, Dispute, Advocacy* (Minneapolis: Augsburg, 1997), 20.

4. Rolf P. Knierim, *Task of Old Testament Theology: Substance, Method, and Cases* (Grand Rapids: Eerdmans, 1995). Knierim in fact hit the problem of normativity head on in this work.

5. Leo Perdue, *Reconstructing Old Testament Theology* (Minneapolis: Fortress, 2005), 340–52, quote at 351.

6. Marvin A. Sweeney, "Biblical Theology in Canonical Perspective: Jewish and Christian Models" (paper presented at the Society of Biblical Literature Annual Meeting, San Antonio, 2016), 1.

7. Sweeney, "Biblical Theology in Canonical Perspective," 2.

Given that "canonical structure plays an important role ... [in determining] the perspectives that interpreters bring to bear in their interpretation," he calls for a critical examination of "the canonical forms of scripture, both Christian and Jewish, to identify their distinctive theological viewpoints and their roles in shaping the ways in which Christians and Jews read scripture." Most significantly, the linear, historical, progressive model of Christian biblical hermeneutics contrasts sharply with the Tanak's "cyclical pattern that entails a statement of ideals in Torah, a portrayal of the disruption of those ideals in the Nevi'im, and a presentation of the potential restoration of those ideals in Ketuvim."[8]

Sweeney notes that, while "Christian interpreters have begun to recognize the implications of [the Christian linear-historical-progressive] model for supersessionist theological perspectives in which Jews are pushed aside as unfaithful obstacles to the recognition of the full plan of divine revelation and love in a suffering world," most of them have done little more than change terminologies and acknowledge the eternal divine covenant with Judaism as being parallel with the Christian model, and "the canonical problem of the interrelationship between the Old Testament and the New Testament has not been fully resolved."[9]

The question of a canon's *normative* function becomes more complex and difficult when this unresolved issue persists unaddressed. The two different canonical structures indeed portray nothing less than a conflict of two radically different worldviews with inevitable consequences for the normative task in canonical context. Even Rolf Rendtorff 's admirable attempt to find a common hermeneutical ground for the two traditions does not succeed in addressing the issue with a full recognition of this fundamental difference.[10] Much work remains to be done to tackle this long-overlooked problem, the results of which could immensely enrich the discourse.

Equally significant, and corollary to the issue just discussed, is the bearing the Shoah has on the normative discourse. To the extent that this deplorable calamity "points to the need to rethink traditional concepts

---

8. Sweeney, "Biblical Theology in Canonical Perspective," 5. See also Rolf P. Knierim, "Cosmos and History in Israel's Theology," in *Task of Old Testament Theology*, 171–224.

9. Sweeney, "Biblical Theology in Canonical Perspective," 8–9.

10. Rolf Rendtorff, *The Canonical Hebrew Bible: A Theology of the Old Testament* (Leiden: Deo, 2005).

of divine presence, power, and righteousness together with traditional notions of human guilt or sin in relation to G-d," not only for the Jews but also for Christians, reading the Hebrew Scriptures/Old Testament normatively presents a radically new challenge.[11] How do the post-Shoah generations live with, much less answer, questions such as: "Does G-d always act responsibly in the world? ... What role must human beings assume when G-d fails to act or when G-d acts sinfully?"[12] Without necessarily invoking reader-response criticism, both canons in the face of the Shoah and its memory already lend themselves to these questions that could run aground on the shore of a theological quagmire for the post-Shoah, post-Hiroshima, or post-1755 Lisbon earthquake generations. How do we indeed read the Hebrew Bible/Old Testament with such questions without jettisoning the canon or giving meager piecemeal "biblical" responses (which is de facto abandonment of the canons)? If, as Sweeney suggests, these questions "call for human beings to take on greater responsibility for the sanctity, well-being, and fundamental justice of the world in which we live,"[13] the *normative function* of the canons takes on a new dimension and requires a new task.

In exploring this side of the normative discourse, one can take a historicist approach in the fashion of Norman Gottwald or Carol Meyers.[14] While

---

11. Sweeney, *Reading the Hebrew Bible after the Shoah* (Minneapolis: Fortress, 2008), 1.

12. Sweeney, *Reading the Hebrew Bible*, 2.

13. Sweeney, *Reading the Hebrew Bible*, 22. See also Rolf P. Knierim, "Hope in the Old Testament," in *Task of Old Testament Theology*, 244–68; Knierim, "On the Contours of Old Testament and Biblical Hamartiology," in *Task of Old Testament Theology*, 416–67: "As the expression of the all-pervasive and ineradicable presence of evil, the primordial chaos sweeps into the creation through human existence and history. After making its way back into the creation, it continually threatens this good order. As long as human existence and history last, the constant containment of and resistance to chaotic influences are, therefore, a basic and inevitable necessity. More is impossible, less unallowable. Containment and resistance are defense mechanisms; they are not ideals. Still, they are realistic mechanisms and cannot be neglected in favor of positive thinking alone, despite the fact that overcoming evil with good is a better way than solely fighting evil. Human initiatives and institutions of all sorts and on all levels are intended to and do serve the purpose of advancing what is good and preventing what is evil" (449).

14. Norman K. Gottwald, *The Tribes of Yahweh: A Sociology of the Religion of Liberated Israel, 1250–1050 BCE* (Maryknoll, NY: Orbis Books, 1979); Carol Meyers, *Dis-*

their works represent the descriptive task more than the normative, they are clearly driven by normative concerns, namely, class and gender issues, as these impact readers negatively.[15] This approach is certainly legitimate and has yielded fruitful results.

Gottwald is so convinced of the indispensable role of the social-historical reading strategy, however, that he goes as far as to declare any biblical theology devoid of social-historical analysis irremediably bankrupt.[16] He then proposes that we substitute biblical *sociology* for biblical *theology*. The unsettled debate over Gottwald's interpretation of archaeological and historical evidence notwithstanding, we can scarcely dismiss the lasting impact of his sweeping methodological proposal.

I would like to submit, however—and I think many of Gottwald's fellow Marxists would argue—that *text* is not external to *history*. As Francis Mulhern aptly observes:

> Textual practice is internal to history, which inhabits it. The tradition of rhetoric assumes just this: linguistic practice is discourse, situated and motivated utterance, organized in and organizing specific relations of culture. To explore the historicity of the text is, then, not simply to relate a frail singularity to the broad design of a period; it is also to investigate its direct social relations..., the formations of writing and reading—and these not as "context" or "background" but as substantive elements of the practice itself.[17]

Louis Althusser had, in fact, plausibly argued that "in ideology the real relation is inevitably invested in the imaginary relation, a relation that *expresses* a *will* (conservative, conformist, reformist or revolutionary), a hope or a nostalgia, rather than describing a reality."[18] Likewise, as Terry

---

covering Eve: Ancient Israelite Women in Context (Oxford: Oxford University Press, 1988).

15."In terms of social and ecclesial contexts, I have moved from vague awareness of biblical hermeneutics as the practice of 'applying' to my own world certain principles or analogies drawn from the Bible to a recognition of the full hermeneutical circle in which my social structural stance and consciousness correlate with biblical readings" (Gottwald, unpublished address to the Society of Biblical Literature Annual Meeting, Kansas City, MO, November 25, 1991).

16. Gottwald, *Tribes of Yahweh*, 665–709.

17. Francis Mulhern, ed., *Contemporary Marxist Literary Criticism* (New York: Longman, 1992), 19.

18. Louis Althusser, *For Marx* (New York: Vintage Books, 1969), 234.

Eagleton notes of the ideological function of language, "it is fundamentally a matter of fearing and denouncing, reverencing and reviling, all of which then sometimes gets coded into a discourse which looks as though it is describing the way things actually are."[19] Eagleton extrapolates on aspects of J. L. Austin's speech act theory that see an important function of language as belonging to the class of speech acts that are thus performative.[20] Language gets something done. That is its function. As Eagleton observes elsewhere:

> [The heart of literary criticism is] its concern for the kind of *effects* which discourses produce, and how they produce them.... It is in fact, the oldest form of "literary criticism" in the world, known as rhetoric. Rhetoric, which was the received form of critical analysis all the way from ancient society to the eighteenth century, examined the way discourses are constructed in order to achieve certain effects. It was not worried about whether its objects of inquiry were speaking or writing, poetry or philosophy, fiction or historiography: its horizon was nothing less than the field of discursive practices in society as a whole, and its particular interest lay in grasping such practices as forms of power and performances.[21]

The concern of these Marxist literary critics is with the function of language itself rather than the sociohistorical context of literary works. While we must always explore the relation between literature and its social context in order to understand the text, they urge us to come to grips with the text's more immediate rhetorical function.

Marxist literary criticism has had its share of contours since its inception in the late nineteenth century.[22] The history of these contours begins

---

19. Terry Eagleton, *Ideology: An Introduction* (New York: Verso, 1991), 19.

20. John L. Austin, *How to Do Things with Words* (Cambridge: Harvard University Press, 1962).

21. Terry Eagleton, *Literary Theory* (Minneapolis: University of Minnesota Press, 1983), 205.

22. See Georg Lukács, *Die Theorie des Romans*, 2nd ed. (Neuwied am Rhein: Luchterhand, 1963) (first published in 1920); Lukács, *Studies in European Realism* (New York: Grosset & Dunlap, 1964) (essays of 1935–1939); Lukács, *The Historical Novel* (London: Merlin, 1962); Fredric Jameson, *Marxism and Form: Twentieth-Century Dialectical Theories of Literature* (Princeton: Princeton University Press, 1974); Jameson, *The Prison-House of Language: A Critical Account of Structuralism and Russian Formalism* (Princeton: Princeton University Press, 1972); Jameson, *The Political Unconscious: Narrative as a Socially Symbolic Act* (New York: Cornell Univer-

even before the October Revolution of 1917 and continues well into the twentieth century, as is well testified by the debate between the two opposing critical schools: the Plekhanovites (Plekhanov and his followers) and the Bogdanovites (Bogdanov and his followers).[23]

The debate surrounds the nature and function of literary art. Plekhanov, along with Trotsky and others, sees the aesthetics as essentially a passive process. He believes an artist unconsciously intuits the world and expresses it without subjecting it to much conscious volition. He therefore wants to leave artists with political freedom in which they would accurately, if passively, render the "objective" reality as they see it. Bogdanov, along with Gorky, and others, on the other hand, takes a more activist view. Borrowing from Tolstoy's notion of emotional "infection," he views literature less as a passive, contemplative reflection of social reality than as a tool for making an impact on society. Thus, he calls upon the artist to play the role of an active agent for social agenda.

The debate continued beyond 1917 and defined the terms of Russian literary disputes for decades to come. Daniel Lucid observed the final outcome of the debate as of the early 1970s, well before the demise of the Soviet Union: "As a result, Soviet Marxist aesthetics has been left with a Bogdanovite literary theory and a Plekhanovite practical criticism, with the theory harping on the tendentious duties of contemporary art, and the criticism *investigating the social origins of past art*."[24]

Gottwald has his own complexities, and we cannot place him at a single spot on the map briefly surveyed without doing him injustice. We can nonetheless detect in Gottwald a trace of certain aspects of the debate. For instance, I doubt that Gottwald believes that the literary agents who produced the Old Testament's extant texts played only a passive, reflective

---

sity Press, 1981); Peter Demetz, *Marx, Engels, and the Poets* (Chicago: University of Chicago Press, 1967); Raymond Williams, *Marxism and Literature* (Oxford: Oxford University Press, 1977); Terry Eagleton, *Criticism and Ideology: A Study in Marxist Literary Theory* (London: Verso, 1985); Eagleton, *Marxism and Literary Criticism* (Oakland: University of California Press, 1976), Eagleton, *The Function of Criticism* (London: Verso, 1984), Eagleton, *Literary Theory*; Eagleton, *Ideology*; Pierre Macherey, *A Theory of Literary Production*, trans. Geoffrey Wall, repr. ed. (London: Routledge, 2006); Mulhern, *Contemporary Marxist Literary Criticism*.

23. For a study on the history of these two schools during this period, see Daniel Peri Lucid, "Preface to Revolution: Russian Marxist Literary Criticism, 1883–1917" (PhD diss., Yale University, 1972).

24. Lucid, "Preface to Revolution," 435, emphasis added.

role, especially when he speaks of their "endeavor to justify Israelite par-
ticularism by recourse to various subterfuges and rationalizations."[25] To
be sure, the agents and the brokers of many of the biblical texts played the
role opposite to what the Bogdanovites would have prescribed for them.
Nevertheless, they were active agents in the fullest sense of the word, and
Gottwald recognizes it. On the other hand, Gottwald's call for substitution
of biblical sociology for biblical theology appears to betray a Plekhanovite
sentiment. Like the Plekhanovites, he wants to use the text primarily for
the purpose of obtaining clues to the social reality that they depict or fail to
depict, that is, to use it mainly as data for sociological understanding of the
world behind the text. While recognizing the text as a product of agenda-
filled activities of the writers and the redactionists, Gottwald's interest lies
ultimately in the text's utility as a clue for ascertaining the social reality and
the origins behind the text.

Pierre Macherey, also a Marxist—although not a literary critic but
a philosopher—develops a theory on this approach that I find helpful.[26]
Building on, and moving beyond, Althusser's theory of the relationship
between literature and ideology, Macherey raises the question of *literary
production*. Against the traditional view, he sees the writer not so much as
the creator as the producer of the text.[27] This means for Macherey that literature is a *material production*. His immediate focus is on the materiality
of the text itself rather than on something preliterary that gives rise to the
text. It is therefore for him

> pointless to look in the texts for the "original" bare discourse of these
> ideological positions, as they were "before" their "literary" realization,
> for these ideological positions can only be formed in the materiality of
> the literary text. That is, they can only appear in a form which provides
> their imaginary solution, or better still, which displaces them by substi-
> tuting imaginary contradictions.[28]

---

25. Gottwald, *Tribes of Yahweh*, 702.

26. I am immensely grateful to Prof. Ted Stolze at California State University at
Hayward at the time of this writing for helping me walk through some of the difficult
aspects of Macherey's theory.

27. Macherey, *Theory of Literary Production*.

28. Étienne Balibar and Pierre Macherey, "On Literature as an Ideological Form,"
trans. Ian McLeod, John Whitehead, and Ann Wordsworth, *OLR* 3 (1978): 4–12.

What Macherey takes most seriously is therefore the immediate reality of the text and its effects: "Literature is not fiction, a fictive image of the real, ... [but] the production ... of a certain reality ... and of a certain social effect.... Literature is not therefore a fiction, but the production of fictions: or better still, the production of fiction-effects."[29] Particularly helpful is Macherey's "theory of literary *reproduction*."[30] With this further nuanced and refined theory he argues that literature is constituted by its material reproduction, which belongs to the very nature of literature. Relying on, and expanding, Marx's notion of "the eternal charm of Greek art," Macherey maintains that:

> In the very constitution ... of the literary work in particular, there is something which condemns it to become outdated and no longer to exist except in the form of a relic in the absence of the social context in relation to which it was produced. It no longer subsists except through the mediation of its material envelope, as a "work" inscribed in the literal body of its own text.... [This] means, in other words, that these "works" have not been produced as such, but precisely have become works in completely different conditions which are those of their production.[31]

Extrapolating on Foucault's admonition that the author should resist the temptation to become "the name, the law, the secret, [and] the measure" of her work, but should let go of his work "to be recopied, fragmented, repeated, simulated, divided, finally to disappear without the one who has happened to produce it ever being able to claim the right to be its master,"[32] Macherey redefines the production-reproduction relationship of a literary work: "The event [of writing], which is everything but the act of a subject who would be its Author, precedes the work, which is itself only the repetition, in a relationship which is not that of massive identity but of insensible difference."[33]

Macherey maintains that the author is never the absolute author but rather "the reader, critic, translator, editor, even ... a simple copyist."

---

29. Balibar and Macherey, "On Literature as an Ideological Form."

30. Macherey, *In a Materialist Way: Selected Essays*, ed. Warren Montag, trans. Ted Stolze (London: Verso, 1998), 42–51.

31. Macherey, *In a Materialist Way*, 43.

32. Michel Foucault, *Historie de la folie à l' âge classique* (Paris: Gallimard, 1972), 7–8, as cited in Macherey, *In a Materialist Way*, 46.

33. Macherey, *In a Materialist Way*, 46–47.

Rather than being produced, then, the works actually "begin to exist only from the moment they are 'reproduced.'" For him there is "a poetics of reproduction functioning as a model of writing." Writing by necessity is done on the previous writing: "One writes on the written." The palimpsest is not so much a literary genre as "the very essence of the literary, which coincides with the movement of its own reproduction…. [T]here is no first writing which is not also a rewriting."[34]

Macherey thus offers a quasi-ontology of literary work, a dialectical ontology that is self-sustaining as a reproduction with a distinct materiality of its own far removed from the "original" extraliterary factors and, most importantly, with an equally distinct *material effect*, the latter point also having been articulated by Eagleton, as we have noted.

Far be it from me to suggest that we can now therefore simply dismiss sociohistorical analysis of the text. We would do so only at our own peril. But I am prepared neither to accept sociohistorical analysis as a *substitute* for biblical theology nor to suspend the practice of biblical theology until it is fully informed by sociohistorical analysis. By definition, the text of the Hebrew Bible/Old Testament seeks to persuade. It intends to achieve a *material effect*—indeed, a *God effect*. This intention is evident and can be assessed quite apart from the sociohistorical context that gave rise to the text.

As I have noted above, it is obvious that concern about material effect of the text is what prompts Gottwald and Meyers to turn to the extratextual world. I suspect the same is true of James Barr. Barr is, of course, correct in observing that when the text presents חרם, for instance, it does not matter whether חרם is fact or fiction because the text presents it to inculcate it as a good model for readers to endorse.[35] But Barr is not ready to argue, as a theologian with a Machereyan bent might, that the theological task is to

---

34. Macherey, *In a Materialist Way*, 47–49. This is of course how the entire Hebrew Bible (in fact, the whole Bible) was written. For one of the best and most recent examples of tradition and redaction criticism at work, see Antony F. Campbell and Mark O'Brien, *Unfolding the Deuteronomistic History: Origins, Upgrades, Present Text* (Minneapolis: Fortress, 2000). For an excellent study on the growth of the book of Joshua toward extermination theology, see Antony F. Campbell, "The Growth of Joshua 1–12 and the Theology of Extermination," in *Reading the Hebrew Bible for a New Millennium: Form, Concept, and Theological Perspective*, ed. Deborah Ellens et al., 2 vols. (Harrisburg, PA: Trinity Press International, 2000), 2:72–88.

35. James Barr, *Biblical Faith and Natural Theology* (Oxford: Clarendon, 1993), 209–10.

confront the material reality of the text as a self-integrated reproduction. Instead, he takes a historicist approach, arguing energetically against the notion that *ḥerem* was justified in view of child sacrifice by the Canaanites, because the supposition that this practice was widespread, or that its occurrence motivates the narratives of *ḥerem*, lacks sound historical grounding.

Barr is in fact unequivocal about his methodology. Accusing biblical interpretation of being "strongly inclined to restrict its sources of guidance to the *internal* relations perceptible within the biblical text itself," he asserts that "interpretation for the modern situation can occur only when you bring to the text other factors, other ideas, other knowledge of situations, which are expressly other than internal content and internal relations of the text."[36] Nonetheless, for Barr, as for Gottwald and Meyers, the concern is none other than material effect of the reproduced text, and because of this concern, he turns to extratextual factors in search of counter evidence.

Macherey's methodological implications would invite us, however, to examine the rhetoric of Joshua's war as *material reproduction of the text* with specific *material effect* without depending primarily on extratextual referents—to raise the question of the *theological validity* of the text and to seek answers from "the *internal* relations perceptible within the biblical text itself."

Literature is a projected reality, a discourse with its own material logic. We are therefore not mandated to judge the *text* of Joshua only in reference to what really happened or did not really happen in history outside the *text* of Joshua. The same applies to other texts as well, such as Exodus, with its understanding of God as acting in history to achieve liberation. The text of Joshua or Exodus produces and reproduces its own world with its own ideological agenda, with the aim of convincing its reader of a truth claim in the name of God. It intentionally exerts a material God effect. It is a reproduced literature with reproduced God effects, not only throughout its traditional and redactional stages but also beyond its final canonical stage—because, and precisely to the extent to which, a canon that includes it is a reproduced literature embodying reproduced God effects. Further, Langdon Gilkey's bombshell "Ontology, Cosmology, and the Travail of Biblical Language" notwithstanding, the text's truth claim with regard to this intended God effects has less to do with whether or not liberation

---

36. Barr, *Biblical Faith and Natural Theology*, 206–7.

from slavery or military conquest of indigenous people happened as the text describes than with whether or not it *should* ever happen, then, now, or in the future—historically or as an imaginary solution to an imaginary historical problem, as Althusser and Macherey would put it.[37]

That the Hebrew Bible/Old Testament contains a plurality and diversity of theologies is a truism. Perhaps less banal and more poignant is the fact that not all of these plural and diverse theologies are harmonious and complementary with each other. The truth claims made by some contradict those made by others; consider, for instance, the distinction between conquest theology on the one hand and liberation or creation theology, on the other. The contradictions are too stark to legitimate any sort of reconciliation or resolution; they leave us with conflicting truth claims in their raw confrontations. It would be an understatement to say that we have a problem.

In our postmodern era, some scholars might deny that this situation poses a problem. Burke Long's "Letting Rival Gods Be Rivals,"[38] for example, comes to mind.[39] Others would acknowledge the problem while proposing a dialogical model that invites different or conflicting theological truth claims to participate in a dialogical roundtable. Some recent examples of this approach are Juliana Claassens's excellent *Journal of Biblical Literature* article introducing the implications of Mikhail Bakhtin's literary theory for biblical theology, Brueggemann's aforementioned volume with the telling subtitle *Testimony, Dispute, Advocacy*, and the more recent work by John W. Rogerson, who takes full cognizance of the fact that the Hebrew Bible/Old Testament retains memories that are not monolithic but diverse, even self-contradicting, but who refuses to

---

37. Langdon Gilkey, "Ontology, Cosmology, and the Travail of Biblical Language," *JR* 41 (1961): 194–205.

38. Burke Long, "Letting Rival Gods Be Rivals: Biblical Theology in a Postmodern Age," in *Problems in Biblical Theology: Essays in Honor of Rolf Knierim*, ed. Henry T. C. Sun, Keith Eades, and James Robinson (Grand Rapids: Eerdmans, 1997), 222–33.

39. Enough warnings have been effectively issued by many against irresponsible use of postmodern deconstructionist approaches, and I do not need to revisit that debate here. See, for example, William A. Beardslee, "Poststructuralist Criticism," in *To Each Its Own Meaning: An Introduction to the Biblical Criticisms and Their Application*, ed. Steven L. McKenzie and Stephen R. Haynes (Louisville: Westminster John Knox, 1993), 221–35; Terence Fretheim and Karlfried Froelich, *The Bible as Word of God in a Postmodern Age* (Minneapolis: Fortress, 1998).

harmonize them and insists on maintaining the creative tension within the canon.[40]

A dialogical model is indeed the place to begin. In fact, I cannot think of any other place to begin the discourse. We cannot simply let different theologies in the Hebrew Bible/Old Testament run along separate tracks, not because we want to search for some false unity or for a *Mitte* that by now has been proven to be nonexistent, but because, as Perdue has put it, an unchallenged Bible ultimately leads to demonic behavior, among other things. Further, to challenge the Bible *biblically*, or better yet, by means of biblical *theology*, we must indeed bring the various theologies found in the Hebrew Bible/Old Testament in dialogue with each other. After all, the Hebrew Bible/Old Testament is not just a collection of monstrous, diabolical theologies. If it were, the real name of the Society of Biblical Literature and the comparable guilds should be Sadists Anonymous. Non-life-giving, destructive theologies can be boldly exposed and challenged, even corrected, by life-giving, constructive theologies also found in the Hebrew Bible/Old Testament.

A dialogical model would provide a space wherein such exposure, challenge, and corrective construction could begin by bringing the diverse theologies into a dialogue across many boundaries.[41] But the model, while indispensable for this reason, is not without limitations and dangers. Such a dialogical model cannot be used, for instance, simply to expose, acknowledge, and respect the polarities and tensions among theologies. It would be unhelpful for us wishfully to think that all will be well as long as these polarities and tensions are kept in dialogue with each other—to hope that if we simply let polarities and tensions be polarities and tensions in dialogue, they will somehow work themselves out for the good of human-

---

40. L. Juliana M. Claassens, "Biblical Theology as Dialogue: Continuing the Conversation on Mikhail Bakhtin and Biblical Theology," *JBL* 122 (2003): 127–44; Brueggemann, *Theology of the Old Testament*; John W. Rogerson, *A Theology of the Old Testament: Cultural Memory, Communication, and Being Human* (Minneapolis: Fortress, 2010). Theological works on the Hebrew Bible/Old Testament of course continue to appear, as they always have, from nondialogical perspectives, and they span a broad range of the ideological spectrum. At the Christian apologetics end, for example, we have Iain Provan's *Seriously Dangerous Religion: What the Old Testament Really Says and Why It Matters* (Waco, TX: Baylor University Press, 2014), which, despite the author's effort to the contrary, ends up being little more than a sophisticated exercise in prooftexting.

41. Claassens, "Biblical Theology as Dialogue," 142–44.

ity through the activity of some sort of invisible hand in the *laissez faire* free market of theologies. This kind of dialogue would do little more than what a canon has already done: to bring varied and conflicting theologies together into a single space. It would add useful and interesting complexity to the descriptive task but little more.

For the model to be genuinely dialogical, it must recognize itself as participating in a speech act, as an intentional rhetoric, as having performative functions. It is essential to be explicit about what any dialogue is designed to achieve—in terms of both theological substance and material effect—and about the norms that will govern it. The model should avoid the fallacy often committed by dialogicians such as Dennis McCann and Charles Strain, who propose "a public discourse free from domination and constraint as well as from commitment to all substantive positions, the only justifiable commitment being the 'readiness to reason together.'" As Anselm Kyongsuk Min points out in criticism, this proposal urges that we "shift the discussion from substantive issues and positions to the formal conditions and criteria for the possibility of authentic discourse about such issues." [42]

"In a world increasingly fragmented and incapable of any consensus on substantive issues yet anxious to avoid violence and dictatorship," Min understands why we are faced with "the temptation to retreat into the purely formal and procedural conditions of genuine dialogue to be respected by all parties despite their substantive differences." Min insists, however, that a concern with process is insufficient. "What if," he asks, "not all the parties to the dialogue agreed to those procedural conditions or were capable of committing themselves to either such conditions or the conclusions of such a dialogue? ... How can parties with radically different horizons engage in a real dialogue, not merely the appearance of one?"[43]

Min then proceeds to advance his liberationist argument and asserts that liberation theology is "not a result of a dialogue with the generals, landlords, and the multinational corporations, any more than capitalism is a result of a dialogue with [minority groups], the unemployed, or those living under the poverty line." "Should Cardinals Lorscheider and Arns," he asks, "have entered into dialogue with Cardinals Trujillo and Obando,

42. Anselm Kyongsuk Min, *Dialectic of Salvation: Issues in Theology of Liberation* (Albany: State University of New York Press, 1989), 43.
43. Min, *Dialectic of Salvation*, 75–76.

the Somozas and the Pinochets?"[44] What about Adolf Hitler and Dietrich Bonhoeffer, we might add? What kind of dialogue could we envision between *them*?

Knierim has described the problem of reading the Hebrew Bible/Old Testament theologically in a similar vein:

> Imagine a symposium of all the theological voices in the Old Testament on the question of Israel's relationship to its neighbors in the land.... I am sure that a considerable number of those theologians would raise their eyebrows and tell the "holy war and get tough with the inhabitants of the land" party that [the party's] position is simply out of tune with what it means to say [YHWH]—and ultimately "Israel".... If they could not persuade the war party, they would rather *risk a schism than yield to this theology and ethos!* Indeed, they would want to give "the Canaanites" their right to exist, their self-determination, and their dignity, because of [YHWH] the God of all, and because of Israel's identity as [YHWH's] people.[45] (emphasis added)

Given the monotheistically (or mono-YHWH-istically) structured worldview shared by all the participants of such an imaginary symposium, we would indeed be hard-pressed to imagine a scenario in which they would simply agree to disagree at the end of the dialogue and then go out to have a beer. Min is correct in maintaining that the fact that

> the difference in perspective and priorities leads to different assessments of the historical situation and its challenges and sets a definite limit to the possibility of dialogue should be quite clear from the debates between capitalists and socialists, Continental philosophers and British analysts, Thomists and Whiteheadians, theists and atheists, and indeed the Vatican and [liberation theologians]. A dialogue only becomes concretely possible either if one party converts to the horizon of the other or both parties rise to a "higher" horizon which they can share. In either case, it is a matter of conversion."[46]

The same is true when it comes to the theologies that confront each other in a canon of the Hebrew Bible/Old Testament. Of course, dialogue does not always call for or aim at conversion, because not all theolo-

---

44. Min, *Dialectic of Salvation*, 76–77.
45. Knierim, *Task of Old Testament Theology*, 320.
46. Min, *Dialectic of Salvation*, 74–75.

gies contained in a canon of the Hebrew Bible/Old Testament contrast as starkly as the positions Min considers. But the proponents of a dialogical model must still acknowledge that dialogue will reach an impasse from time to time because some theologies are irreconcilably at odds with others because of their radically different horizons, perspectives, and priorities. When it does, dialogue will have done its job by sharply exposing irreconcilable contradictions and irresolvable conflicts. In such cases, proponents of a dialogical model must accept its limitation in order to allow room for a dialectical verdict.

Brueggemann's court model and trial metaphor could have taken us beyond the limits of dialogical model, had he taken this step. But it seems that his desire to be faithful to postmodern mandates deflects him from boldly embracing the dialectical task as Knierim does. As Margaret Odell astutely points out, "[Brueggemann's] metaphor of the trial court undercuts his goals of sustaining the plurality of testimony and dispute. In court, a testimony or a cluster of testimonies is declared 'true' while others are rejected as less 'true'"—or, indeed, simply false or wrong.[47]

Fundamental to the frame of reference within which Knierim's methodology operates is the observation that the Hebrew Bible/Old Testament contains theological contradictions that directly challenge the assumption of a monotheistic structure of reality implied in their various monotheistic claims. Not all biblical contradictions need to be or can be resolved, to be sure, monotheistic structure or not. Nor can they, however, all be reduced to ironies that we must live with or somehow eventually become synthesized in Hegelian sense. As Marx noted in his 1843 *Critique of Hegel's Philosophy of Right*, certain "essential contradictions, contradictions between elements that did not need each other and could not be mediated … [or] did not lead to completeness or harmony," remain contradictions.[48]

I would argue that this is the case with many of the Hebrew Bible/Old Testament—and, indeed, biblical—contradictions embedded within their

---

47. Margaret Odell, review of *Theology of the Old Testament*, by Joel S. Kaminsky, Margaret S. Odell, and Rolf Rendtorff, *RBL* (1999), presented at a Society of Biblical Literature panel review.

48. Karl Marx, *Critique of Hegel's Philosophy of Right*, ed., intro., and notes by Joseph O'Malley, trans. Annette Jolin and Joseph O'Malley (Cambridge: Cambridge University Press, 1970); Lawrence Wild, "Logic: Dialectic and Contradiction," in *The Cambridge Companion to Marx*, ed. Terrell Carver (Cambridge: Cambridge University Press, 1991), 288.

diverse monotheistic assumptions. After all, "how do we know that [the different monotheistic claims] lead to the same God, and not to many gods?" as Knierim would put it.[49] If there is any validity to Yehezkel Kaufmann's claim that the monotheistic YHWH is radically different and independent from the morally neutral "metadivine realm" of the neighboring polytheistic traditions, ancient or modern, then the question posed by Knierim indeed emerges in a sharp relief from the surrounding plane of biblical theology and hermeneutics.[50]

If the hermeneutical task of biblical theology that we carry on is based on the worldview that claims there is integrity to reality because it is monotheistically structured, then we should be prepared to deal with the inner contradictions embedded in our theological claims that will erode and eventually undermine that structure if left unaddressed.

These contradictions, of course, will never be resolved, even in a non-synthesized way; the materiality of the biblical texts and their theologies, the materiality of the "monotheistically structured" worldview, even the materiality of the monotheistic YHWH herself/himself will always remain dialectically open despite our best efforts to provide hermeneutical closure, perpetually demanding a dialectical encounter, reading us as we read them (à la Jacques Derrida).[51] In other words, the demand that ensues such an encounter is not a closure (certainly not Knierim's aim, contra some of his critics' misunderstanding) but an open dialectic—not as an endless play but as a relentless dialectical intervention. The task is nothing less than daunting.

Elaborating further on his imagined symposium, Knierim explains what he means by such a simulation: "The Old Testament, with the plurality of its voices, is on its way, a restless way, to a better [*and dialectical,* I should add,] understanding of God and his people in the world. Precisely because its voices are diverse, they call upon us to read them with discernment."[52] Such "discernment" for Knierim requires more than a dia-

---

49. Knierim, *Task of Old Testament Theology*, 6.

50. Yehezkel Kaufmann, *The Religion of Israel*, trans. Moshe Greenberg (New York: Schocken, 1972).

51. Jacques Derrida, *Writing and Difference* (Chicago: University of Chicago Press, 1978); see also Derrida, *Of Grammatology*, 40th anniversary ed. (Baltimore: Johns Hopkins University Press, 2016) (originally published 1978).

52. Knierim, *Task of Old Testament Theology*, 320.

logical model. Exemplified in his own methodological proposal, it calls for a dialectical model that is adjudicating, prioritizing, and verdict rendering.

It is worth noting that the current Marxist philosophical discourse on "materialist and idealist tendencies" recognizes—setting aside the onto-logical question and focusing on the epistemological question alone, with its implications for practice—the ever-present category of idealist tenden-cies as a necessary component of philosophical debate.

> Marxism is not a "finished theory, with its system of prepared responses and fossilized concepts" but is instead a "knot of simple and concrete problems." … Althusser's project to establish a philosophical practice that would be appropriate for Marxism did not simply consist of iden-tifying and defending a "materialist" position in philosophy against external "idealist" challenges or threats. On the contrary, it recognized that there exists an interminable struggle between inextricably linked but ever-shifting materialist and idealist tendencies—a struggle that operates as a defining feature in the history of philosophy.[53]

Jean-Toussaint Desanti in fact argued in his *Introduction à l'histoire de la philosophie* that the struggle between idealism and materialism has been "the center of the entire history of philosophy" and is "the very essence of philosophy: it is the expression of the process of knowledge by concepts at the heart of society."[54] Furthermore, Althusser reiterated that "every idealist philosophy necessarily includes in it materialist arguments, and vice-versa." Insisting that no philosophy is "pure, meaning completely ide-alist or materialist," he maintained that "Marxist materialist philosophy can itself never claim to be completely materialist, for it would then have aban-doned the struggle, giving up the preventative seizure of positions occupied by idealism."[55] Stolze thus concludes that "philosophy cannot overcome its internal struggle between materialist and idealist tendencies because it exists

---

53. Ted Stolze, "What Is a Philosophical Tendency?," *Historical Materialism* 23.4 (2015): 4–5.

54. Jean-Toussaint Desanti, *Introduction à l'histoire de la philosophie*, 2nd ed. (Paris: Presses universitaires de France, 2006), 80, as quoted in Stolze, "What Is a Phil-osophical Tendency?," 9.

55. Louis Althusser, *Initiation à la philosophie pour les non-philosophes*, ed. G. M. Goshgarian (Paris: Presses Universitaires de France, 2014) 325, as quoted by Stolze, "What Is a Philosophical Tendency?," 14.

and operates only by reproducing actually existing external social conflicts and scientific disputes that continually reemerge in mediated forms."[56]

While the heart of the materialist-idealist tension is "an ontological dispute between two philosophical tendencies over the nature of Being [*ousia*]" that goes back to Plato, Stolze reminds us that Plato himself "envisioned not the eradication of either tendency but the preservation of both in a perpetual state of mutual tension."[57] So, "just as Marxists have not created class struggle but only take sides within it, so too must they defend positions within an already-existing struggle of philosophical tendencies.... Moreover, realism need not imply direct access to the world but is compatible with extensive conceptual mediation and multiple interpretative and evaluative stances."[58]

This means that, although the materialist tendencies recognize that the idealist tendencies overdraw from their ontological account, for the materialist tendencies the focus of philosophy remains on this side of ontological claims; as a result, they are able to engage the idealist tendencies on their terms. In other words, while

> idealist tendencies signify the ways in which philosophies embody the relentless desire to know even in excess of what can be known and, as Smolin puts it, "are just making stuff up".... Macherey has never regarded science as providing the only, or even the primary, model for philosophy to emulate. Indeed, literature is an equally appropriate medium for encountering "philosophy without philosopher."[59]

Finally, and most germane to the argument of my essay, Stolze insists that it is thus

> quite possible—and even desirable—to maintain a robust ontological commitment to realism, as Lenin did in Materialism and Empirio-Criticism, with an equally robust epistemological commitment to nonreductive materialism regarding the process of intellectual

---

56. Stolze, "What Is a Philosophical Tendency?," 17.
57. Stolze, "What Is a Philosophical Tendency?," 23.
58. Stolze, "What Is a Philosophical Tendency?," 27–28.
59. Stolze, "What Is a Philosophical Tendency?," 29, quoting Lee Smolin, *Time Reborn: From the Crisis in Physics to the Future of the Universe* (New York: Mariner, 2014), 11.

production and practical commitment to the priority of practice over theory.[60]

True to the heart of Marxist philosophy, Stolze reiterates the Marxist's central tenet that is more fundamental than ontology and epistemology, namely, the question of *action*. While not abandoning their ontological commitment to materialism,

> the most important question for Marxists is not "What exists?" or "How can one know it?" but "How should one act?" ... [A]s Macherey has stressed, materialism is ultimately "not a doctrine, not a theory, not a body of knowledge, but rather a manner of intervention, a philosophi- cal *position*.... A position is not the theory of an object, the discourse within which the latter is at once represented and constituted; it is the manifestation, the affirmation of an orientation, of a tendency, of a way of moving through, not *reality*, which is not an object of philosophy, but the philosophical field itself, grasped in the concrete complexity of its internal conflicts as the specific site of this intervention."[61]

It bears repeating what Stolze reminds us: "Just as Marxists have not cre- ated class struggle but only take sides within it, so too must they defend positions within an already-existing struggle of philosophical tenden- cies.... Moreover, realism need not imply direct access to the world but is compatible with extensive conceptual mediation and multiple interpreta- tive and evaluative stances."[62] By the same token and analogy, one does not have to have a direct access to the world that precedes the text of the Hebrew Bible but has to engage in "the extensive conceptual mediation and multiple interpretive and evaluative stances" of the text in an inter- vening way.

A "reductive materialist way" would privilege sociology of the mate- rial conditions of the world that generated biblical texts as the primary epistemological locus, letting the texts devolve into a counterevidence providing at best aid for that sociology and at worst evidence of idealistic overdrawing or corruption. Yet Marxism, well tuned to the complex real-

---

60. Stolze, "What Is a Philosophical Tendency?," 7.

61. Stolze, "What Is a Philosophical Tendency?," 30–31, quoting Macherey, "In a Materialist Way," trans. Lorna Scott Fox, in *Philosophy in France Today*, ed. Alan Mon- tefiore (Cambridge: Cambridge University Press, 1983), 137.

62. Stolze, "What Is a Philosophical Tendency?," 27–28.

ity of the philosophical tendencies, "never regards[s] science as providing the only, or even the primary, model for philosophy to emulate." Indeed, it considers "literature an equally appropriate medium for encountering 'philosophy without philosopher.'" Such Marxism is well aware that the very debate of these tendencies is precisely the location for an action of intervention. It intervenes within the world of the text, with or without the author or philosopher, with or without a full knowledge of sociology, for a better literary effect—yes, even God effect, if the text is a theological production and preproduction.

I should also note in conclusion that for Macherey literary production and reproduction do not operate smoothly, without internal antagonisms, which is all the more reason to challenge a dialogical model of biblical theology.[63] Internal to the text—and not just external and detected by sociological method—are "normative contradictions" between alternative theologies. The role of the dialectical biblical theologian, then, would be to engage in both negative criticism of indefensible theologies (based, e.g., on conquest, patriarchy, domination of nature) and positive reconstruction of more defensible theologies (based, e.g., on liberation, equality, steward-ship of nature).

I am not sure if any model that is less than dialectical, adjudicating, and verdictive could serve as a satisfactory response to Prior, whose rivet-ing challenge is here to stay, for his appeal is an unrelenting reminder that our task of doing Hebrew Bible/Old Testament theology must include facing up to the dark shadows of the book we so love—which turn out to be our own shadows as well. The only viable response to his legiti-mate criticism would be one that would take us dialectically beyond those shadows to a better understanding of God and her world—with caution, to be sure, but without undue hesitation or lack of daring methodological clarity.[64]

---

63. Macherey, *Theory of Literary Production*, 152–74.

64. At the time of his writing Prior does not seem to have read Knierim (this is not an accusation or judgment. One cannot possibly read everything!), who knows precisely the limits of the dialogical model and proposes a methodology that moves beyond those limits. Knierim's influence on my thinking is obvious in this essay, but exploring his proposal is a subject for another time.

Bibliography

Althusser, Louis. *For Marx*. New York: Vintage Books, 1969.

———. *Initiation à la philosophie pour les non-philosophes*. Edited by G. M. Goshgarian. Paris: Presses Universitaires de France, 2014.

Austin, John L. *How to Do Things with Words*. Cambridge: Harvard University Press, 1962.

Balibar, Étienne, and Pierre Macherey. "On Literature as an Ideological Form." Translated by Ian McLeod, John Whitehead, and Ann Wordsworth. *OLR* 3 (1978): 4–12.

Barr, James. *Biblical Faith and Natural Theology*. Oxford: Clarendon Press, 1993.

Beardslee, William A. "Poststructuralist Criticism." Pages 221–35 in *To Each Its Own Meaning: An Introduction to the Biblical Criticisms and Their Application*. Edited by Steven L. McKenzie and Stephen R. Haynes. Louisville: Westminster John Knox, 1993.

Brueggemann, Walter. *Theology of the Old Testament: Testimony, Dispute, Advocacy*. Minneapolis: Augsburg, 1997.

Campbell, Antony F. "The Growth of Joshua 1–12 and the Theology of Extermination." Pages 2:72–88 in *Reading the Hebrew Bible for a New Millennium: Form, Concept, and Theological Perspective*. Edited by Deborah Ellens, Michael Floyd, Wonil Kim, and Marvin Sweeney. 2 vols. Harrisburg, PA: Trinity Press International, 2000.

Campbell, Antony F., and Mark A. O'Brien. *Unfolding the Deuteronomistic History: Origins, Upgrades, Present Text*. Minneapolis: Fortress, 2000.

Claassens, L. Juliana M. "Biblical Theology as Dialogue: Continuing the Conversation on Mikhail Bakhtin and Biblical Theology." *JBL* 122 (2003): 127–44.

Collins, John. "The Zeal of Phinehas: The Bible and the Legitimation of Violence." *JBL* 122 (2003): 3–21.

Creach, Jerome F. D. *Violence in Scripture: Resources for the Use of Scripture in the Church*. Louisville: Westminster John Knox, 2013.

Crenshaw, James. *Defending God: Biblical Responses to the Problem of Evil*. Oxford: Oxford University Press, 2005.

Demetz, Peter. *Marx, Engels, and the Poets*. Chicago: University of Chicago Press, 1967.

Derrida, Jacques. *Of Grammatology*. 40th anniversary ed. Baltimore: Johns Hopkins University Press, 2016.

———. *Writing and Difference*. Chicago: University of Chicago Press, 1978

Desanti, Jean-Toussaint. *Introduction à l'histoire de la philosophie*. 2nd ed. Paris: Presses universitaires de France, 2006.

Eagleton, Terry. *Criticism and Ideology: A Study in Marxist Literary Theory*. London: Verso, 1985.

———. *The Function of Criticism*. London: Verso, 1984.

———. *Ideology: An Introduction*. New York: Verso, 1991.

———. *Literary Theory*. Minneapolis: University of Minnesota Press, 1983.

———. *Marxism and Literary Criticism*. Oakland: University of California Press, 1976.

Foucault, Michel. *Historie de la folie à l' âge classique*. Paris: Gallimard, 1972.

Fretheim, Terence, and Karlfried Froelich. *The Bible as Word of God in a Postmodern Age*. Minneapolis: Fortress, 1998.

Gilkey, Langdon. "Ontology, Cosmology, and the Travail of Biblical Language." *JR* 41 (1961): 194–205.

Gottwald, Norman K. *The Tribes of Yahweh: A Sociology of the Religion of Liberated Israel, 1250–1050 BCE*. Maryknoll, NY: Orbis Books, 1979.

Jameson, Fredric. *Marxism and Form: Twentieth-Century Dialectical Theories of Literature*. Princeton: Princeton University Press, 1974.

———. *The Political Unconscious: Narrative as a Socially Symbolic Act*. New York: Cornell University Press, 1981.

———. *The Prison-House of Language: A Critical Account of Structuralism and Russian Formalism*. Princeton: Princeton University Press, 1972.

Kaufmann, Yehezkel. *The Religion of Israel*. Translated by Moshe Greenberg. New York: Schocken, 1972.

Kelle, Brad, and Frank Ames, eds. *Writing and Reading War: Rhetoric, Gender, and Ethics in Biblical and Modern Contexts*. Atlanta: Society of Biblical Literature, 2008.

Kim, Wonil. "Biblical Theology in Canonical Perspective: Jewish and Christian Models." Society of Biblical Literature presentation, San Antonio, Texas, 2016.

Knierim, Rolf P. "Cosmos and History in Israel's Theology." Pages 171–224 in *The Task of Old Testament Theology: Substance, Method, and Cases*. Grand Rapids: Eerdmans, 1995.

———. "Hope in the Old Testament." Pages 244–68 in *The Task of Old Testament Theology: Substance, Method, and Cases*. Grand Rapids: Eerdmans, 1995

———. "On the Contours of Old Testament and Biblical Hamartiology." Pages 416–67 in *The Task of Old Testament Theology: Substance, Method, and Cases*. Grand Rapids: Eerdmans, 1995.

———. *The Task of Old Testament Theology: Substance, Method, and Cases*. Grand Rapids: Eerdmans, 1995.

Long, Burke. "Letting Rival Gods Be Rivals: Biblical Theology in a Postmodern Age." Pages 222–33 in *Problems in Biblical Theology: Essays in Honor of Rolf Knierim*. Edited by Henry T. C. Sun, Keith Eades, and James Robinson. Grand Rapids: Eerdmans, 1997.

Lucid, Daniel Peri. "Preface to Revolution: Russian Marxist Literary Criticism, 1883–1917." PhD diss., Yale University, 1972.

Lukács, Georg. *Die Theorie des Romans*. 2nd ed. Neuwied am Rhein: Luchterhand, 1963.

———. *The Historical Novel*. London: Merlin, 1962.

———. *Studies in European Realism*. New York: Grosset & Dunalp, 1964.

Macherey, Pierre. *In a Materialist Way: Selected Essays*. Edited by Warren Montag. Translated by Ted Stolze. London: Verso, 1998.

———. "In a Materialist Way." Translated by Lorna Scott Fox. Pages 136–54 in *Philosophy in France Today*. Edited by Alan Montefiore. Cambridge: Cambridge University Press, 1983.

———. *A Theory of Literary Production*. Translated by Geoffrey Wall. Repr. ed. London: Routledge, 2006.

Marx, Karl. *Critique of Hegel's Philosophy of Right*. Edited with an introduction and notes by Joseph O'Malley. Translated by Annette Jolin and Joseph O'Malley. Cambridge: Cambridge University Press, 1970.

Meyers, Carol. *Discovering Eve: Ancient Israelite Women in Context*. Oxford: Oxford University Press, 1988.

Min, Anselm Kyongsuk. *Dialectic of Salvation: Issues in Theology of Liberation*. Albany: State University of New York Press, 1989.

Mulhern, Francis, ed. *Contemporary Marxist Literary Criticism*. New York: Longman, 1992.

Niditch, Susan. *War in the Hebrew Bible: A Study in the Ethics of Violence*. Oxford: Oxford University Press, 1993.

Odell, Margaret. Review of *Theology of the Old Testament*, by Joel S. Kaminsky, Margaret S. Odell, and Rolf Rendtorff. *RBL*, November 8, 1999.

Perdue, Leo. *Reconstructing Old Testament Theology*. Minneapolis: Fortress, 2005.

Prior, Michael. "A Land Flowing with Milk, Honey, and People (the Lattey Lecture 1997)." *Spring Britain* 28 (1998): 2–17.

Provan, Iain. *Seriously Dangerous Religion: What the Old Testament Really Says and Why It Matters*. Waco, TX: Baylor University Press, 2014.

Rendtorff, Rolf. *The Canonical Hebrew Bible: A Theology of the Old Testament*. Leiden: Deo, 2005.

Rogerson, John W. *A Theology of the Old Testament: Cultural Memory, Communication, and Being Human*. Minneapolis: Fortress, 2010.

Smolin, Lee. *Time Reborn: From the Crisis in Physics to the Future of the Universe*. New York: Mariner, 2014.

Stolze, Ted. "What Is a Philosophical Tendency?" *Historical Materialism* 23.4 (2015): 3–38.

Sweeney, Marvin A. "Biblical Theology in Canonical Perspective: Jewish and Christian Models." Paper presented at the Society of Biblical Literature Annual Meeting, San Antonio, 2016.

———. *Reading the Hebrew Bible After the Shoah*. Minneapolis: Fortress, 2008.

Wild, Lawrence. "Logic: Dialectic and Contradiction." Pages 275–95 in *The Cambridge Companion to Marx*. Edited by Terrell Carver. Cambridge: Cambridge University Press, 1991.

Williams, Raymond. *Marxism and Literature*. Oxford: Oxford University Press, 1977.

Making a Place for Metaphor
in Biblical Theology

Andrea L. Weiss

When I initially received an invitation to contribute to a conversation on "What Is Biblical Theology?" I agreed to participate not because I knew the answer to this question but because I did not. As a rabbinic student at the Hebrew Union College–Jewish Institute of Religion in New York, I took courses in medieval Jewish philosophy and modern Jewish thought, but not biblical theology. At the University of Pennsylvania, I studied Deuteronomy, Kings, and other biblical books, but not biblical theology. Finally, not surprisingly, in my position as a Bible professor at the Hebrew Union College–Jewish Institute of Religion, I teach courses on the prophets, Psalms, and other subjects, but not biblical theology. Nevertheless, since much of my research focuses on biblical metaphors for God, I had a hunch that I would have something to say about biblical theology.

1. Biblical Theology in a Jewish Context

A review of the evolving history of the field of biblical theology reveals why it makes sense that I did not formally study biblical theology in rabbinical school in the late 1980s and early 1990s and then in subsequent years in a doctoral program in which I studied mainly with Jewish professors. In a 1987 essay, "Tanakh Theology," Moshe Goshen-Gottstein observes that, in contrast to Christian colleagues, "no Jewish Bible scholar came to the academic scene as a trained 'theologian.'" He asserts: "'Theology' was something that simply did not exist for Tanakh scholarship."[1] In the title

---

1. Moshe Goshen-Gottstein, "Tanakh Theology: The Religion of the Old Testament and the Place of Jewish Biblical Theology," in *Ancient Israelite Religion: Essays in Honor of Frank Moore Cross*, ed. Patrick D. Miller Jr., Paul D. Hanson, and S. Dean

of another article published that same year, Jon D. Levenson states matter-of-factly, "Why Jews Are Not Interested in Biblical Theology."[2] Levenson offers a number of reasons for this lack of interest, including what he characterizes as "the intense anti-Semitism evident in many of the classic works in the field," the view of Old Testament theology as "a preparatory exercise for the study of the New Testament," an active Protestant agenda, and the "impulse to systematize."[3]

Ten years later, however, the tenor of the conversation began to change, in part due to a 1996 University of Chicago conference on "Jewish Biblical Theology" organized by Michael Fishbane and Tikva Frymer-Kensky. Marc Zvi Brettler, a participant in that conference, published a 1997 article in which he describes Jewish biblical theology as an "emerging enterprise."[4] He speculates that in another ten years it might be necessary to revise Levenson's title to read, "Why Jews *Were* Not Interested in Biblical Theology."[5] In another article that appeared in 1997, Marvin A. Sweeney also plays on Levenson's title, calling his piece, "Why Jews Should Be Interested in Biblical Theology."[6] Likewise, Frymer-Kensky claims that, in the not too distant past, writing on Jewish biblical theology would have been "unthinkable" or "incomprehensible"; the title of her 2000 article, "The Emergence of Jewish Biblical Theologies," signals a significant shift.[7]

In 2012, twenty-five years after Levenson's influential essay, the publication of two full-length books on this subject proves that, in fact, Jews now are interested in and writing about biblical theology. The first, *Tanak* by Sweeney, aims to chart the course for a distinctively Jewish biblical

---

McBride (Philadelphia: Fortress, 1987), 621. He aims to fill this gap by advocating for what he describes as "a hitherto nonexisting area of academic study … the theology of the Tanakh" (617).

2. Jon D. Levenson, "Why Jews Are Not Interested in Biblical Theology," in *The Hebrew Bible, the Old Testament and Historical Criticism: Jews and Christians in Biblical Studies* (Louisville: Westminister John Knox, 1993), 33–61.

3. Levenson, "Why Jews Are Not Interested," 40, 39, 45–51.

4. Marc Zvi Brettler, "Biblical History and Jewish Biblical Theology," *JR* 77 (1997): 564.

5. Brettler, "Biblical History and Jewish Biblical Theology," 565.

6. Marvin A. Sweeney, "Why Jews Should Be Interested in Biblical Theology," *CCAR* 44 (1997): 67–75.

7. Tikva Frymer-Kensky, "The Emergence of Jewish Biblical Theology," in *Jews, Christians, and the Theology of the Hebrew Scriptures*, ed. Alice Ogden Bellis and Joel S. Kaminsky (Atlanta: Society of Biblical Literature, 2000), 109.

theology.[8] The second, *Jewish Biblical Theology*, edited by Isaac Kalimi, collects the work of fifteen Jewish scholars writing about various theological issues and topics.[9]

Interestingly, one of these essays challenges the above narrative arc. Ehud Ben Zvi asserts that the "social memory in which there was no Jewish biblical theology before the present … deemphasizes or 'erases' … a relatively large corpus of data," including medieval theologians such as Saadia Gaon and Maimonides, as well as twentieth-century thinkers such as Martin Buber and Abraham Joshua Heschel.[10] He contends that because much of the contemporary theological work has been written by liberal Jews, it has been marginalized, thus leading to the misperception that Jewish engagement in biblical theology is a recent phenomenon. Sweeney likewise finds it "somewhat ironic" that Jews are perceived as "relative newcomers to the modern critical and theological study of the Bible."[11] He argues that Jews have participated in the field of biblical theology since the Enlightenment.[12]

In a survey of influential figures in the field of contemporary Jewish biblical theology, Sweeney highlights the work of twenty-three scholars whose work appeared since the 1980s. He asserts that, despite Levenson's claim that Jews should not be interested in biblical theology, and "despite the fact that [Levenson] views his work as the history of Israelite religion, not biblical theology," Levenson himself made "substantive contributions to the field."[13] Some of the individuals Sweeney cites intentionally write

---

8. Marvin A. Sweeney, *Tanak: A Theological and Critical Introduction to the Jewish Bible* (Minneapolis: Fortress, 2012).

9. Isaac Kalimi, ed., *Jewish Biblical Theology: Perspectives and Case Studies* (Winona Lake, IN: Eisenbrauns, 2012).

10. Ehud Ben Zvi, "Constructing the Past: The Recent History of Jewish Biblical Theology," in Kalimi, *Jewish Biblical Theology*, 41.

11. Marvin A. Sweeney, "Jewish Biblical Theology," in *The Hebrew Bible: New Insights and Scholarship*, ed. Frederick E. Greenspahn (New York: New York University Press, 2008), 192.

12. Sweeney, *Tanak*, 11. Similarly, in a chapter on "Dialogical Biblical Theology: A Jewish Approach to Reading Scripture Theologically," Benjamin D. Sommer endeavors "to show that Jewish interest in this field had in fact been vigorous even before the publication of Levenson's article" (in *Biblical Theology: Introducing the Conversation*, ed. Leo G. Perdue, Robert Morgan, Benjamin D. Sommer [Nashville: Abingdon, 2009], 3).

13. Sweeney, *Tanak*, 15.

about biblical theology, such as Benjamin D. Sommer, who has published articles on "Revelation at Sinai in the Hebrew Bible and in Jewish Theology" and "Dialogical Biblical Theology."[14] In other cases, scholars may "take up various important issues relevant to Jewish biblical theology," but they may not explicitly classify their work as "biblical theology."[15] According to Sweeney, what these various scholars have in common is their attention to the defining feature of biblical theology: "a concern with the construction of G-d as presented in the Bible."[16] Given that definition, in the case of my own research, I may not have been engaged consciously in the enterprise of biblical theology, but as a scholar of biblical metaphor with a particular interest in metaphors for God, I have, in fact, been part of the emerging field of Jewish biblical theology.

2. Biblical Theology in a Metaphoric Context

If, according to John J. Collins, biblical theology should involve "the critical evaluation of biblical speech about God" and the "open-ended and critical inquiry into the meaning and function of God-language," then the study of metaphors for God should be central to biblical theology.[17] Sallie McFague recognizes the potential contribution of metaphor in her 1982 book, *Metaphorical Theology: Models of God in Religious Language*. Challenging the dominance of certain core metaphors such as God the Father, she asserts that "a metaphorical theology will insist that *many* metaphors and models are necessary, that a piling up of images is essential, both to avoid idolatry and to attempt to express the richness and variety of the divine-human relationship."[18]

In the thirty-seven years since the publication of McFague's book, few scholars have deliberately wedded the fields of biblical theology and metaphor studies. Walter Brueggemann stands out as one of the few bibli-

---

14. Sweeney, *Tanak*, 18, referring to Sommer, "Revelation at Sinai in the Hebrew Bible and in Jewish Theology," *JR* 79 (1999): 422–51, and Sommer, "Dialogical Biblical Theology."

15. See, for example, the works cited by Jacob Milgrom and Dalit Rom-Shiloni, Sweeney, *Tanak*, 19–20.

16. Sweeney, *Tanak*, 26.

17. John J. Collins, "Is a Critical Biblical Theology Possible?" in *Encounters with Biblical Theology* (Minneapolis: Fortress, 2005), 18, 22.

18. Sallie McFague, *Metaphorical Theology: Models of God in Religious Language* (Philadelphia: Fortress, 1982), 20.

cal theologians to address the topic of metaphor. In *Theology of the Old Testament*, Brueggemann argues that "the 'what' of Israel's God-talk is completely linked to the 'how' of that speech."[19] He explains:

> To cite God as the subject of theology, however, is to take only the *theos* of theology. There is also the speech (*logos*) element of theology. Thus our proper subject is *speech about God*, suggesting yet again that our work has to do with rhetoric. The question that will guide our work is, How does ancient Israel, in this text, speak about God?[20]

Addressing what he sees as "insufficient attention to the ways of Israel's rhetoric" in Old Testament theology, Brueggemann divides his analysis of Israel's "practice of testimony" into three categories: verbal sentences, adjectival claims about God, and nouns.[21]

The chapter on "Nouns: Yahweh as Constant" focuses on "The Testimony of Metaphor," starting with the following assertion: "Metaphors are nouns that function in Israel in order to give access to the Subject of verbs, who is endlessly elusive." The chapter goes on to explore "Metaphors of Governance," such as God as king, warrior, judge, and father, and "Metaphors of Sustenance," such as God as an artist, gardener, mother, and shepherd. Throughout the chapter Brueggemann calls attention to the multiplicity of metaphors in the Bible, a point he links to McFague's earlier work. He observes that "the Old Testament employs many metaphors for Yahweh because no single metaphor can say all that Israel has to say about their God." Brueggemann insists that "the sheer multiplicity and polyvocality of the nouns ... are necessary in order to speak Yahweh fully and faithfully."[22]

It is important to note that, although Brueggemann equates metaphors with nouns and often uses the two terms interchangeably, divine metaphors manifest themselves in multiple grammatical guises. Although we use English nouns such as *shepherd* or *husband* to label biblical metaphors for God, that does not mean that those metaphors appear exclusively in nominal form in the Bible. Some metaphors are found only in verbal constructions, while still others are expressed through both

---

19. Walter Brueggemann, *Theology of the Old Testament: Testimony, Dispute, Advocacy* (Minneapolis: Fortress, 1997), 119.

20. Brueggemann, *Theology of the Old Testament*, 117, emphasis original.

21. Brueggemann, *Theology of the Old Testament*, 119 n. 5.

22. Brueggemann, *Theology of the Old Testament*, 230–32, 262.

nouns and verbs.[23] Furthermore, Brueggemann concentrates exclusively on human analogies for God, thereby omitting from the discussion the many nonhuman divine analogies that frequent the Bible, such as God as a rock, shield, dew, or lion. Published in 1997, *Theology of the Old Testament* appeared just before the steady growth in research on metaphor in the Bible, as biblical scholars began to engage seriously in metaphor theory and then apply those insights to the Bible.[24] By insisting that we explore both what and how ancient Israel spoke about God, Brueggemann makes a compelling argument for metaphor's place in the field of biblical theology, yet a more sophisticated understanding of how biblical metaphors operate and interact requires attention not just to rhetoric but also to linguistics and metaphor theory. The following examples aim to illustrate how this type of close reading of biblical metaphors can inform and advance the theological endeavor.

3. Theological Metaphors in a Biblical Context

Amidst more familiar biblical metaphors such as God as king and shepherd, the Hebrew Bible contains a diverse array of analogies that articulate

---

23. Metaphors of God as an eagle, for example, appear only using the corresponding noun (e.g., Exod 19:4; Deut 32:11). In contrast, metaphors of God as a farmer are constructed from verbs and other linguistic elements that depict the actions of a farmer, without ever using a nominal label for that metaphoric role (e.g., Isa 5:1–7). In other cases, a given metaphor may appear in both forms: compare the instances of God as a king formed from a verb (e.g., Exod 15:18) versus a noun (e.g., Zech 14:9).

24. Several full-length books about metaphor in the Bible came out in 1989–1990, including Marc Zvi Brettler, *God Is King: Understanding an Israelite Metaphor* (Sheffield: Sheffield Academic, 1989), and Peter Macky, *The Centrality of Metaphors to Biblical Thought: A Method for Interpreting the Bible* (Wales: Mellen, 1990), both of which followed the seminal work by George Lakoff and Mark Johnson, *Metaphors We Live By* (Chicago: University of Chicago Press, 1980). In the years immediately following the publication of *Theology of the Old Testament*, increasing numbers of articles and books on the subject began to appear, some with a particular focus on metaphors for God, such as Marc Zvi Brettler, "The Metaphorical Mapping of God in the Hebrew Bible," in *Metaphor, Canon and Community: Jewish, Christian and Islamic Approaches*, ed. Ralph Bisschops and James Francis (Oxford: Lang, 1999), 219–32; Bernhard Oestreich, *Metaphors and Similes for Yahweh in Hosea 14:2–9* (Frankfurt am Main: Lang, 1998). For a review of research on metaphor in the Bible, see Andrea L. Weiss, *Figurative Language in Biblical Prose Narrative: Metaphor in the Book of Samuel* (Leiden: Brill, 2006), 20–32.

different messages about who God is and how God operates in the world, particularly in relationship with the people Israel. Take, for example, the poem in Deut 32 that compares God to a rock (32:4), father (32:6), eyelid (32:10), eagle (32:11), and nursing mother (32:13)—all within the span of only ten verses.[25] Each metaphor serves to make a different point: about God's steadfast loyalty, God's role as Israel's creator, God's protective powers, and God's loving, abundant provision of Israel in the promised land. The text makes no attempt to reconcile the conflicting aspects of these analogies: how God can be perceived as both father and mother, as both an animal and a concrete object. Instead, each metaphor communicates a separate aspect of the larger message about God's early relationship with Israel and how that relationship eventually goes awry. Deuteronomy 32 reinforces Brueggemann's observation that the "fluid and porous" metaphors in the Bible resist reductionism: "They do not all fit conveniently or smoothly together, and Israel did not seem bothered about the awkwardness created by the richness."[26]

Multiple metaphors appear not only within the same book or the same pericope but often within the same verse. Due in part to the dynamics of poetic parallelism, numerous biblical verses pair metaphors that relate to one another with varying degrees of semantic equivalence and contrast. Jeremiah 14:8–9, for instance, places two metaphoric word pairs side-by-side:

Hope of Israel,
its rescuer in times of trouble,
why are You like a *sojourner* in the land,
and like a *traveler* who turns aside to lodge?
Why are You like a *helpless man*,[27]

---

25. For a discussion of these metaphors in light of conceptual metaphor theory and ancient Near Eastern iconography, see Izaak J. de Hulster and Brent A. Strawn, "Figuring YHWH in Unusual Ways: Deuteronomy 32 and Other Mixed Metaphors for God in the Old Testament," in *Iconographic Exegesis of the Hebrew Bible/Old Testament: An Introduction to Its Method and Practice*, ed. I. de Hulster, B. Strawn, and R. Bonfiglio (Göttingen: Vandenhoeck & Ruprecht, 2015), 117–33.

26. Brueggemann, *Theology of the Old Testament*, 262.

27. While a certain degree of uncertainty surrounds the *hapax legomenon* נדהם, Jack R. Lundbom argues convincingly that the expression refers to "a helpless man." He explains: The verb "is commonly taken to mean, 'be astonished, surprised,' based largely on a comparison with Arabic. But the word has shown up on a late seventh-

like a *hero who cannot rescue?*
But You are in our midst, YHWH,
and Your name upon us is called.
Do not leave us!

The nonfigurative declarations that frame the passage express confidence in God's nearness and power to save, but through metaphor the two intervening questions introduce a clear sense of anxiety about the veracity of those assertions. The first metaphoric pair uses two related images—God as a temporary sojourner and an itinerant traveler—to depict the general notion of God as a wayfarer, a transient being. The second pair envisions God as a valiant hero who does not live up to expectations and cannot rescue those in need. While Jer 14:8–9 casts God in markedly different human roles, together both sets of metaphors reveal the people's fear of not experiencing God's lasting, efficacious presence. Thus, through figurative language the people confront God with the reality of their spiritual lives. Although they refer to God in direct address as their "rescuer in times of trouble" (14:8), they worry that God "cannot rescue" (14:9). Although they acclaim that God is in their midst (14:9), they bemoan God's ephemeral presence (14:8). Metaphor provides a means to give voice to doubts and insecurities that lurk behind more familiar and more formulaic pronouncements about God.

Elsewhere in Jeremiah another group of metaphoric word pairs suggests that the misgivings go both ways. In Jer 2:31–32, God expresses concern about Israel's commitment to the relationship:

Have I become like a *wilderness* for Israel,
or a *land of darkness?*
Why do my people say, "We roam freely
and we will not come again to you"?
Shall a young woman forget her *jewels,*
a bride her *sashes?*
But my people have forgotten me,
days without number.

In 2:31, the first metaphoric pair suggests that God resembles a dark, desolate wilderness, the kind of foreboding place one would shun and

---

century ostracon from Yavneh-Yam, in the N-stem, where the meaning appears to be 'helpless (to save),' the exact opposite of 'savior'" (*Jeremiah 1–20*, AB 21A [New York: Doubleday, 1999], 702). Translations are my own.

"not come [to] again." In contrast, the metaphoric pair in 2:32 compares God to treasured, sought-after material objects. The verse raises the unexpected possibility that a woman might neglect her jewels or wedding finery, just as one would avoid or neglect inhospitable territory. Through metaphors, the prophet accuses the people of neglecting God, the same message expressed in the non-figurative statement at the end of 2:32: "But my people have forgotten me, days without number." These unusual, unexpected images vividly communicate God's disappointment and vulnerability. They do so in a way that aims to motivate Israel to repair the strained relationship, similar to the way the metaphors in Jer 14:8–9 seek to soften God's heart and ensure that God will respond favorably to the plea: "Do not leave us."

The metaphoric word pairs in these two passages from Jeremiah illustrate one way that metaphors interact in the Bible. Less frequently we encounter another notable form of metaphoric interaction: "metaphoric clusters" that contain four or more metaphoric utterances for the same referent in a compact unit with a limited number of consecutive poetic lines. For example, in Ps 18:3 the speaker establishes his special relationship with God through a lengthy list of divine epithets: "YHWH is my *crag*, and my *stronghold*, and my deliverer, my God, my *rock* where I shelter, my *shield*, and the *horn* of my rescue, my *fortress*."[28] If terseness is a defining feature of biblical poetry, why use so many words to cram together so many metaphors in such a confined poetic unit? Konrad Schaefer offers one answer when he wonders: "How can God resist the litany of titles which invoke personal strength and protection?"[29] His remark suggests that the metaphors and nonfigurative terms strung together in this verse perform a persuasive function, intended to move the addressee to take action on the speaker's behalf. The effusive praise also reflects something about the challenge of trying to articulate in human language the complexity and immensity of the divine.

More often we find single metaphors: instances where an analogy in one half of a bi- or tricolon stands alone and is not paired with a corresponding metaphor elsewhere in the poetic verse. Examples abound as biblical authors utilize the known—all aspects of the world around them—to explore the unknown: God's role in the universe, God's expec-

---

28. Other examples of metaphoric clusters include Hos 13:7–8; Ps 18:5–6; 31:3–5; 62:7–8; 144:1–2.

29. Konrad Schaefer, *Psalms* (Collegeville, MN: Liturgical Press, 2001), 43.

tations for humanity, God's special connection to the people Israel. The book of Hosea showcases the metaphoric creativity, sophistication, and diversity found in the Bible. In this prophetic corpus and elsewhere in the Bible, metaphors for God involve corresponding analogies for Israel. If Israel is an unfaithful wife, then God is a jealous, vengeful husband (Hos 2). If Israel is a senseless dove flittering between Egypt and Assyria, then God is a bird catcher ready to swoop his net down on the unsuspecting bird (Hos 7:11–12). If Israel is a pampered child, then God is a loving parent (Hos 11:1–4). If Israel is a verdant plant, then God is the dew that enables the plant to thrive (Hos 14:6–8). These examples remind us of the dynamic and reciprocal nature of the divine-human relationship. Explaining his notion of divine pathos, Abraham Joshua Heschel writes: "God is involved in the life of man. A personal relationship binds Him to Israel; there is an interweaving of the divine in the affairs of the nation."[30] According to Goshen-Gottstein, Tanak theology should explore "what Tanakh is about." In his view, the Tanak is all about "God's way with Israel and Israel's way with God" or "the central ongoing binary relationship between God and Israel."[31] Metaphors play a pivotal role in communicating what it means to be engaged in this relationship.

We need multiple metaphors, in the Bible and in our lives, because no single comparison can encapsulate all that needs to be said about God and the complexity of the divine-human connection. Reflecting on the reason biblical texts present a mix of divine images, Brent A. Strawn concludes: "One metaphor alone by itself ... cannot, in the words of Brueggemann, get this God said right. The elusive nature of Yahweh is, in fact, what leads to the use of metaphorical language ... in the first place."[32] After studying the juxtaposition of different metaphors throughout the book of Hosea, Göran Eidevall proposes that the purpose of such a "plurality of perspectives" is not simply stylistic variation. He posits: "The effect is radical relativization. No model is given a monopolistic position ... which hints at the insight that all kinds of 'anthropomorphism' are, in the final analysis,

---

30. Abraham Joshua Heschel, *The Prophets* (New York: Perennial Classics, 2001), 29.

31. Goshen-Gottstein, "Tanakh Theology," 628.

32. Brent A. Strawn, *What Is Stronger Than a Lion? Leonine Image and Metaphor in the Hebrew Bible and the Ancient Near East* (Fribourg: Academic Press Fribourg; Göttingen: Vandenhoeck & Ruprecht, 2005), 271.

hopelessly inadequate as representations of the deity: 'for I am God, and not human' (11:9)."[33]

Multivocality proves to be a prominent feature of not only how ancient Israel spoke about God (*logos*) but also how Jewish scholars speak about biblical theology (*theos*). Levenson writes:

> The effort to construct a systematic, harmonious theological statement out of the unsystematic and polydox materials in the Hebrew Bible fits Christianity better than Judaism because systematic theology in general is more prominent and more at home in the church than in the *bet midrash* (study house) and the synagogue.[34]

Building on this observation, Brettler claims that "any Jewish biblical theology needs to be attuned to polydoxy or polyphony" and should be "a *Mitte*-less theology."[35] Likewise, when Sommer considers the question "what sort of biblical theology *would* interest Jews?" he concludes: "Such a theology would accept the multivocality of the biblical text and would eschew attempts to privilege any particular biblical voice."[36] Metaphors contribute to the multivocal nature of the Bible as they capture the diverse ways people in ancient Israel imagined and spoke about God. As a result, metaphor deserves a more prominent place in the field of biblical theology.

Bibliography

Ben Zvi, Ehud. "Constructing the Past: The Recent History of Jewish Biblical Theology." Pages 31–50 in *Jewish Biblical Theology: Perspectives and Case Studies*. Edited by Isaac Kalimi. Winona Lake, IN: Eisenbrauns, 2012.

---

33. Göran Eidevall, *Grapes in the Desert: Metaphors, Models, and Themes in Hosea 4–14* (Stockholm: Almqvist & Wiksell International, 1996), 229.

34. Levenson, "Why Jews Are Not Interested in Biblical Theology," 51.

35. Marc Zvi Brettler, "Psalms and Jewish Biblical Theology," in *Jewish Biblical Theology: Perspectives and Case Studies*, 189. Brettler refers here to the focus on finding the *Mitte* or "center" of biblical theology. See also Frymer-Kensky, "Emergence of Jewish Biblical Theology," 114–21; Sommer, "Dialogical Biblical Theology," 4, 13.

36. Sommer, "Dialogical Biblical Theology," 13, italics original. Also see Sweeney's notion of the "dialogical character of the Bible" produced by the diversity of concerns it raises and the various viewpoints it espouses (*Tanak*, 32–33).

Brettler, Marc Zvi. "Biblical History and Jewish Biblical Theology." *JR* 77 (1997): 564.

———. *God Is King: Understanding an Israelite Metaphor.* Sheffield: Sheffield Academic, 1989.

———. "The Metaphorical Mapping of God in the Hebrew Bible." Pages 219–32 in *Metaphor, Canon and Community: Jewish, Christian and Islamic Approaches.* Edited by Ralph Bisschops and James Francis. Oxford: Lang, 1999.

———. "Psalms and Jewish Biblical Theology." Pages 187–97 in *Jewish Biblical Theology: Perspectives and Case Studies.* Edited by Isaac Kalimi. Winona Lake, IN: Eisenbrauns, 2012.

Brueggemann, Walter. *Theology of the Old Testament: Testimony, Dispute, Advocacy.* Minneapolis: Fortress, 1997.

Collins, John J. "Is a Critical Biblical Theology Possible?" Pages 11–23 in *Encounters with Biblical Theology.* Minneapolis: Fortress, 2005.

Eidevall, Göran. *Grapes in the Desert: Metaphors, Models, and Themes in Hosea 4–14.* Stockholm: Almqvist & Wiksell International, 1996.

Frymer-Kensky, Tikva. "The Emergence of Jewish Biblical Theology." Pages 109–21 in *Jews, Christians, and the Theology of the Hebrew Scriptures.* Edited by Alice Ogden Bellis and Joel S. Kaminsky. Atlanta: Society of Biblical Literature, 2000.

Goshen-Gottstein, Moshe. "Tanakh Theology: The Religion of the Old Testament and the Place of Jewish Biblical Theology." Pages 617–44 in *Ancient Israelite Religion: Essays in Honor of Frank Moore Cross.* Edited by Patrick D. Miller Jr., Paul D. Hanson, and S. Dean McBride. Philadelphia: Fortress, 1987.

Heschel, Abraham Joshua. *The Prophets.* New York: Perennial Classics, 2001.

Hulster, Izaak J. de, and Brent A. Strawn. "Figuring YHWH in Unusual Ways: Deuteronomy 32 and Other Mixed Metaphors for God in the Old Testament." Pages 117–33 in *Iconographic Exegesis of the Hebrew Bible/Old Testament: An Introduction to Its Method and Practice.* Edited by Izaak de Hulster, Brent Strawn, and Ryan Bonfiglio. Göttingen: Vandenhoeck & Ruprecht, 2015.

Kalimi, Isaac, ed. *Jewish Biblical Theology: Perspectives and Case Studies.* Winona Lake, IN: Eisenbrauns, 2012.

Lakoff, George, and Mark Johnson. *Metaphors We Live By.* Chicago: University of Chicago Press, 1980.

Levenson, Jon D. "Why Jews Are Not Interested in Biblical Theology." Pages 33–61 in *The Hebrew Bible, the Old Testament and Historical Criticism: Jews and Christians in Biblical Studies*. Louisville: Westminister John Knox, 1993.

Lundbom, Jack R. *Jeremiah 1–20*. AB 21A. New York: Doubleday, 1999.

Macky, Peter. *The Centrality of Metaphors to Biblical Thought: A Method for Interpreting the Bible*. Wales: Mellen, 1990.

McFague, Sallie. *Metaphorical Theology: Models of God in Religious Language*. Philadelphia: Fortress, 1982.

Oestreich, Bernhard. *Metaphors and Similes for Yahweh in Hosea 14:2–9*. Frankfurt am Main: Lang, 1998.

Schaefer, Konrad. *Psalms*. Collegeville, MN: Liturgical Press, 2001.

Sommer, Benjamin D. "Dialogical Biblical Theology: A Jewish Approach to Reading Scripture Theologically." Pages 1–53 in *Biblical Theology: Introducing the Conversation*. Edited by Leo G. Perdue, Robert Morgan, Benjamin D. Sommer. Nashville: Abingdon, 2009.

———. "Revelation at Sinai in the Hebrew Bible and in Jewish Theology." *JR* 79 (1999): 422–51.

Strawn, Brent A. *What Is Stronger Than a Lion? Leonine Image and Metaphor in the Hebrew Bible and the Ancient Near East*. Fribourg: Academic Press Fribourg; Göttingen: Vandenhoeck & Ruprecht, 2005.

Sweeney, Marvin A. "Jewish Biblical Theology." Pages 191–208 in *The Hebrew Bible: New Insights and Scholarship*. Edited by Frederick E. Greenspahn. New York: New York University Press, 2008.

———. *Tanak: A Theological and Critical Introduction to the Jewish Bible*. Minneapolis: Fortress, 2012.

———. "Why Jews Should Be Interested in Biblical Theology." *CCAR* 44 (1997): 67–75.

Weiss, Andrea L. *Figurative Language in Biblical Prose Narrative: Metaphor in the Book of Samuel*. Leiden: Brill, 2006.

A Theology of Creation—Critical and Christian

Jacqueline E. Lapsley

1. Christian, Jewish, Critical?

The title of the panel for which this essay was prepared was "Biblical Theology in Context: Jewish, Christian, and Critical Approaches to the Theology of the Hebrew Bible." It is worth reflecting a bit on the title itself, each part of which is worthy of an essay unto itself. Out of curiosity I went to Wikipedia to see if there was an entry on *biblical theology* and, if so, what it said. There is indeed an entry on biblical theology, which is defined as follows:

> Biblical theology for the most part is a Christian approach in which the theologian studies the Bible from the perspective of understanding the progressive history of God revealing Himself to humanity following the Fall and throughout the Old Testament and New Testament.[clarification needed] It particularly focuses on the epochs of the Old Testament in order to understand how each part of it ultimately points forward to fulfillment in the life mission of Jesus Christ.[1]

This definition of biblical theology is unrecognizable to me, and I think of myself as primarily a biblical theologian. I suspect it is also unrecognizable to many others. My favorite part of this formulation is the superscript editorial note from the Wikipedia editors in the middle of the text that says "clarification needed." Clarification is indeed needed. I will return to the problem of defining biblical theology below.

---

1. "Biblical Theology," Wikipedia, http://en.wikipedia.org/wiki/Biblical_theology, accessed October 30, 2014.

But first the second part of the panel title: "Jewish, Christian, and Critical Approaches to the Theology of the Hebrew Bible." This formulation suggests that Jewish and Christian approaches are somehow to be contrasted with critical approaches. Does a critical approach inhabit some neutral, objective space because it is nonconfessional? This seems strange indeed. Every approach is confessional in some way; that is, everyone has a worldview that informs her or his reading—atheists and agnostics are also confessional in this sense. Critical reading might be defined as readings that take seriously the various dimensions of the texts, their historical and cultural embeddedness. Critical readings use the methodologies and approaches in the biblical scholar's tool belt in order to illumine the texts. Logically, then, there are Jewish readings, Christian readings, agnostic readings, atheistic readings, and so on. Some of these are also critical readings, and some are not.

Since its origins, the nature of the task of biblical theology has been contested: Should biblical theology be descriptive or constructive? Descriptive biblical theology seeks to elucidate the theological claims of ancient Israelite writers; it essentially describes ancient Israelite religion.[2] Describing Israelite religion is an important task and a prerequisite for constructive biblical theology; descriptive biblical theology is one of the tools biblical theologians may use in constructive biblical theology. This leaves us with the question of how to define *constructive* biblical theology; this is to ask not only what it does but also what its purpose is. The topic here is more narrowly the theology of the Hebrew Scriptures, or Old Testament theology, in its Christian formulation.

2. Sculpting Old Testament Theology

My purpose here is not to recite the long history of discussion over the nature of biblical theology, from Johann Philipp Gabler, up through the mid-twentieth-century theologies of Walther Eichrodt, Gerhard von Rad, and Brevard S. Childs, to the present day with the major contributions of

---

2. James Barr tries to keep these distinct in *The Concept of Biblical Theology: An Old Testament Perspective* (Minneapolis: Fortress, 1999), but as Jon D. Levenson notes in his review, such a distinction collapses (review of *The Concept of Biblical Theology: An Old Testament Perspective*, by James Barr, First Things, February 2000, https://tinyurl.com/SBL03100a).

Walter Brueggemann and R. W. L. Moberly, among others.[3] Suffice it to say that biblical theology has been on somewhat less sure footing since the mid-twentieth-century attempts to discover a central theme around which to organize. In contrast to the multivolume works of von Rad, Eichrodt, and others in the glory days of biblical theology, contemporary biblical theologies usually pursue less ambitious programs for unifying their works. Biblical theologians are more cautious in their claims, and there is more recognition that factoring in the diversity of the texts is important.

Still, even as diversity is now widely accepted, the idea that biblical theology needs to have a certain coherence and be holistic is still widely assumed.[4] Many biblical theologians, including almost all feminist biblical theologians, resist the idea that a holistic or comprehensive treatment is necessary to qualify for the title "biblical theology" or "Old Testament theology." Indeed, many believe that a holistic, comprehensive Old Testament Theology is a unicorn: a creature that one can imagine and try to draw but never see because it does not exist. Rather, much biblical theology today undertakes readings of individual texts, explicit engagement with present-day social and political realities, reflection on themes occurring in a minority of texts, and so on—these are the purview of biblical theology, without apology. Feminist biblical theologians, among others, have pointed out that the totalizing schemas of traditional biblical theology have tended to reflect androcentric bias, and they sometimes engage in abstractions that are far from the needs and concerns of confessional communities, who are, or should be, the principle audience for constructive biblical theologies.

Over twenty years ago Carol A. Newsom reflected on the nature of biblical theology in a way that still resonates today. She begins by recount-

---

3. Walther Eichrodt, *Theologie des Alten Testaments*, 3 vols. (Leipzig: Hinrichs, 1933–1939); Gerhard von Rad, *Theologie des Alten Testaments*, 2 vols. (Munich: Kaiser, 1957–1960); Brevard S. Childs, *Biblical Theology of the Old and New Testaments: Theological Reflection on the Christian Bible* (Minneapolis: Fortress, 1993); Walter Brueggemann, *Theology of the Old Testament: Testimony, Dispute, Advocacy* (Minneapolis: Fortress, 1997); R. W. L. Moberly, *Old Testament Theology: Reading the Hebrew Bible as Christian Scripture* (Grand Rapids: Baker Academic, 2013).

4. For example, biblical theology and Old Testament theology offers a "coherent and wholistic presentation of the faith claims of the canonical text, in a way that satisfies the investigations of historical-critical scholarship and the confessional-interpretive needs of ongoing ecclesial communities" (Walter Brueggemann, *Old Testament Theology: An Introduction* [Nashville: Abingdon, 2010], 5).

ing a scene from a job interview in a Christian seminary: a candidate for a position in Old Testament reached an impasse with a theologian on the committee over how to read the Bible. The theologian inquired about the Hebrew Scriptures' theological center or primary theme. The biblical scholar resisted repeatedly, insisting on the diversity of texts in the biblical material, which prompted the theologian to blurt out in exasperation, "I'm just trying to find something that theology can work with."[5]

In her account, Newsom quotes a series of renowned biblical theologians from the past who gave theology something it could work with, but at the expense of distorting the Bible's own nature. The difficulty is that the Bible and its theological concerns are distorted by the modern West's propensity for monologic truth. Drawing from Mikhail Bakhtin's "Discourse in the Novel" and *Problems of Dostoevsky's Poetics*, Newsom offers instead a description of dialogical, or polyphonic, truth capable of negotiating the compositional and ideological complexity of biblical texts.[6] Dialogic truth "exists at the point of intersection of several unmerged voices," as a conversation among different consciousnesses embodied as persons. It is not systematic, but rather is manifest in *event*, in the dynamic interaction of perspectives that do not merge with one another and remain open, *unfinalizable*. Many scholars have since then also entered into biblical theology through Bakhtin's dialogic doors.[7]

Bakhtin gave Fyodor Mikhailovich Dostoevsky credit for creating such dialogic events in his novels. Within the Bible, Newsom acknowledges, only the book of Job shows evidence of similar orchestration. However, the biblical redactors' practice of leaving the voices of source materials unmerged, although it may frustrate a seeker of monologic truth, invites investigation into the (usually implicit but occasionally explicit) dialogues among texts and their authors. By way of example, Newsom notes side-by-side creation accounts, interpolated flood narratives, and repeated and varied treatments of such themes as identity, land, and outsiders in the

---

5. Carol A. Newsom, "Bakhtin, the Bible, and Dialogic Truth," *JR* 76 (1996): 290.

6. Mikhail Bakhtin, "Discourse in the Novel," in *The Dialogic Imagination*, ed. M. Holquist, trans. C. Emerson and M. Holquist (Austin: University of Texas Press, 1981), 259–422; Bakhtin, *Problems of Dostoevsky's Poetics*, ed. and trans. C. Emerson (Minneapolis: University of Minnesota Press, 1984).

7. Two examples are Carleen Mandolfo, *God in the Dock: Dialogic Tension in the Psalms of Lament* (London: Sheffield Academic, 2002); L. Juliana M. Claassens, *The God Who Provides: Biblical Images of Divine Nourishment* (Nashville: Abingdon, 2004).

patriarchal narratives. "Would it be possible," Newsom asks, "for biblical theology to 'play Dostoevsky' to the various ideas and worldviews of the biblical text? There are many implicit quarrels in the Bible which need only a little prodding to make them explicit." A biblical theologian's role, then, "would not be to inhabit the voice, as the novelist does, but rather to pick out the assumptions, experiences, entailments, embedded metaphors, and so on, that shape each perspective and to attempt to trace the dotted line to a point at which it intersects the claims of the other" and to "self-consciously go beyond what the texts themselves explicitly say to draw out the implications of their ideas."[8]

But the complaint of the theologian in that interview still rings in our ears. Tracing out the trajectories of competing voices until we see where they intersect may not be necessary or desirable for some forms of biblical theology. Dennis Olson has argued that one can engage in "provisional monologization," an act that both recognizes the dialogic nature of truth embedded in the Scriptures and also acknowledges that sometimes one simply must make some claims about what is being said in order to engage in constructive ethical and theological reflection.[9] It is possible to acknowledge the noncomprehensive, nonholistic nature of all biblical theologies and at the same time seek to hear the signal amid the noise in terms of a particular set of issues for a particular context.

People of faith have long puzzled over how they should interpret the Bible given its enormous diversity, that is, what kind of hermeneutical orientation, or overarching interpretive framework, they should adopt. As early as the fourth century, Augustine of Hippo, still an enormously influential Christian theologian for biblical theologians, famously affirmed: "Whoever, then, thinks that he understands the Holy Scriptures, or any part of them, but puts such an interpretation upon them as does not tend to build up this twofold love of God and our neighbor, does not yet understand them as he ought" (*Doctr. chr.* 1.3.3). So love of God and love of neighbor should be the interpretive framework within which all biblical interpretation occurs. Many Christians have found this to be a powerful and positive hermeneutic for reading the Bible. The difficulty is that loving God and loving neighbor have been notoriously difficult to define.[10] The

---

8. Newsom, "Bakhtin, the Bible, and Dialogic Truth," 305.

9. Dennis Olson, "Biblical Theology as Provisional Monologization: A Dialogue with Childs, Brueggemann and Bakhtin," *BibInt* 6 (1998): 162–80.

10. See the discussion in Richard S. Briggs, *The Virtuous Reader: Old Testament*

language of love is too slippery and, of late, too vacuous. Those who have used the Bible as a weapon in the debates over homosexuality, for example, repeatedly say that they are "loving their neighbor" with their "hate the sin, love the sinner" mantra, but the neighbors addressed do not experience it as love but as hate. Love is too fuzzy to be of use in our current context.

A recent volume of essays by biblical scholars and ethicists takes a different tack. The essays in *Restorative Readings*, edited by L. Juliana M. Claassens and Bruce C. Birch, center on a hermeneutic of human dignity as the necessary interpretive framework for biblical interpretation. Ethically informed, "restorative readings may contribute to the larger vision of the promotion of human dignity that manifests itself in the call to resist violence, injustice, and xenophobia that on a daily basis threaten the well-being of individuals and groups in different parts of the world."[11] The claim that human dignity is inherent and a central principle is, of course, derived from the Bible itself (see Gen 1:26; Gal 3:28; Col 3:11) even as it also becomes the lens by which to interpret the Bible—a hermeneutical circle that still makes a salutary journey.

With Claassens's definition in mind, one might, with all due respect, emend Augustine a bit: the fulfillment and end of Scripture is the love of God and the dignity of every human being. Human dignity may seem pretty basic, but it is critical to affirm in an era when it is under such acute threat around the world. Far from a departure from Christian tradition, the emphasis on human dignity is in continuity with the traditional emphasis in the Jewish and Christian traditions on the central role of humanity within creation. But by defining human dignity as entailing a call to resist violence, injustice, and xenophobia, Claassens gives a clearer substance to Augustine's "love" ethic.

3. Creational Theology

Yet as Patricia K. Tull and others have shown, an emphasis on human dignity without a clear understanding of humanity within the context of the rest of creation is destructive for nonhuman creation. Furthermore, human dignity itself is diminished and distorted from its true form unless

---

Narrative and Interpretive Virtue (Grand Rapids: Baker Academic, 2010), 136–37.

11. L. Juliana Claasens, introduction to *Restorative Readings: The Old Testament, Ethics, and Human Dignity*, ed. L. Juliana Claassens and Bruce C. Birch (Eugene, OR: Wipf & Stock, 2014), xxiv.

humanity is situated within its interdependent relationships with the rest of creation. Bruce Birch gets at this affirmation in his essay in *Restorative Readings* by focusing on the dignity of human beings within the context of creation in the Old Testament.[12] Human dignity can only be understood within a context of creational dignity.

While many biblical theologies would be welcome in our current context, creational theologies are urgently needed for several reasons. First, there is the matter of climate change. The most recent United Nations report uses the most dire language yet:

> Failure to reduce emissions, the group of scientists and other experts found, could threaten society with food shortages, refugee crises, the flooding of major cities and entire island nations, mass extinction of plants and animals, and a climate so drastically altered it might become dangerous for people to work or play outside during the hottest times of the year.[13]

Given the convulsions and threats that climate change and environmental degradation pose, human dignity must be set within its proper context, that is, within the dignity that all creation, every part of the created order, inherently possesses. Second, this task is even more pressing in a Christian context because there is evidence that American Christians, at least, are less environmentally aware than American non-Christians.[14]

A number of biblical scholars and theologians have begun to argue that an emphasis on human dignity without a clear understanding of humanity *within the context of the rest of creation* is destructive for non-human creation, as well as human beings. The work of Terence Fretheim was an initial and important effort in this task, and more recently Richard Bauckham, Ellen F. Davis, William Brown, and Patricia K. Tull, among others, have made significant contributions.[15] Human dignity itself is

---

12. Bruce C. Birch, "The Moral Trajectory of the Old Testament: Creation, Exodus, Exile," in Claassens and Birch, *Restorative Readings*, 3–18.

13. Justin Gillis, "U.N. Panel Issues Its Starkest Warning Yet on Global Warming," *New York Times*, November 2, 2014, https://tinyurl.com/SBL03100b, accessed February 13, 2017.

14. Katherine Mast, "Watershed Disciples," *Christian Century*, October 29, 2014, 13.

15. Terence E. Fretheim, *God and World in the Old Testament: A Relational Theology of Creation* (Nashville: Abingdon, 2005); Patricia K. Tull, *Inhabiting Eden: The Bible, Christians, and the Ecological Crisis* (Louisville: Westminster John Knox, 2013);

diminished and distorted from its true form unless humanity is situated within its interdependent relationships with the rest of creation. The ongoing ecological disaster is a result of this disequilibrium. Human dignity must always be placed within the larger framework of creational dignity.

The traditional view of the relationships among God, humanity and the rest of creation looks something like this:

God
humanity

animals (rest of creation)

On this traditional view, humanity is distant from other animals and higher up in the hierarchy, close to God; in fact, because of the *imago dei*, only humans bear the imprint of God's image. Yet this idea is under scrutiny and revision by biblical theologians.[16] In a creational theology, informed by the Scriptures and especially the Hebrew Scriptures, human beings are understood to be fundamentally connected to other animals. Much of the biblical evidence suggests, much as modern scientific evidence does, that humans belong within the category of animals.

The Bible posits the larger gap not between animals and humans but between animals (including humans) and God. The picture is being redrawn to reflect the biblical witness more faithfully:

God

animals (including humans)

Tull suggests that the *imago dei* in human beings means mirroring "God's priorities and intents" as they appear in Scripture: "playing God" is thus

---

Richard Bauckham, *The Bible and Ecology: Rediscovering the Community of Creation* (Waco, TX: Baylor University Press, 2010); Ellen F. Davis, *Scripture, Culture, and Agriculture: An Agrarian Reading of the Bible* (Cambridge: Cambridge University Press, 2008). Bruce Birch also moves in this direction in his contribution to *Restorative Readings*, "Moral Trajectory of the Old Testament."

16. See esp. Celia Deane-Drummond, *The Wisdom of the Liminal: Evolution and Other Animals in Human Becoming* (Grand Rapids: Eerdmans, 2014); David Clough, *Systematic Theology*, vol. 1 of *On Animals* (London: Bloomsbury, 2012).

not an appropriate interpretation.[17] Pushing even further, David S. Cunningham argues that "all flesh" is a better category than humanity for the imprint of the *imago dei*. The Christian doctrine of incarnation takes on new resonance when it is not limited to humanity but is refracted through creation.[18]

To be sure, human beings are different from other animals in having a unique capacity to change the environment for better and, mostly of late, for worse. Within the biblical witness, human beings have a unique role to fill within God's creation. The precise nature of the human role within creation, how it should exercise its unique power, is not entirely clear. The old mode of exercising *dominion*, which was and is a form of exploitation, is unsustainable. It can be argued that what makes human beings distinctive among creation currently is our hubris. But it does not have to be so: defining the contours of humanity's unique role within the rest of creation is an ongoing task, but there is promise for a role that emerges from a clearer understanding of our finitude, our interconnectedness with the rest of creation, and a humble sense of our limits. This requires either a new definition of stewardship or abandoning the concept altogether.[19]

However the human role is configured, the desired result is the flourishing of all creation. To flourish for any creature is to live in a context in which the fulfillment of its God-given potential is made possible, even if not actualized. God's speech from the whirlwind evokes this flourishing well; as Samuel E. Balentine observes, in the poetic imagery of Job 38–39, animals "frolic in the freedom of being exactly who they are."[20] This does not necessitate a romantic view of creation, but it does mean that most of the practices of agribusiness are violations of a creational ethic and are deleterious for the planet and the creatures that live here.

---

17. Tull, *Inhabiting Eden*, 21–23.

18. David S. Cunningham, "The Way of All Flesh: Rethinking the *Imago Dei*," in *Creaturely Theology: On God, Humans and Other Animals*, ed. Celia Deane-Drummond and David Clough (London: SCM, 2009).

19. Richard Bauckham discusses numerous problems with dominion and stewardship as they are traditionally conceived: (1) they express hubris, (2) they exclude God's activity in the world, (3) they lack specific content, (4) they set humans over creation, not within it, and (5) they tend to isolate one Scriptural text (*Bible and Ecology*, 1–12).

20. Samuel E. Balentine, "Ask the Animals and They Will Teach You," in *"And God Saw That It Was Good": Essays on Creation and God in Honor of Terence E. Fretheim*, ed. Frederick J. Gaiser and Mark A. Throntveit (Minneapolis: Word & World, 2006), 9.

In conclusion, as Douglas Lawrie says in his essay on restoring human dignity in Judg 19–21, the Bible is akin to fire: it can be either "useful or dangerous."[21] The pressing question for biblical theology, at least for this biblical theologian, is how it can be read so that it is useful. The need for Christian biblical theologies of creation is urgent, but these theologies must reach their target audience: Christians and others who have ears to hear who do not otherwise find environmental issues of pressing concern but who may well be persuaded if shown that the Scriptures themselves support care for creation—as indeed they do.

Bibliography

Bakhtin, Mikhail. "Discourse in the Novel." Pages 259–422 in *The Dialogic Imagination*. Edited by Michael Holquist. Translated by Caryl Emerson and Michael Holquist. Austin: University of Texas Press, 1981.

———. *Problems of Dostoevsky's Poetics*. Edited and translated by Caryl Emerson. Minneapolis: University of Minnesota Press, 1984.

Balentine, Samuel E. "Ask the Animals and They Will Teach You." Pages 3–11 in *"And God Saw That It Was Good": Essays on Creation and God in Honor of Terence E. Fretheim*. Edited by Frederick J. Gaiser and Mark A. Throntveit. Minneapolis: Word & World, 2006.

Barr, James. *The Concept of Biblical Theology: An Old Testament Perspective*. Minneapolis: Fortress, 1999.

Bauckham, Richard. *The Bible and Ecology: Rediscovering the Community of Creation*. Waco, TX: Baylor University Press, 2010.

Birch, Bruce C. "The Moral Trajectory of the Old Testament: Creation, Exodus, Exile." Pages 3–18 in *Restorative Readings: The Old Testament, Ethics, and Human Dignity*. Edited by L. Juliana Claassens and Bruce C. Birch. Eugene, OR: Wipf & Stock, 2014.

Briggs, Richard S. *The Virtuous Reader: Old Testament Narrative and Interpretive Virtue*. Grand Rapids: Baker Academic, 2010.

Brueggemann, Walter. *Old Testament Theology: An Introduction*. Nashville: Abingdon, 2010.

———. *Theology of the Old Testament: Testimony, Dispute, Advocacy*. Minneapolis: Fortress, 1997.

---

21. Douglas Lawrie, "Outrageous Terror and Trying Texts: Restoring Human Dignity in Judges 19–21," in Claassens and Birch, *Restorative Readings*, 68.

Childs, Brevard S. *Biblical Theology of the Old and New Testaments: Theological Reflection on the Christian Bible.* Minneapolis: Fortress, 1993.

Claassens, L. Juliana M. *The God Who Provides: Biblical Images of Divine Nourishment.* Nashville: Abingdon, 2004.

———. Introduction to *Restorative Readings: The Old Testament, Ethics, and Human Dignity.* Edited by L. Juliana Claassens and Bruce C. Birch. Eugene, OR: Wipf & Stock, 2014.

Clough, David. *Systematic Theology.* Vol. 1 of *On Animals.* London: Bloomsbury, 2012.

Cunningham, David S. "The Way of All Flesh: Rethinking the *Imago Dei.*" Pages 100–17 in *Creaturely Theology: On God, Humans and Other Animals.* Edited by Celia Deane-Drummond and David Clough. London: SCM, 2009.

Davis, Ellen F. *Scripture, Culture, and Agriculture: An Agrarian Reading of the Bible.* Cambridge: Cambridge University Press, 2008.

Deane-Drummond, Celia. *The Wisdom of the Liminal: Evolution and Other Animals in Human Becoming.* Grand Rapids: Eerdmans, 2014.

Eichrodt, Walther. *Theologie des Alten Testaments.* 3 vols. Leipzig: Hinrichs, 1933–1939.

Fretheim, Terence E. *God and World in the Old Testament: A Relational Theology of Creation.* Nashville: Abingdon, 2005.

Gillis, Justin. "U.N. Panel Issues Its Starkest Warning Yet on Global Warming." *New York Times,* November 2, 2014. https://tinyurl.com/SBL03100b. Accessed February 13, 2017.

Lawrie, Douglas. "Outrageous Terror and Trying Texts: Restoring Human Dignity in Judges 19–21." Pages 37–54 in *Restorative Readings: The Old Testament, Ethics, and Human Dignity.* Edited by L. Juliana Claassens and Bruce C. Birch. Eugene, OR: Wipf & Stock, 2014.

Levenson, Jon D. Review of *The Concept of Biblical Theology: An Old Testament Perspective,* by James Barr. First Things, February 2000. https://tinyurl.com/SBL03100a.

Mandolfo, Carleen. *God in the Dock: Dialogic Tension in the Psalms of Lament.* London: Sheffield Academic, 2002.

Mast, Katherine. "Watershed Disciples." *Christian Century,* October 29, 2014.

Moberly, R. W. L. *Old Testament Theology: Reading the Hebrew Bible as Christian Scripture.* Grand Rapids: Baker Academic, 2013.

Newsom, Carol A. "Bakhtin, the Bible, and Dialogic Truth." *JR* 76 (1996): 290–306.

Olson, Dennis. "Biblical Theology as Provisional Monologization: A Dialogue with Childs, Brueggemann and Bakhtin." *BibInt* 6 (1998): 162–80.

Rad, Gerhard von. *Theologie des Alten Testaments*. 2 vols. Munich: Kaiser, 1957–1960.

Tull, Patricia K. *Inhabiting Eden: The Bible, Christians, and the Ecological Crisis*. Louisville: Westminster John Knox, 2013.

Toward a Constructive
Jewish Biblical Theology of the Land

David Frankel

1. Jewish Biblical Theology in Israel: The Fundamental Tension

One of the most important principles in traditional Judaism is תלמוד
תורה, the study of torah. While the centrality of this precept has rarely
been contested, the question of its meaning has occasioned considerable
debate. According to one talmudic passage (b. Qidd. 40b), a group of rabbinic authorities determined, somewhat paradoxically, that torah study
is greater than works because it is torah study that leads to works.[1] This
passage apparently reflects the understanding that the purpose of torah
is to serve as a catalyst and guide, both for the individual and for Israel as
a whole, in the realm of works and proper living. One studies Scripture
following this understanding in order to do. Other traditional texts, however, clearly see torah study as superior to works, with which it stands in
tension. Indeed, torah study may actually serve as a means for retreating
from the world of action, allowing the student to inhabit the world of intellectual contemplation. According to one talmudic passage, for example (y.
Pes. 3:7), the torah student should refrain from involvement in communal
needs. Torah study is to be interrupted only if there is no one else to tend

---

1. The classic passage reads as follows: "Rabbi Tarfon and the Elders were once
reclining in the upper story of Nithza's house in Lydda when this question was raised
before them: Is study greater, or practice? Rabbi Tarfon answered and said: Practice
is greater. Rabbi Akiva answered saying: Study is greater. Then they all answered and
said: Study is greater for it leads to action." All translations of nonbiblical Hebrew texts
are mine.

to the communal need.[2] The torah, in sum, is far loftier than a handbook for mundane living, and its study is pursued as an end unto itself.[3]

Something of this ancient controversy pertains, *mutatis mutandis*, in the new realm of Jewish biblical theology that has recently sprung forth in academic circles both in Israel and in the United States.[4] Perhaps the first Jewish thinker to have embarked on a scholarly project that may be associated with this category is Martin Buber. A major concern of Buber's biblical scholarship was to show the relevance of biblical thought for modern humanity as well as for Israel as a people. Buber did not eschew the academic and historical approach to the biblical text or the need to understand it against the backdrop of its ancient environment. At the same time, however, he called upon people to read it, or listen to it, with an open heart and with a readiness to be moved and enlightened by its words and

---

2. For a discussion of the issue, see Ephraim E. Urbach, *The Sages: Their Concepts and Beliefs*, trans. Israel Abrahams (Cambridge: Harvard University Press, 1987), 603–20.

3. This conflict over the significance of Scripture and the purpose of its study continued in one form or another throughout Jewish history. For Maimonides, study of the Talmud was chiefly oriented toward action. He referred to the technical and theoretical disputes between the talmudic authorities Rava and Abaya as דבר קטן, matters of little import (Mishneh Torah 4:13). His main interest in the often long-winded talmudic discussions about biblical law was with the bottom line, that is, with determining which opinions were legally binding. His codification of talmudic law in a succinct and highly accessible format, and his refusal to cite the talmudic sources upon which he made his determinations reflect his fairly clear attempt to actually supplant talmudic study altogether. For a recent discussion, see Moshe Halbertal, *Maimonides: Life and Thought*, trans. Joel Linsider (Princeton: Princeton University Press, 2014), 164–96. For countless other rabbinic authorities, however, Talmud study was an end unto itself, an end of the highest possible order. The same opposition can be found in the various Jewish approaches to Bible commentary. Homiletic commentators like Rashi highlighted those midrashim that expounded the practical ethical and religious lessons that can be derived, however unnaturally, from the biblical text. In contrast, other biblical commentators such as Rashi's grandson, Rashbam, focused on issues of grammar, syntax, and textual coherence, largely, if not completely, leaving aside the question of how the text might enrich daily life.

4. The literature in this field is growing. See, e.g., Isaac Kalimi, ed., *Jewish Bible Theology: Perspectives and Case Studies* (Winona Lake, IN: Eisenbrauns, 2012); Marvin A. Sweeney, *Tanak: A Theological and Critical Introduction to the Jewish Bible* (Minneapolis: Fortress, 2012); Benjamin D. Sommer, "Dialogical Biblical Theology: A Jewish Approach to Reading Scripture Theologically," in *Biblical Theology: Introducing the Conversation*, ed. Leo G. Perdue (Nashville: Abingdon, 2009), 1–15.

meanings. In spite of his recognition of the theological diversity that can be found in the Bible, he insisted that the Hebrew Bible is a fundamentally unified work, reflecting what he referred to as "religious humanism." He also grounded much of his unique "theo-political" version of Zionism and his teachings about God, humans, Israel, and human society more generally in the enduring teachings of the Bible as he understood it.[5] For Buber, then, torah study and biblical scholarship was anything but a retreat from concern with proper living both for the individual and for society.

Buber's theologically and politically oriented biblical scholarship did not escape criticism. Some pointed out that his reading of the biblical corpus in terms of religious humanism is extremely selective and that Buber conveniently ignored major aspects of biblical teaching that were anything but humanistic in orientation.[6] Yehezkel Kaufmann maintained that the "unparalleled theological message" that Buber claimed to have found in the Bible—that a human in his or her totality is called upon to serve the deity in all realms of life—is in fact a most commonplace presupposition of the Bible and paganism alike.[7] Underlying Kaufmann's scathing

---

5. For Martin Buber's major biblical studies, see Buber, *The Prophetic Faith*, trans. Carlyle Witton-Davies (New York: Macmillan, 1949); Buber, *Kingship of God*, trans. Richard Scheimann (New York: Harper Row, 1967); Buber, *Moses: The Revelation and the Covenant* (New York: Harper, 1958). For a convenient collection of some of Buber's most important biblical essays, see Buber, *On the Bible: Eighteen Studies*, ed. Nahum N. Glatzer (New York: Schocken, 1968). A more extensive collection in Hebrew is Buber, *Darko shel miqra* (Jerusalem: Bialik, 1964). For an important study of Buber's hermeneutic, see Steven Kepnes, *The Text as Thou: Martin Buber's Dialogical Hermeneutics and Narrative Theology* (Bloomington: Indiana University Press, 1992). For Buber's conception and promotion of biblical theocracy, see Samuel Brody, *This Pathless Hour: Messianism, Anarchism, Zionism, and Martin Buber's Theopolitics Reconsidered* (Chicago: University of Chicago, The Divinity School, 2013). See also Buber, *Land of Two Peoples: Martin Buber on Jews and Arabs*, ed. Paul Mendes-Flohr (Chicago: University of Chicago Press, 2005).

6. See Yisrael Eldad, "The Ethics of the Conquerors of Canaan" [Hebrew], in *Hegionot ha-mikra* (Jerusalem: Sulam, 1958), 11–24. For critique from a later period, see Benyamin Uffenheimer, "Buber and Modern Biblical Scholarship," in *Martin Buber: A Centenary Volume*, ed. Ḥayim Gordon and Jochanan Bloch (New York: Ktav, 1984), 205–8; Uffenheimer, "Buber's Socialist and Political Views: A Critique," in *Thinkers and Teachers of Modern Judaism*, ed. Raphael Patai and Emanuel S. Goldsmith (New York: Paragon, 1994), 67–82. See also Manfred Vogel, "Buber and the Arab-Jewish Conflict," in Patai and Goldsmith, *Thinkers and Teachers*, 43–65.

7. Yehezkel Kaufmann, *Mikhivshonah shel haytsirah hamiqrait: Collected Essays*

point-by-point critique of Buber's biblical theology is the repeated insinu-
ation that Buber was an overly engaged reader. His passionate concern to
present the Bible as a unique and compelling guide toward meaningful
living, particularly for the society emerging in Zion, led to the unwitting
distortion of its overall import.[8] Indeed, for Kaufmann, many of Buber's
close readings of biblical texts basically stood "on the border of *derash*."[9]
Following somewhat similar lines, the great Israeli scholar of kabbalah,
Gershom Scholem, unleashed an even more biting critique of Buber's
interpretation of the meaning of Hasidism.[10]

Turning now to the contemporary scene in the Israeli academy, I think
it is fair to say that the overwhelming majority of those who work in the
field of biblical thought and theology, and I count myself among them, do
not follow in the footsteps of Buber. Most of us emphasize the far-reaching
theological diversity that the biblical corpus exhibits and speak little of any
purported unity.[11] Further, as academics we tend to recoil from attempts to
present biblical teaching as authoritative or instructive for contemporary

---

(Tel Aviv: Dvir, 1966), 256–80. This essay presents a detailed critique of Buber's book,
Prophetic Faith. For his critique of Buber's *Kingship of God*, see Yehezkel Kaufmann,
review of *Königtum Gottes*, by Martin Buber, *Kirjath Sepher* 10 (1933–1934): 62–66;
Kaufmann, *Toledot ha'emunah hayisra'elit*, 4 vols. (Jerusalem: Bialik & Dvir, 1960),
1:703–6 and n. 25.

8. Of course, the same criticism can most easily be leveled against Kaufmann
himself. See, e.g., Isaac Leo Seeligmann, "Certain of His Truth and Independent of
Other Opinions," in *On the Late Professor Y. Kaufmann*, ed. Benjamin Mazar et al.
(Jerusalem: Magnes, 1964), 16–28.

9. Kaufmann, review of *Königtum Gottes*, 66.

10. See on this controversy, Jerome Gellman, "Buber's Blunder: Buber's Replies
to Scholem and Schatz-Uffenheimer," *MJ* 20 (2000): 20–40; Rachel White, "Recovering the Past, Renewing the Present: The Buber-Scholem Controversy over Hasidism
Reinterpreted," *JSQ* 14 (2007): 364–92.

11. One notable exception to this trend is Joshua Berman, *Created Equal: How
the Bible Broke with Ancient Political Thought* (Oxford: Oxford University Press, 2008).
The title of Berman's book, however, is quite misleading. It gives the impression that
the book demonstrates that "the Bible" as a whole presents a unified political outlook
that rejects class distinctions reflected in the "ancient world" that does not include the
Bible. In actuality, Berman treats the Pentateuch alone and fails to give due weight
to the fact that significant portions of the Bible outside the Pentateuch highlight the
divine or near-divine status of the king. For a more balanced discussion of political
thought in the Bible, see Yair Lorberbaum, *Disempowered King: Monarchy in Classical
Jewish Literature*, trans. Jonathan Chipman (London: Continuum, 2011), 1–36.

Jewish and/or Israeli life, let alone for humankind in general. Somewhat like the rabbis of the talmudic debate, we see our study as an end in itself. The new emphasis on the wide diversity of opinion within biblical thought has, of course, its own underlying, if unstated and sometimes unwitting, agenda: to legitimate and promote a practically unlimited theological and ideological pluralism. This has the concomitant effect of severely diminishing the ability to invoke Scripture in a meaningfully authoritative way. If one can identify in the Bible thoroughly divergent and even contradictory approaches to such central issues as God's essential character, nationalism versus universalism, the relation between ritual and ethics, and so on, then no contemporary position on these or related matters can make a strong claim to having biblical sanction. This is why many Israeli rabbis and religious authorities who do speak in the name of the Bible nearly always ignore its diversity, not to mention the ambiguities and complexities involved in translating ancient texts for the contemporary situation.[12] As academics committed to the ideals of intellectual integrity, we can hardly allow ourselves to participate in such distortion. Indeed, one prominent Israeli Bible scholar has recently called for a shunning of all Buber-like attempts to find meaning and relevance in the biblical corpus or to bring its contents to bear on contemporary matters. The Bible must remain situated in its ancient historical context, and its distance must be maintained at all times if its variegated contents are to be understood properly.[13] Of

---

12. See Yosef Aḥituv, "State and Army According to the Torah: Realism and Mysticism in the Circles of 'Merkaz HaRav,'" in *Religion and State in Twentieth Century Jewish Thought* [Hebrew], ed. Aviezer Ravitzky (Jerusalem: The Israeli Institute for Democracy, 2005), 449–72.

13. Yair Zakovitch, "*Rihuq tsorekh qirvah*," *TE* 4 (1995): 7–17. Zakovitch actually directs his critique at Zvi Adar and his followers, who seek to use the Bible as an educational tool for the promotion of humanistic values. See, e.g., Zvi Adar, *Humanistic Values in the Bible*, trans. Victor Tcherikover (New York: Reconstructionist, 1967). One of the few contemporary Israeli Bible scholars who do seek to bring biblical literature to bear on contemporary affairs is Uriel Simon. See the collection of his essays in Uriel Simon, *Seek Peace and Pursue It: Topical Issues in the Light of the Bible; The Bible in the Light of Topical Issues* (Tel Aviv: Yediot Aharonot, 2002). Of course, mention must also be made of the late Moshe Greenberg, who frequently employed his skills as a biblical scholar to help promote humanistic values. For a recent appreciation of Greenberg's work, see Marc Zvi Brettler, "Concepts of Scripture in Moshe Greenberg," in *Jewish Concepts of Scripture: A Comparative Introduction*, ed. Benjamin D. Sommer (New York: New York University Press, 2012), 247–66. For the overall decline of the position of the Bible in contemporary Israeli society, see Simon,

course, beyond this appeal's stated concern with the accurate understanding of biblical literature also lie continuing tensions in Israeli society between the religious and the secular, as well as fears—which can indeed be fully appreciated—that religion will progressively encroach upon the public domain.

2. The Need for a New Jewish-Biblical Theology in Israel

While I find myself in partial sympathy with calls of this sort, I believe that we must be wary of throwing out the baby with the bathwater. In this context, I would like to cite the words of Scholem, who was both a staunch religious anarchist and a rigorously historical scholar of religion. In a lecture that he gave in 1975 entitled "The People of the Book," he asked,

> Today, when the unethical seems so self-evident, does the Bible still address us with its call? And is the people of the book still able to do something with its book? Is it possible that a time will come when it will fall silent? I am convinced that the existence of this nation depends upon the answer to this question far more decisively than it does upon the ups and downs of politics.[14]

What Scholem was saying, I believe, is that for any nation to survive, it must cultivate its sense of identity and unique place in the world. The collective, like the individual, cannot long endure, and surely cannot thrive, without some fundamental conception of its distinctive qualities. For the "people of the book," the Jews of Israel and of the world at large, this sense of self can never be completely severed from the biblical cannon or, I would add, the later tradition that both determined its precise contents and confines and built upon it. To insist that the ancient writings be read as addressed to the ancients alone is to deprive the living Jewish people of its roots and identity and hence of its spiritual orientation toward the future.[15]

"The Place of the Bible in Israeli Society: From National Midrash to Existential Peshat," *MJ* 19 (1999): 155–77.

14. See Gershom Scholem, *On the Possibility of Jewish Mysticism in Our Time and Other Essays*, ed. Avraham Shapira, trans. Jonathan Chipman (Philadelphia: Jewish Publication Society of America, 1997), 175.

15. Simon Rawidowicz emphasized this point in a compelling way. See Simon Rawidowicz, "On Interpretation," in *Studies in Jewish Thought*, ed. Nahum N. Glatzer (Philadelphia: Jewish Publication Society of America, 1974), 45–80.

A cogent argument can be made for the thesis that Judaism has always been so diverse in terms of its beliefs that it eludes strict definition in terms of any alleged *essence*.[16] This is all the more so today, with the advent of modernity and postmodernity and the growth of secular-national, cultural, socialist, and various other nonreligious versions of Jewish identity. Perhaps we may state that that which unifies Judaism or Jewish thought in all its diversity is not any specific content but rather its structure as an exegetical organism. Nigh all forms of Judaism, regardless of how radically antithetical they may be in terms of belief and practice, ground their understandings of what it means to be Jewish in the interpretation of Jewish texts, the most prominent of which is the Hebrew Bible.[17] If this thesis is broadly accurate, then the call of Israeli academics to leave the Bible out of contemporary debates concerning Israeli society and the values that should guide it so that a more accurate and unbiased understanding of biblical literature can be achieved is ultimately a call for the collapse of a meaningful Israeli Judaism. Ironically, it also goes against the grain of much of the biblical text and those Jews who formed the Jewish canon. The biblical text often presents itself as addressing both "those that are with us here today and those that are not with us here today" (cf. Deut 29:14) and, as the rabbis of the Talmud rightly maintained (b. Meg. 14a), those who formed the canon preserved only those oracles שנצרכו לדורות, whose relevance was felt to extend beyond their immediate historical context.

It is perfectly legitimate to read biblical texts exclusively as addressed to their earliest audiences. This is the study of ancient Israelite literature. It is also legitimate, however, to read those same texts as additionally addressing the Jewish people throughout the generations and particularly as addressing the queries of our own generation today. When we read the texts in this way, we read them as Jewish Bible. There need not be an insurmountable clash between these different reading strategies. Thus in the

---

16. For two Israeli explications of this position, see Yeshayahu Leibowitz, *Judaism, Human Values, and the Jewish State*, ed. Eliezer Goldman (Cambridge: Harvard University Press, 1992), 3–12; Gershom Scholem, "Judaism," in *Twentieth Century Jewish Religious Thought: Original Essays on Critical Concepts, Movements and Beliefs*, ed. Arthur A. Cohen and Paul Mendes-Flohr (Philadelphia: Jewish Publication Society of America, 2009), 505–8. Leibowitz ultimately defines Judaism exclusively in terms of halakic praxis. Scholem, without explicitly referring to Leibowitz, considers this idea "utter nonsense."

17. See Moshe Halbertal, *People of the Book: Canon, Meaning and Authority* (Cambridge: Harvard University Press, 1997), 1–2.

traditional debate reviewed at the beginning of this essay over whether Scripture should be employed in the service of societal needs and goals or whether it should be studied as an end unto itself, I would insist on endorsing *both* positions. The complete subordination of the biblical text to the spiritual needs and ethical challenges of contemporary society risks distorting the biblical witness and apologetically converting the sacred text into a univocal reflection of that which we seek to find. The complete isolation of Scripture from the needs and goals of contemporary society preserves the independent integrity of the texts but threatens to render torah thoroughly irrelevant and the very title *torah*, that is, teaching and guidance, a misnomer. Both approaches to the text are thus needed, and a dialectical tension should be maintained between the two, with each one keeping the other in check.

3. A Jewish Biblical Critique of the Religious-Nationalist Approach to the Land

My own work in the realm of biblical thought includes a book entitled *The Land of Canaan and the Destiny of Israel: Theologies of Territory in the Hebrew Bible*.[18] As implied by the title, the book presents widely divergent biblical approaches to various issues surrounding the theological significance of the land. In accordance with prevailing academic convention, at least in Israel, I do not take a personal theological stance in the book, though I do make some brief comments in the book's epilogue.[19] It is clearly no accident, however, that the book was written by an observant Jew who lives in Israel. Obviously, the topics discussed in the book with studied detachment are also of pressing personal and existential concern. This existential concern is heightened by the fact many religious authorities in Israel today are actively involved in promoting an ultranationalist, biblical theology of the land with anything but dispassion and academic detachment. For a growing coalition of religious Zionists, one of a more fundamentalist stripe, Jewish sovereignty over all of the biblical land of Israel is a cardinal element of Jewish faith. God promised the land in the Bible to the nation of Israel alone, and that promise has now been realized in historical reality. We are living, many affirm, in the era of the final mes-

---

18. David Frankel, *The Land of Canaan and the Destiny of Israel: Theologies of Territory in the Hebrew Bible*, Siphrut 4 (Winona Lake, IN: Eisenbrauns, 2011).

19. Frankel, *Land of Canaan*, 382–400.

sianic redemption, and any form of territorial compromise would hinder or halt this redemptive process. Forfeiting parts of the holy land that was given to the Jews would be a sinful affront to the God of Israel. For not a few of these ideologues (and their secular supporters), complete democratic equality does not seem to be deemed a vital imperative.[20]

To frankly state what by now is surely obvious, I find this biblical-political approach to the contemporary situation in the land of the Bible both theologically and morally disturbing and politically dangerous. As intimated above, the attempt to respond to religious (or, for that matter, secular-nationalist) ideologies of this sort by calling for an isolation of biblical study from contemporary life is self-defeating and inadequate. What is required, in my view, is a return of sorts to Buber's project of presenting a constructive Jewish biblical theology that promotes religious humanism and the sanctity and dignity of the human being at its center, one that can serve as an alternative to the absolutism and fundamentalism of the above-mentioned approach to the land and the other in the land. This return would have to avoid, however, replicating the weaknesses that mar Buber's biblical-theological writings. It would entail highlighting the humanistic thrust of much of the Hebrew Bible and the Jewish tradition that developed from it, without denying the diversity of the tradition and the fact that other voices can indeed be heard in it. Indeed, it would have to include a frank and unapologetic critique of those other voices. It would also have to speak chiefly in the realm of values, recognizing the ambiguities involved in any attempt to translate ultimate values into concrete policies of action within the daunting complexities of the real world. Finally, it would have to eschew fanciful interpretations of biblical texts that belong more properly in the realm of *derash*.

---

20. For a presentation and critique of this school of thought, see, inter alia, Aviezer Ravitzky, *Messianism, Zionism and Jewish Religious Radicalism*, trans. Michael Swirsky and Jonathan Chipman, CSHJ (Chicago: University of Chicago Press, 1996), 79–144; Ehud Luz, *Wrestling with an Angel: Power, Morality and Jewish Identity*, trans. Michael Swirsky (New Haven: Yale University Press 2003), 221–37; Shai Held, "What Zvi Yehuda Kook Wrought: The Theopolitical Radicalization of Religious Zionism," in *Rethinking the Messianic Idea in Judaism*, ed. Michael L. Morgan and Steven Weitzman (Bloomington: Indiana University Press, 2015), 229–55. See also the recent Hebrew publication of Yosef Aḥituv, *A Critique of Contemporary Religious Zionism: Selected Writings*, ed. Yakir Englander and Avi Sagi (Ein Zurim: Shalom Hartman Institute and Yaacov Herzog Center for Jewish Studies, 2013). For the strong dependence of this school on biblical precedent in determining policy, see Aḥituv, "State and Army."

In this context, I would like to offer my own critique, from the perspective of an alternative kind of Jewish biblical theology, of the messianic approach to the land mentioned above.[21] It is hoped that this will provide something of an indication of some of the directions in which a new Jewish biblical theology of the land might proceed.

3.1. Pragmatic and Dispassionate Thinking

As noted above, many of those who reject on principle all forms of territorial compromise insist that we are now living in the messianic era. One of the main dangers of this absolute conviction is that it fosters a decision-making process in the political realm that ignores, or deemphasizes, the importance of realistic and pragmatic calculation. We need not worry about the possible repercussions of the actions that we take, for in the imminent future the messiah will appear to vindicate us. This contravenes a clear rabbinic principle: "One must not rely on miracles" (y. Yoma 1:4). This rabbinic principle is not a late development but epitomizes the thinking reflected in much, though not all, of biblical narrative. To cite just one example of many, when God tells Samuel to go anoint David to be king over Israel, Samuel responds by asking God the impudent yet legitimate question, "How can I go? When Saul hears of it he will kill me!" (1 Sam 16:2, my trans.). Samuel does not simply obey God's dangerous command in humble faith, trusting that God will protect his own emissary. Rather, he elicits from God a practical scheme that will allow him to circumvent

---

21. The following critique is inspired by Moshe Greenberg, "On the Political Use of the Bible in Modern Israel: An Engaged Critique," in *Pomegranates and Golden Bells: Studies in Biblical, Jewish, and Near Eastern Ritual, Law, and Literature in Honor of Jacob Milgrom*, ed. David P. Wright, David Noel Freedman, and Avi Hurvitz (Winona Lake, IN: Eisenbrauns, 1995), 461–71. Though many scholars have attacked the ideology of messianic religious Zionism, few have used the Bible itself as the central ground from which to launch their critiques. For example, Menachem Kellner seeks to employ Maimonides as a counterbalance to the violent texts of the Bible. See Kellner, "'And the Crooked Shall be Made Straight': Twisted Messianic Visions, and a Maimonidean Corrective," in *Rethinking the Messianic Idea in Judaism*, ed. Michael L. Morgan and Steven Weitzman (Bloomington, IN: Indiana University Press, 2015), 108–40, esp. 114–15. Many others turn chiefly to rabbinic literature for counterbalance. I believe that it is vital to locate and highlight the counterbalance in biblical texts and to show how the more moderate postbiblical voices continue biblical currents.

the danger.[22] Faith and piety are no substitute for pragmatism in the theology of this and other passages.[23]

In truth, most religious ideologues who insist on maintaining Jewish sovereignty over all of the land do not claim to ignore the demands of pragmatic politics. On the contrary, most of them are convinced that a pragmatic and objective political analysis only supports their religious-political convictions. They believe that relinquishing political and military control over parts of the land poses a mortal threat to Israel's very existence, and no form of accommodation to Israel's security needs could alter that fact. Strategic analysis thus happily supports the dictates of the religious-nationalist, messianic worldview. The Jewish state must maintain control over all of the land, as the Bible supposedly dictates, and territorial compromise is both politically foolhardy and religiously sinful.

Here, I believe, the danger of the fusion of religious-nationalist ideology with contemporary politics is more subtle and therefore even greater. Many torah passages are sensitive to the fact that even our deepest moral and religious instincts cloud our judgment and assessment of the facts. Thus we find the repeated insistence that judges diligently be on guard against the tendency to compassionately favor the case of the poor (Exod 23:3; Lev 19:15). In light of this, I would raise the following question: Can we really trust our political assessments to be sound and balanced, particularly when we have a fervent religious-political agenda tipping the scales of our judgment in a certain direction?[24]

---

22. See the commentary of Rabbi David Kimchi on the verse. Kimchi cites a host of similar passages to illustrate the same point.

23. In biblical times, the pragmatic approach was sometimes contested by prophets who called for absolute trust in God's salvation. See Gerhard von Rad, *Old Testament Theology*, vol. 2, trans. David M. G. Stalker (New York: Harper & Row, 1965), 158–61; Buber, *Prophetic Faith*, 135–39; Sara Japhet, *The Ideology of the Book of Chronicles and Its Place in Biblical Thought*, trans. Anna Barber, BEATAJ 9 (Frankfurt am Main: Lang, 1989), 255–58. What is so striking about the text of 1 Sam 16 is that it presents the very Godhead as recognizing the need for pragmatism in carrying out God's own program! In any event, as I will argue below, a nonmessianic approach to prophetic texts that preach complete reliance on God would highlight the fact that we live today in a postprophetic era and consequently can rarely be certain of God's current will.

24. Of course, people on all sides of the political debate should foster a healthy sense of suspicion toward their political assessments of reality. For all of us, the interpretation of complex reality and the decision to highlight certain elements thereof and

This, I suggest, is one of the lessons we might learn from the report of Josiah's death in the battle at Megiddo in 2 Kgs 23:29–30. According to the book of Kings, King Josiah upheld all the words of the torah. He destroyed all forms of idolatry throughout the land and made a covenant over the torah with all the subjects of his kingdom. There was no king either before him or after him who returned to the Lord with all his heart, soul, and might like him. However, when Josiah set out to Megiddo to deflect the Egyptian military from reaching Assyria and aiding his arch enemy, the pious king was killed on the spot. Why did Israel's most pious king die in battle? Did he give no consideration to Egypt's military might? The text in Kings gives no explicit answer, but the juxtaposition of the report of his death with the report of the extreme zealousness with which he carried out his religious and nationalist reforms suggests a possible interpretation. An even-tempered assessment of the balance of powers might have kept Josiah from embarking on too dangerous a venture. Josiah's religious and political fervor, however, clouded his assessment of the facts on the ground and led him to interpret reality in a way that supported his nationalist aspirations.[25] Needless to say, this fatal error of judgment did not affect Josiah alone. It brought Judah a significant step closer to the final fall and destruction of Jerusalem.

The need for dispassionate analysis of political and public affairs and the importance of questioning one's own judgment in such matters is emphasized in several passages in the book of Proverbs. In Prov 15:22, for example, we read, "Plans fail for lack of counsel, but with many advisors they succeed" (my trans.). Why does honest counsel with many advisors increase the likelihood of success? Reality is extremely complex, and no

---

to minimize or ignore other aspects thereof are influenced by our social context and world of values. This is why, as I stated above, biblical theology should focus on values rather than on how those values should be translated into policies.

25. The Talmud (b. Ta'an. 22b) offers a striking interpretation that proceeds somewhat along the lines I am suggesting. It claims that Josiah refused to consult with Jeremiah and mistakenly relied on the biblical promise that "the sword shall not pass through your land" (Lev 26:6, my trans.). The Talmud does not imply, of course, that the biblical verse is in need of correction. It was Josiah who was at fault for thinking that he knew that the verse applied specifically in his time and in relation to the specific political situation at hand. The lesson of Josiah's death for the rabbis, however, is not so much that Josiah failed to take counsel in his strategic analysis. His sin consisted of his arrogant assumption that he had the capacity to translate prophetic texts into a contemporary political program.

single individual can claim to attain a reliable, comprehensive, and objective perspective on it. Dangerous and destructive political decisions are best avoided when decision makers earnestly listen to as wide and divergent a range of well-informed analyses as possible.[26] Rehoboam's foolish fixation on the hard-line advice of his younger advisors and his failure to give serious consideration to the more conciliatory approach of his seasoned advisers led to the secession of the northern tribes from Judah and the collapse of the united kingdom (1 Kgs 12).[27] According to the rabbis, who may be seen as following here in the path of the book of Proverbs, Moses committed a grievous sin when he told the judges whom he appointed over Israel to bring to him the difficult cases.[28] In spite of Moses's extraordinary wisdom, his trust in his ability to judge by himself was sinful because it reflected hubris.[29] Distrust of one's own judgments and evaluations is thus a biblical and rabbinic virtue.

3.2. God's Absolute Freedom

Another critical point must be raised. The conviction that we are living in the messianic era and that history will imminently proceed in a clear direction reflects the dubious assumption that God must act in particular ways.[30] This contravenes the fundamental theological principle of God's absolute freedom. This freedom is affirmed in God's words to Moses in

---

26. Menahem Hameiri (in his commentary on Prov 15:22) emphasizes the great importance of prolonged consultation with "elders" and on exercising great caution before taking the kinds of action that will have serious repercussions. See Menahem Meshi, *Perush haMeiri ʿal Sefer Mishley*, ed. Menahem M. Meshi Zahav (Jerusalem: Otzar haPosqim, 1969), 153.

27. For the editorial character of 1 Kgs 12:15, which radically changes the significance of the "older narrative," see Gary N. Knoppers, *The Reign of Solomon and the Rise of Jeroboam*, vol. 1 of *Two Nations under God: The Deuteronomistic History of Solomon and the Dual Monarchies*, HSM 52 (Atlanta: Scholars Press, 1993), 218–23.

28. See Rashi on Deut 1:17.

29. Though not explicitly stated, Moses's superior wisdom is probably implied by the fact that the other judges were to be chosen on the basis of their intellectual capacities and by the fact that Moses makes no mention of his turning the difficult case over to God. Moses's superior wisdom is also implied in Deut 34:9–10. For the superior wisdom of Moses in rabbinic thought, see b. Meg. 13a. See also Acts 7:22.

30. For a critique of messianic inevitability from a scholar who affirms modern Israel's messianic status, see Shubert Spero, "Does Traditional Jewish Messianism Imply Inevitability? Is There a Political Role for Messianists in Israel Today?," *MJ* 8

Exod 33:19: "I will be gracious to whom I will be gracious, and I will have compassion on whom I will have compassion" (my trans.).[31] Similarly, the prophet of Isaiah castigates those who refuse to believe that God could possibly appoint Cyrus of Persia as his messiah with the words: "Woe to him who strives with his maker, an earthen vessel with the potter! Does the clay say to him who fashions it, 'What are you making?'" (Isa 45:9 RSV). Jews affirm this principle in their daily liturgy: "You made the heavens and the earth, the sea and all that is in them. Who is there from among all your creatures in the upper or lower worlds who can tell you what to do and how to act?"[32] Even when God makes promises, we must not deny God's basic right to go back on those promises. It must openly be acknowledged that this idea goes against the grain of many biblical texts.[33] At the same time, it is clearly implied, for example, in the oracle to Eli in 1 Sam 2:27–36. God, we are told, appeared to Eli's ancestors in Egypt and chose his father's house to serve as priests for Israel. However, in light of the sins of Eli and his sons, God decides to destroy his household and raise up a new priestly house in its place. The wording of 2:30 is particularly significant: "Thus says the Lord, the God of Israel, 'It is true that I said, "Your house and the house of your father shall serve before me forever." But now, declares the Lord, far be it from me! For I honor those who honor me, but those who spurn me shall be dishonored'" (my trans.). I do not mean to imply that Jews (or Christians) should despair of biblical promises. But we should

---

(1988): 271–85. Also relevant from a biblical point of view is Uriel Simon, "The Biblical Destinies: Conditional Promises," *Tradition* 17 (1978): 84–90.

31. See Umberto Cassuto, *A Commentary on the Book of Exodus*, trans. Israel Abrahams (Jerusalem: Magness, 1967), 436.

32. See Philip Birnbaum, ed., *The Daily Prayer Book: Sephardic* (New York: Hebrew Publishing, 1969), 29. It is significant to note that this line is immediately followed by the prayer that God might be so gracious as to keep his promise to bring the people of Israel back to their land. Even though the ingathering of the exiles is referred to as a divine promise, God is understood as being under no duress to keep his promises. If he would choose to keep his promises, it would have to be appreciated as an act of grace.

33. See, e.g., Num 23:19; 1 Sam 15:29. For a discussion of these texts, see Alexander Rofé, *The Prophetical Stories: The Narratives about the Prophets in the Hebrew Bible, Their Literary Types and History* (Jerusalem: Magnes, 1988), 99–105, 164–70. See also Joel S. Kaminsky, "Can Election Be Forfeited?" in *The Call of Abraham: Essays on the Election of Israel in Honor of Jon D. Levenson*, ed. Gary A. Anderson and Joel S. Kaminsky (Notre Dame: University of Notre Dame Press, 2013), 44–66.

never think God has completely boxed himself in to a particular scheme of history that we can define. As Abraham Joshua Heschel wrote, "No word is God's last word."[34]

3.3. Maimonides and the Demotion of Messianism

A classic medieval text that speaks against the entire approach of religious-political messianism is that of Maimonides (*Mishneh Torah*, Laws of Kings 11).[35] Maimonides was undoubtedly the most prominent Jewish theologian of the middle ages, and his biblical interpretations may be employed (to be sure, with critical caution) in a contemporary Jewish-biblical theology. I will try to briefly explicate this Maimonidean text and to show both how it continues significant strands of biblical and rabbinic thought and how it reflects a coherent and important theological stance.

After mentioning various possible scenarios for how the final redemption might take place, Maimonides states:

> Concerning all of these matters, and similar ones, no one knows how they will be until they happen. For the matters are hidden with the prophets.... One should never deal with the words of the stories [about the redemption], nor spend any length of time on the rabbinic interpretations that deal with these and similar issues. One should not make them central, for they bring neither love of God nor fear of God.

Maimonides clearly indicates here that people should not scrutinize biblical and rabbinic texts about the end of days. People must not speculate about the messianic era, nor should they allow such matters to distract them from the major task at hand: the love and fear of God in the world as it is. Maimonides's assertion that "these matters are hidden with the prophets" has a firm biblical basis in the book of Daniel. From Dan 9 we learn that prophecy is anything but clear and transparent. Only when Daniel is granted a prophetic vision of his own can he understand the true meaning of Jeremiah's ostensibly unambiguous prophecy concerning redemption

---

34. Abraham Joshua Heschel, *The Insecurity of Freedom* (New York: Schocken, 1972), 182.

35. For analysis of Maimonides's messianic vision, see Aviezer Ravitzky, "'To the Utmost of Human Capacity': Maimonides on the Days of the Messiah," in *Perspectives on Maimonides*, ed. Joel L. Kraemer (London: Littman Library of Jewish Civilization, 1996), 221–56; Kellner, "And the Crooked Shall Be Made Straight."

after seventy years.[36] The implication of this seems rather plain. Since we are not prophets like Daniel, we can never be sure of our interpretations of prophetic texts.[37] Nor do we have prophetic figures to whom we might turn.[38] We cannot know that we are living in the messianic era. Rabbi Akiva interpreted the passage in Num 24:17 as a messianic reference to Bar Kokhba and helped bring untold disaster upon Israel and the land. Prophetic writing, we may well extrapolate, should be read chiefly as religious and ethical instruction, not as imminently relevant eschatological information that may be used to inform decisions of policy.

Maimonides's demotion of prophetic eschatology is firmly rooted in Scripture itself. Of central significance in this context is the editorial passage at Mal 3:22: "Remember the torah of Moses my servant that I commanded him at Horeb for all Israel, laws and decrees" (my trans.). As indicated already by Michael Fishbane, the intention of this remark, which comes at the end of the entire corpus of the literature of the prophets, is to emphasize the priority of the law of Moses in relation to the prophets.[39] Particularly in light of the verse's appearance within the context of oracles concerning the eschatological day of the Lord, the verse's emphasis on the torah of Moses serves as a warning against speculation concerning the future that might distract the community of faith from the stable structures of the law in the world as it is. Marvin A. Sweeney has noted that, while the Christian Old Testament culminates in the Prophets, which points forward to the time of Christ as depicted in the New Testament, the Jewish Bible ends with Ketuvim, or the Writings, wherein the restoration of Israel is depicted.[40] I would add that wisdom literature constitutes a major component of the Writings section. The placement of wisdom following the Prophets in the Jewish Bible may thus also reflect a shift away

---

36. It must be emphasized that this reflects a uniquely late understanding of the nature of prophecy. See Michael Fishbane, *Biblical Interpretation in Ancient Israel* (Oxford: Clarendon, 1988), 479–99.

37. This is precisely the lesson the rabbis drew from the story of Josiah's death. See n. 25 above.

38. For a fascinating analysis of the role of renewed prophecy in certain messianic-nationalist circles, see Shlomo Fischer, "Religious Zionism at the Threshold of the Third Millennium: Two Cultures of Faith" [Hebrew], *Akdamot* 22 (2009): 9–38.

39. See Michael Fishbane, *The Garments of Torah: Essays in Biblical Hermeneutics* (Bloomington: Indiana University Press, 1989), 75.

40. Marvin A. Sweeney, "Jewish Biblical Theology and Christian Old Testament Theology," *TLZ* 134 (2009): 397–410.

from eschatological speculation and expectation toward enhanced human initiative and responsibility in the world as it is. In this context one might consider rendering Prov 14:15, פתי יאמין לכל דבר, as "The fool believes every prophetic word."[41] As the rabbis put it most succinctly, חכם עדיף מנביא, "The Sage carries more weight than the Prophet" (b. B. Bat. 12a).[42]

3.4. The Importance of Prioritizing Religious Values

It is important to emphasize that Maimonides in no way intends to reject messianism or the study of biblical prophecies relating to it. What Maimonides does seek to do is to create a principle whereby different religious values and activities found in Scripture can be evaluated in terms of their relative importance. In Maimonides's estimation, involvement with prophetic statements about the future contributes little or nothing to the ultimate principle of the love of God. Thus heightened involvement with prophetic eschatology is downplayed not merely because it is politically dangerous; it is also downplayed because it reflects a misguided sense of religious priorities. Concern with the end of days has its place in Jewish life, but that place is at the bottom of the hierarchy rather than at the top.

Maimonides's concern with the proper prioritizing of religious values is again well rooted in both biblical and rabbinic sources. Biblical texts that account for the exile in terms of Sabbath desecration (Jer 17:21–27), intermarriage with foreigners (Ezra 9:1–14), or failure to allow the land to lie fallow every seven years (Lev 26:34–35) do not simply deal with the issue of theodicy as justification of God's acts in the past. Rather, each of these texts seeks to define the most important issue that must be focused on *in*

---

41. For דבר as prophetic word, see, for example, Jer 18:18. On the overall tension between wise men and prophets, see the discussion in Raymond C. Van Leeuwen, "The Sage in the Prophetic Literature," in *The Sage in Israel and the Ancient Near East*, ed. John G. Gammie and Leo G. Perdue (Winona Lake, IN: Eisenbrauns, 1990), 295–306.

42. On the reserved messianic posture of the rabbis, particularly in wake of the Bar Kokhba debacle, see Joseph Heinemann, "The Messiah of Ephraim and the Premature Exodus of the Tribe of Ephraim," *HTR* 52 (1959): 1–15. For a recent diachronic analysis, see Philip S. Alexander, "The Rabbis and Messianism," in *Redemption and Resistance: The Messianic Hopes of Jews and Christians in Antiquity*, ed. Markus Bockmuehl and James Carleton Paget (London: T&T Clark, 2009), 227–44. On the rabbinic approach to prophetic inspiration and Jewish law, see Ephraim E. Urbach, *The World of the Sages: Collected Studies* [Hebrew] (Jerusalem: Magnes, 2002), 21–27.

the present in order to restore the fractured relationship with God. Many of the prophets, as is well known, emphasized the primacy of morality and social justice and their precedence over involvement with the cult.[43] Hillel the Elder, in basic continuity with the prophets, considered the entire torah to be subsumed under the standard and principle of דעלך סני לחברך לא תעביד, "That which is hateful to you, do not do unto your fellow" (b. Šabb. 31a). He said of this principle, זו היא כל התורה כולה ואידך פירושה הוא, זיל גמור, "This is all of the torah. The rest is its interpretation. Go and learn." Hillel, it seems, understands the idea of not harming others not only as the *essence* of torah but as a kind of hermeneutical principle as well. It is on the basis of this hermeneutical principle that one must "go and learn." The details of the torah must thus be interpreted such that they conform to the principle. Finally, when Rabbi Akiva declared that "You shall love your neighbor as yourself" (Lev 19:18) is the greatest principle of the torah, Ben Azzai said, "This is the book of the generations of man, when God created man he made him in the likeness of God (Gen 5:1)—that is an even greater principle" (Sipra on Lev 19:18).[44]

Prioritization and the attempt to determine a hierarchy of religious values is thus an incessant biblical and Jewish preoccupation.[45] It stems from the important recognition that diverse religious values and activities do not just compete with each other in terms of the allocation of time and resources. The complexities of life are such that they may actively clash and undermine one another, as when inordinate trust in the efficacy of the cult encourages the perpetuation of social injustice or, as the Talmud warns, when excessive emphasis on absolute justice undermines the ability to facilitate compromise (see b. San. 6b). The exclusive or disproportional emphasis on that which is secondary may thus be not only inept and misguided but actually detrimental to the accomplishment of that which is primary.

---

43. For a recent treatment of this theme, see John Barton, "The Prophets and the Cult," in *Temple and Worship in Biblical Israel*, ed. John Day, LHBOTS 422 (London: T&T Clark, 2005), 111–22.

44. For a beautiful exposition of this debate within the context of a discussion of human dignity and equality in Jewish sources, see Menachem Elon, *Jewish Law: History, Sources, Principles*, trans. Bernard Auerbach and Melvin J. Sykes, 4 vols. (Philadelphia: Jewish Publication Society of America, 1994), 4:1850–54.

45. This is equally true in the realm of halakah. Note, for example, the well-known principle asserting that preservation of life outweighs Sabbath observance (b. Šabb. 151b). Similarly, according to another talmudic source (b. Ber. 19b), concern for human dignity outweighs Torah prohibitions.

3.5. Territorial Completeness Is Not Essential

I believe that the above mentioned assessment pertains to the excessive emphasis on the entirety of the land and the biblically based, a priori rejection of all territorial compromise. A constructive Jewish-biblical theology of the land would emphasize that, while national life in the land is unquestionably central to the conception of "Israel" in the Jewish Bible (and the ongoing tradition), nowhere does this literature present territorial *completeness* as critical, situated at the top of the hierarchy of values.[46] According to Judg 2:19–21, in the period of the judges, God decided to punish Israel for its unabated sinfulness by putting an end to the conquest project, in spite of the fact that it was far from completed in the time of Joshua.[47] Thus no prophet subsequent to Judg 2 ever calls upon an Israelite or Judean leader or king to take up and continue Joshua's unfinished conquest of the land, nor does any prophet castigate them for failing to do so. The complete possession of the entirety of the land is thus presented as or presumed, in at least much of biblical literature, an irretrievably lost ideal.[48]

---

46. I formulated this sentence under the influence of Greenberg, "On the Political Use," 469, where he writes: "Scripture knows of no general injunction of lasting validity to settle the land and expel its inhabitants.… On the contrary, the injunctions to take the land are embedded in narrative and give the appearance of being addressed to a specific generation, like the commandment to annihilate or expel the natives of Canaan, which refers specifically to the seven Canaanite nations." Relevant to this point is also Warren Zeev Harvey, "Rabbi Reines on the Conquest of Canaan and Zionism," in *The Gift of the Land and the Fate of the Canaanites in Jewish Thought*, ed. Katell Berthelot, Joseph E. David, and Marc G. Hirshman (Oxford: Oxford University Press, 2014), 386–98. In his review of this paper, Peter Pettit called me to task for claiming that territorial completeness is "nowhere" presented in the text as an essential principle, noting that so many people clearly do find the primacy of this principle in the text. Perhaps it would have been better to state that nowhere in the biblical text is the principle of the completeness of the land *explicitly* placed above all others. There is, however, a midrashic text that places living in the land on par with the other commandments (Sipre Deut 80). Further, in speaking of the principle of completeness of the land, I refer to the *communal task* of achieving and maintaining political hegemony over all of the land.

47. For a clear analysis of this easily misunderstood text, see Moshe Weinfeld, *The Promise of the Land: The Inheritance of the Land of Canaan by the Israelites* (Berkeley: University of California Press, 1993), 156–67.

48. For further sources and discussion, see Frankel, *Land of Canaan*, 33–35. It must be admitted, of course, that parts of Joshua insist that the land in its entirety was

In broad accordance with this, many prophecies of redemption foresee a restoration for Zion and Judah alone (e.g., Zeph 3:14–20; Joel 4:18–20).[49] At least in these texts of future redemption, the entire land of Canaan need not be restored in order for Israel to stand in a proper relationship with her God.

Responsible living under the guidance of wisdom within the complexities of the world requires realistic evaluation of the relative gains and losses of the choices that we make regarding the land, its borders, and its extremities. The singular emphasis on the entirety of the land not only taps on material resources that could go elsewhere; it also undermines more primary *spiritual* values such as, to quote from the prophet Micah (6:8), that which God seeks most of all, the love of kindness and walking humbly with God.

3.6. The Land Is Not Innately Holy

For many ideologues within the religious-nationalist camp, the land is holy by its very constitution. This belief probably bolsters the conviction that territorial compromise is sacrilege. When accompanied by the additional belief that the people of Israel are also innately holy, the conception of the innate holiness of the land can nurture religiously motivated aspirations to remove non-Jews from the land or to treat them as having less than equal rights in the land.[50] Not unexpectedly, the writings of Maimonides have been invoked to defend an alternative, less crude conception of the sanctity of the land.[51] From a biblical perspective, I would

---

indeed conquered by Joshua. See Nili Wazana, "'Everything Was Fulfilled' versus 'The Land That Yet Remains': Contrasting Conceptions of the Fulfillment of the Promise in the Book of Joshua," in Berthelot, David, and Hirshman, *Gift of the Land*, 13–35.

49. See Frankel, *Land of Canaan*, 37. Again, this is not to deny that some utopian prophecies foresee a restoration of Israel and Judah together. See, e.g., David C. Greenwood, "On the Jewish Hope for a Restored Northern Kingdom," *ZAW* 88 (1976): 376–85.

50. See Adrian Hastings, "Holy Lands and their Political Consequences," *NN* 9 (2003): 29–54. For a chilling work expounding extreme racist positions with regard to non-Jews in the land, see Yitzhak Shapira and Yosef Elitsur, *Torat Hamelekh* (Yitshar: Yeshivat 'od Yosef Hay, 2010).

51. For a discussion of the Maimonides's nomistic conception of the sanctity of the land, see Menachem Kellner, *Maimonides' Confrontation with Mysticism* (Oxford: Littman Library of Jewish Civilization, 2006), 107–15; for a list of earlier studies, see

like to emphasize two points. First, while one can find slight biblical support for the idea that the land as a whole is holy, this conception is rarely made explicit and is extremely marginal within biblical literature as a whole.[52] Much more dominant is a rather secular conception of the land. Thus none of the divine promises to the patriarchs in Genesis refers to the land as either holy or particularly unique in any way. The land is chiefly presented in functional terms, as a place for the future descendents of the patriarchs to live on. Starting with the book of Exodus, references to the land as "good" or "flowing with milk and honey" appear. Most famously, we read in Deut 8:7–9:

> For the LORD your God is bringing you into a good land, a land of brooks of water, of fountains and springs, flowing forth in valleys and hills, a land of wheat and barley, of vines and fig trees and pomegranates, a land of olive trees and honey, a land in which you will eat bread without scarcity, in which you will lack nothing, a land whose stones are iron, and out of whose hills you can dig copper. (RSV)

In these and many other passages, the uniqueness of the land is thoroughly material and not spiritual.[53] The land, we may say, is designed to promote the welfare of the people. It has no sacral significance in and of itself.

Furthermore, even in texts that attribute a unique spiritual character to the land, this character is neither holy nor innate. In the literature that

---

107 n. 68; and for Kellner's own use of Maimonides's approach within the context of the contemporary debate on the situation in Israel, see 294.

52. The term "holy land" appears almost exclusively in postbiblical literature. For a discussion, see W. D. Davies, *The Gospel and the Land: Early Christianity and Jewish Territorial Doctrine* (Berkeley: University of California Press, 1974), 29–30 and n. 27. For "holy land" in the Bible, Davies points to Ps 78:54 and Zech 2:16. See also James Kugel, "The Holiness of Israel and the Land in Second Temple Times," in *Texts, Temples and Traditions: A Tribute to Menahem Haran*, ed. Michael V. Fox et al. (Winona Lake, IN: Eisenbrauns, 1996), 21–32. Kugel suggests that the late conception in Ezra of Israel as "holy seed" contributed to the development of a similar essentialist conception with regard to the land.

53. The one exception to this is Deut 11:12, which affirms that the eyes of the Lord are continuously focused on the land. This "spiritual" uniqueness is, however, a double-edged sword. While it implies that God will be sure to provide for the land if those living on it behave properly, it also implies that misbehavior will not be overlooked. This is the force of the continuation of the passage in Deut 11:13–21. Most important, the "eyes of God" remain in heaven and are not present within the land.

scholars attribute to the Holiness school, God sanctifies the sanctuary (Exod 29:44; Lev 21:23), the priests (Lev 22:9), and the Sabbath (Exod 20:11). God never sanctifies, or calls upon Israel to sanctify, the land.[54] The land, it is true, is uniquely sensitive to sin and impurity and can be *contaminated*, as any object (Lev 18:24–28). However, since it was never made *sacred*, it can never be *profaned*, as can the sanctuary (Lev 21:12), the priests (Lev 21:15), or the Sabbath (Exod 31:14). The land's special sensitivity to impurity is a function or consequence of God's presence in the sanctuary (Num 35:34). God will not remain present in an impure environment. This, however, has nothing to do with the land itself. Israel had to be just as careful about sin and impurity when it wandered about in the wilderness, encamped around the portable divine tabernacle. In sum, there is no conception in all of this material of the holiness of the land or of its *innate* spiritual character.[55] On the most fundamental level, the approach that scholars attribute to Maimonides is, once again, well rooted in the texts of the Bible. It should not be conceived of as a radical innovation.

4. A Nonmessianic Hermeneutic of Biblical Texts: Accommodation versus Justice

Rejection of the messianic orientation toward contemporary issues concerning Israel and the land need not imply that messianic texts should be ignored. On the contrary, I would posit that a Jewish and religious-humanist approach toward Israel's relation to the land has much to learn from messianic (and other) biblical texts, if we read them with a nonmessianic hermeneutic. Messianic texts speak, for example, of the final achievement of absolute justice in the world. According to the famous vision of Isaiah (2:1–4), for example, in the end of days all the nations of the world will come up to Jerusalem to learn of God's ways. God will adjudicate between the competing claims of the warring nations of the world, determine which claims are just and which are not, and thereby bring about peace on earth.

---

54. It is telling that Israel is called upon in Lev 25:10, 12 to sanctify the jubilee year, when all agricultural work ceases and slaves are released to return to their inheritances. In spite of the land-centered character of this law, it is the time period that is sanctified rather than the land.

55. See Jan Joosten, *The People and the Land in the Holiness Code: An Exegetical Study of the Ideational Framework of the Law in Leviticus 17–26*, VTSup 67 (Leiden: Brill, 1996), 123–24, 178–79.

The implication of this prophecy, when read from a nonmessianic perspective, is that only God (and, according to other texts, his messiah) can determine justice absolutely. So long as we live in the world as it is, with all its complexities, the ability of any human being to definitively determine absolute justice will necessarily elude us. Humility before God requires that we acknowledge our inability to rise above our limited and situated perspectives and look out from some objective and all-encompassing vantage point.[56] Thus, if conflicting parties insist on speaking in the name of absolute truth and justice, no understanding will ever be achieved. Each side will bring a long list of grievances and claim that justice is completely with them.[57] The assertion of Prov 16:2, "A person's own paths are pure in his eyes" (my trans.), applies as much to groups, nations, and religions as it does to individuals. Rather than speaking the eschatological language of absolute justice, contesting parties should employ the pragmatic discourse of compromise and mutual accommodation.

This is the positive model provided by Abraham, who lived, as we do today, in an unredeemed world. When Abraham's herdsmen quarreled with the herdsmen of Lot, he did not attempt to adjudicate between them. Presumably he recognized that this would lead only to deadlock and hostility. Instead, he offered a pragmatic solution that allowed for the needs of both parties to be met. Abraham and Lot separated from one another, and each group settled in its own part of the land (Gen 13:5–12). Isaac employed an even more accommodating strategy. When Isaac's herdsmen dug and found a well of spring water by the wadi of Gerar and the herdsman of Gerar claimed it as their own, Isaac did not argue with them in the name of justice. He simply moved on and dug another well. When this well, too, was contested by the herdsmen of Gerar, Isaac continued to move even farther. When Isaac's rights to the third well were finally recognized, he called the well Rehoboth, saying, "Now at last the Lord has granted us ample space to increase in the land" (26:22). The Lord made space for Isaac in the land after Isaac chose to make space for others.[58]

---

56. This may be the most basic implication of the divine response to Job. Human beings can never make absolute claims to knowledge of truth since their perspectives are always partial and situated within a specific context.

57. Suffering from this deficiency, in my evaluation, are many of the essays in Nur Masalha and Lisa Isherwood, eds., *Theologies of Liberation in Palestine-Israel: Indigenous, Contextual, and Postcolonial Perspectives* (Eugene, OR: Pickwick, 2014).

58. In the contemporary context, I would extend the lesson of this verse to the

Isaac had the extraordinary inner strength to let go not only of territory that was rightly his but also of his sense of just entitlement.[59] Perhaps it was Isaac's heroic ability to do so that eventually elicited the Gerarites' reconciliation to his presence in the land.

5. Conclusion: Foregrounding "Texts of Tolerance"

Unfortunately, there are some who point to "texts of terror" in the Bible in order to justify the unethical in Israel today. I believe that it is particularly incumbent upon Jewish scholars of the Bible, both in Israel and abroad, to counter this trend by finding and foregrounding what we might refer to as "texts of tolerance." Allow me, in conclusion, to point to one of these: the story of Josiah's death at the hands of the Egyptian army, alluded to above. As opposed to the laconic report of this event presented in the book of Kings, the book of Chronicles presents an extended and unique version of the matter.

> After Josiah did all this for the Temple, Neco king of Egypt led an army to attack Carchemish, a town on the Euphrates River. And Josiah marched out to fight against Neco. But Neco sent messengers to Josiah, saying, "King Josiah, there should not be war between us. I did not come to fight you but my enemies. *Elohim told me to hurry. Cease opposing Elohim who*

---

theological realm as well. God makes space for those in the land who make not only physical space for the other but also theological space.

59. One way of reading Isaac's retreat is to see it as indicating an abdication of his conviction that justice is on his side. Isaac concedes that he may have dug a well on Gerarite property. Another reading would suggest that Isaac does not give up his sense that justice is on his side. Rather, he refrains from pursuing his just claim and translating it into concrete ownership. This is the lesson I would draw from Job's final submission to God after the divine speeches out of the whirlwind (both of which, admittedly, can be read in a wide variety of ways). Some critics find Job's final submission disappointingly cowardly and lacking in promethean defiance. Others go so far as to interpret the text of Job 42:1–6 as depicting Job as defiant to the very end. I do not find either of these readings convincing. It is important to note that, even in the end, Job never states that his suffering was due to sin (as his friends maintained), just as God never asserts in his speeches that Job was punished for his sins. Nor does Job affirm God's justice in afflicting him. What Job forfeits in his submission, I would suggest, is his sense that he is entitled to receive an explanation from God. Of relevance to the general theme is Avi Sagi, *Facing Others and Otherness: The Ethics of Inner Retreat* [Hebrew] (Tel Aviv: Hakibbutz Hameuchad, 2012).

is with me, or he will destroy you." But Josiah did not go away. He wore different clothes so no one would know who he was. *Refusing to listen to the words of Neco from the mouth of Elohim, Josiah went to fight on the plain of Megiddo.* In the battle King Josiah was shot by archers. He told his servants, "Take me away because I am badly wounded." So they took him out of his chariot and put him in another chariot and carried him to Jerusalem. There he died and was buried in the graves where his ancestors were buried. All the people of Judah and Jerusalem were very sad because he was dead. (2 Chr 35:20–24, my trans.)

Chronicles presents us with a remarkable account. Why did Josiah die in battle? Because he refused to pay heed to the Egyptian king's claim to be acting at God's behest. This passage is rather astonishing. Why should Josiah have given credence to the theological claims of Neco? This is especially perplexing since he speaks in the name of "Elohim who is with me," which, as some of the rabbis noted, most naturally refers to Neco's pagan god(s).[60] The apocryphal 1 Esdras introduces two important changes into its account. First, it has Neco speak in the name of *the Lord* God, not in the name of the ambiguous term אלהים. Second, it reformulates 2 Chr 34:22 to state, "He did not heed *the words of Jeremiah the prophet from the mouth of the Lord*" (1 Esd 1:26). Josiah's sin, accordingly, was not that he refused to heed the divine words of Neco but that he refused to heed the divine words of Jeremiah! Yet the text in Chronicles says nothing like this!

It seems to me that the passage in Chronicles offers us a profound lesson in the need to pay heed to the others that we meet. We need to listen carefully and sympathetically to their beliefs and their stories even when they are very different from our own. Neco may have spoken in the name of his pagan deity, but this still contained an echo of the word of the true God.[61] God can speak in many voices and through many traditions, and we must keep ourselves open to hearing his word in unexpected places.

I believe that peace will come to our tormented land when we learn not only to tell our stories but also to listen to the stories of others and when we accept that God is not only to be found in our own faith but is also to be found in the faith of others.

---

60. See the debate on this verse in t. Ta'an. 2.

61. So, at least implicitly, Sara Japhet, *I and II Chronicles: A Commentary*, OTL (London: SCM Press, 1993), 1056–57. For various types of theological pluralism in Genesis, see Frankel, *Land of Canaan*, 326–37.

Bibliography

Adar, Zvi. *Humanistic Values in the Bible*. Translated by Victor Tcherikover. New York: Reconstructionist, 1967.

Aḥituv, Yosef. *A Critique of Contemporary Religious Zionism: Selected Writings*. Edited by Yakir Englander and Avi Sagi. Ein Zurim: Shalom Hartman Institute and Yaacov Herzog Center for Jewish Studies, 2013.

———. "State and Army According to the Torah: Realism and Mysticism in the Circles of 'Merkaz HaRav.'" Pages 449–72 in *Religion and State in Twentieth Century Jewish Thought* [Hebrew]. Edited by Aviezer Ravitzky. Jerusalem: The Israeli Institute for Democracy, 2005.

Alexander, Philip S. "The Rabbis and Messianism." Pages 227–44 in *Redemption and Resistance: The Messianic Hopes of Jews and Christians in Antiquity*. Edited by Markus Bockmuehl and James Carleton Paget. London: T&T Clark, 2009.

Barton, John. "The Prophets and the Cult." *Temple and Worship in Biblical Israel*. Edited by John Day. LHBOTS 422. London: T&T Clark, 2005.

Berman, Joshua. *Created Equal: How the Bible Broke with Ancient Political Thought*. Oxford: Oxford University Press, 2008.

Birnbaum, Philip, ed. *The Daily Prayer Book: Sephardic*. New York: Hebrew Publishing, 1969.

Brettler, Marc Zvi. "Concepts of Scripture in Moshe Greenberg." Pages 247–66 in *Jewish Concepts of Scripture: A Comparative Introduction*. Edited by Benjamin D. Sommer. New York: New York University Press, 2012.

Brody, Samuel. *This Pathless Hour: Messianism, Anarchism, Zionism, and Martin Buber's Theopolitics Reconsidered*. Chicago: University of Chicago, The Divinity School, 2013.

Buber, Martin. *Darko shel miqra*. Jerusalem: Bialik, 1964.

———. *Kingship of God*. Translated by Richard Scheimann. New York: Harper Row, 1967.

———. *Land of Two Peoples: Martin Buber on Jews and Arabs*. Edited by Paul Mendes-Flohr. Chicago: University of Chicago Press, 2005.

———. *Moses: The Revelation and the Covenant*. New York: Harper, 1958.

———. *On the Bible: Eighteen Studies*. Edited by Nahum N. Glatzer. New York: Schocken, 1968.

———. *The Prophetic Faith*. Translated by Carlyle Witton-Davies. New York: Macmillan, 1949.

Cassuto, Umberto. *A Commentary on the Book of Exodus*. Translated by Israel Abrahams. Jerusalem: Magness, 1967.

Davies, W. D. *The Gospel and the Land: Early Christianity and Jewish Territorial Doctrine*. Berkeley: University of California Press, 1974.

Eldad, Yisrael. "The Ethics of the Conquerors of Canaan" [Hebrew]. Pages 11–24 in *Hegionot ha-mikra*. Jerusalem: Sulam, 1958.

Elon, Menachem. *Jewish Law: History, Sources, Principles*. Translated by Bernard Auerbach and Melvin J. Sykes. 4 vols. Philadelphia: Jewish Publication Society of America, 1994.

Fischer, Shlomo. "Religious Zionism at the Threshold of the Third Millennium: Two Cultures of Faith" [Hebrew]. *Akdamot* 22 (2009): 9–38.

Fishbane, Michael. *Biblical Interpretation in Ancient Israel*. Oxford: Clarendon, 1988.

———. *The Garments of Torah: Essays in Biblical Hermeneutics*. Bloomington: Indiana University Press, 1989.

Frankel, David. *The Land of Canaan and the Destiny of Israel: Theologies of Territory in the Hebrew Bible*. Siphrut 4. Winona Lake, IN: Eisenbrauns, 2011.

Gellman, Jerome. "Buber's Blunder: Buber's Replies to Scholem and Schatz-Uffenheimer." *MJ* 20 (2000): 20–40.

Greenberg, Moshe. "On the Political Use of the Bible in Modern Israel: An Engaged Critique." Pages 461–71 in *Pomegranates and Golden Bells: Studies in Biblical, Jewish, and Near Eastern Ritual, Law, and Literature in Honor of Jacob Milgrom*. Edited by David P. Wright, David Noel Freedman, and Avi Hurvitz. Winona Lake, IN: Eisenbrauns, 1995.

Greenwood, David C. "On the Jewish Hope for a Restored Northern Kingdom." *ZAW* 88 (1976): 376–85.

Halbertal, Moshe. *Maimonides: Life and Thought*. Translated by Joel Linsider. Princeton: Princeton University Press, 2014.

———. *People of the Book: Canon, Meaning and Authority*. Cambridge: Harvard University Press, 1997.

Harvey, Warren Zeev. "Rabbi Reines on the Conquest of Canaan and Zionism." Pages 386–98 in *The Gift of the Land and the Fate of the Canaanites in Jewish Thought*. Edited by Katell Berthelot, Joseph E. David, and Marc G. Hirshman. Oxford: Oxford University Press, 2014.

Hastings, Adrian. "Holy Lands and their Political Consequences." *NN* 9 (2003): 29–54.

Heinemann, Joseph. "The Messiah of Ephraim and the Premature Exodus of the Tribe of Ephraim." *HTR* 52 (1959): 1–15.

Held, Shai. "What Zvi Yehuda Kook Wrought: The Theopolitical Radicalization of Religious Zionism." Pages 229–55 in *Rethinking the Messianic Idea in Judaism*. Edited by Michael L. Morgan and Steven Weitzman. Bloomington: Indiana University Press, 2015.

Heschel, Abraham Joshua. *The Insecurity of Freedom*. New York: Schocken, 1972.

Japhet, Sara. *I and II Chronicles: A Commentary*. OTL. London: SCM Press, 1993.

———. *The Ideology of the Book of Chronicles and Its Place in Biblical Thought*. Translated by Anna Barber. BEATAJ 9. Frankfurt am Main: Lang, 1989.

Joosten, Jan. *The People and the Land in the Holiness Code: An Exegetical Study of the Ideational Framework of the Law in Leviticus 17–26*. VTSup 67. Leiden: Brill, 1996.

Kalimi, Isaac, ed. *Jewish Bible Theology: Perspectives and Case Studies*. Winona Lake, IN: Eisenbrauns, 2012.

Kaminsky, Joel S. "Can Election Be Forfeited?" Pages 44–66 in *The Call of Abraham: Essays on the Election of Israel in Honor of Jon D. Levenson*. Edited by Gary A. Anderson and Joel S. Kaminsky. Notre Dame: University of Notre Dame Press, 2013.

Kaufmann, Yehezkel. *Mikhivshonah shel haytsirah hamiqrait: Collected Essays*. Tel Aviv: Dvir, 1966.

———. Review of *Königtum Gottes*, by Martin Buber. *Kirjath Sepher* 10 (1933–1934): 62–66.

———. *Toledot ha'emunah hayisra'elit*. 4 vols. Jerusalem: Bialik & Dvir, 1960.

Kellner, Menachem. "'And the Crooked Shall Be Made Straight': Twisted Messianic Visions, and a Maimonidean Corrective." Pages 108–40 in *Rethinking the Messianic Idea in Judaism*. Edited by Michael L. Morgan and Steven Weitzman. Bloomington: Indiana University Press, 2015.

———. *Maimonides' Confrontation with Mysticism*. Oxford: Littman Library of Jewish Civilization, 2006.

Kepnes, Steven. *The Text as Thou: Martin Buber's Dialogical Hermeneutics and Narrative Theology*. Bloomington: Indiana University Press, 1992.

Knoppers, Gary N. *The Reign of Solomon and the Rise of Jeroboam*. Vol. 1 of *Two Nations under God: The Deuteronomistic History of Solomon and the Dual Monarchies*. HSM 52. Atlanta: Scholars Press, 1993.

Kugel, James. "The Holiness of Israel and the Land in Second Temple Times." Pages 21–32 in *Texts, Temples and Traditions: A Tribute to*

Menahem Hara. Edited by Michael V. Fox, Victor Avigdor Hurowitz, Avi Hurvitz, Michael L. Klein, Baruch J. Schwartz, and Nili Shupak. Winona Lake, IN: Eisenbrauns, 1996.

Leibowitz, Yeshayahu. *Judaism, Human Values, and the Jewish State.* Edited by Eliezer Goldman. Cambridge: Harvard University Press, 1992.

Lorberbaum, Yair. *Disempowered King: Monarchy in Classical Jewish Literature.* Translated by Jonathan Chipman. London: Continuum, 2011.

Luz, Ehud. *Wrestling with an Angel: Power, Morality and Jewish Identity.* Translated by Michael Swirsky. New Haven: Yale University Press 2003.

Masalha, Nur, and Lisa Isherwood, eds. *Theologies of Liberation in Palestine-Israel: Indigenous, Contextual, and Postcolonial Perspectives.* Eugene, OR: Pickwick, 2014.

Meshi, Menahem. *Perush haMeiri ʿal Sefer Mishley.* Edited by Menahem M. Meshi Zahav. Jerusalem: Otzar haPosqim, 1969.

Rad, Gerhard von. *Old Testament Theology.* Vol. 2. Translated by David M. G. Stalker. New York: Harper & Row, 1965.

Ravitzky, Aviezer. *Messianism, Zionism and Jewish Religious Radicalism.* Translated by Michael Swirsky and Jonathan Chipman. CSHJ. Chicago: University of Chicago Press, 1996.

———. " 'To the Utmost of Human Capacity': Maimonides on the Days of the Messiah." Pages 221–56 in *Perspectives on Maimonides.* Edited by Joel L. Kraemer. London: Littman Library of Jewish Civilization, 1996.

Rawidowicz, Simon. "On Interpretation." Pages 45–20 in *Studies in Jewish Thought.* Edited by Nahum N. Glatzer. Philadelphia: Jewish Publication Society of America, 1974.

Rofé, Alexander. *The Prophetical Stories: The Narratives about the Prophets in the Hebrew Bible, Their Literary Types and History.* Jerusalem: Magnes, 1988.

Sagi, Avi. *Facing Others and Otherness: The Ethics of Inner Retreat* [Hebrew]. Tel Aviv: Hakibbutz Hameuchad, 2012.

Scholem, Gershom. "Judaism." Pages 505–8 in *Twentieth Century Jewish Religious Thought: Original Essays on Critical Concepts, Movements and Beliefs.* Edited by Arthur A. Cohen and Paul Mendes-Flohr. Philadelphia: Jewish Publication Society of America, 2009.

———. *On the Possibility of Jewish Mysticism in Our Time and Other Essays.* Edited by Avraham Shapira. Translated by Jonathan Chipman. Philadelphia: Jewish Publication Society of America, 1997.

Seeligmann, Isaac Leo. "Certain of His Truth and Independent of Other Opinions." Pages 16-28 in *On the Late Professor Y. Kaufmann* [Hebrew]. Edited by Benjamin Mazar et al. Jerusalem: Magnes, 1964.

Shapira, Yitzhak, and Yosef Elitsur. *Torat Hamelekh.* Yitshar: Yeshivat 'od Yosef Hay, 2010.

Simon, Uriel. "The Biblical Destinies: Conditional Promises." *Tradition* 17 (1978): 84–90.

———. "The Place of the Bible in Israeli Society: From National Midrash to Existential Peshat." *MJ* 19 (1999): 155–77.

———. *Seek Peace and Pursue It: Topical Issues in the Light of the Bible; The Bible in the Light of Topical Issues.* Tel Aviv: Yediot Aharonot, 2002

Sommer, Benjamin D. "Dialogical Biblical Theology: A Jewish Approach to Reading Scripture Theologically." Pages 1–53 in *Biblical Theology: Introducing the Conversation.* Edited by Leo G. Perdue. Nashville: Abingdon, 2009.

Spero, Shubert. "Does Traditional Jewish Messianism Imply Inevitability? Is There a Political Role for Messianists in Israel Today?" *MJ* 8 (1988): 271–85.

Sweeney, Marvin A. "Jewish Biblical Theology and Christian Old Testament Theology." *TLZ* 134 (2009): 397–410.

———. *Tanak: A Theological and Critical Introduction to the Jewish Bible.* Minneapolis: Fortress, 2012.

Uffenheimer, Benyamin. "Buber and Modern Biblical Scholarship." Pages 163–211 in *Martin Buber: A Centenary Volume.* Edited by Ḥayim Gordon and Jochanan Bloch. New York: Ktav, 1984.

———. "Buber's Socialist and Political Views: A Critique." Pages 67–82 in *Thinkers and Teachers of Modern Judaism.* Edited by Raphael Patai and Emanuel S. Goldsmith. New York: Paragon, 1994.

Urbach, Ephraim E. *The Sages: Their Concepts and Beliefs.* Translated by Israel Abrahams. Cambridge: Harvard University Press, 1987.

———. *The World of the Sages: Collected Studies* [Hebrew]. Jerusalem: Magnes, 2002.

Van Leeuwen, Raymond C. "The Sage in the Prophetic Literature." Pages 295–306 in *The Sage in Israel and the Ancient Near East.* Edited by John G. Gammie and Leo G. Perdue. Winona Lake, IN: Eisenbrauns, 1990.

Vogel, Manfred. "Buber and the Arab-Jewish Conflict," Pages 43–65 in *Thinkers and Teachers of Modern Judaism.* Edited by Raphael Patai and Emanuel S. Goldsmith. New York: Paragon, 1994.

Wazana, Nili. "'Everything Was Fulfilled' versus 'The Land That Yet Remains': Contrasting Conceptions of the Fulfillment of the Promise in the Book of Joshua." Pages 13–35 in *The Gift of the Land and the Fate of the Canaanites in Jewish Thought*. Edited by Katell Berthelot, Joseph E. David, and Marc G. Hirshman. Oxford: Oxford University Press, 2014.

Weinfeld, Moshe. *The Promise of the Land: The Inheritance of the Land of Canaan by the Israelites*. Berkeley: University of California Press, 1993.

White, Rachel. "Recovering the Past, Renewing the Present: The Buber-Scholem Controversy over Hasidism Reinterpreted." *JSQ* 14 (2007): 364–92.

Zakovitch, Yair. "*Rihuq tsorekh qirvah*." *TE* 4 (1995): 7–17.

Characterizing Chiastic Contradiction: Literary Structure, Divine Repentance, and Dialogical Biblical Theology in 1 Samuel 15:10–35

Benjamin J. M. Johnson

1. Introduction

According to the Book of Proverbs, the proper response to "a fool" can be described as follows: "Do not answer fools according to their folly, or you will be a fool yourself. Answer fools according to their folly, or they will be wise in their own eyes" (Prov 26:4–5 NRSV). The contradiction between these two statements is blatant and obvious. However, as much as there are various ways that this contradiction is understood, it is apparent that this contradiction is not a problem. Rather, the conflicting statements are clearly intentional and cause the reader or hearer to reflect on the nature of engaging with a fool.[1] It is my suggestion that this contradictory pair of proverbs is an excellent example of dialogical truth. Each statement is true on its own, as far as it goes. However, together, in conversation, the two opposing and contradictory statements paint a bigger and fuller picture of the truth of the proper response to a fool.

This kind of thinking is, I suggest, similar to what Russian literary theorist Mikhail M. Bakhtin terms dialogical. For Bakhtin all texts (and all truths for that matter) are dialogical. "This means that no word or text can

---

1. For discussion stressing the ambiguity of this contradiction, see Roland E. Murphy, *Proverbs*, WBC 22 (Nashville: Nelson, 1998), 203. Michael V. Fox thinks that Prov 26:5 has the final say (*Proverbs 10–31: A New Translation with Introduction and Commentary*, AB 18B [New Haven: Yale University Press, 2009], 793–94). However, his discussion still highlights the dialogical nature of this contradiction.

be heard or read in isolation. Each word or utterance responds in one form or another to utterances that precede it."[2] The meaning of a text for Bakhtin exists in the dialogue between a text and another text (or context).[3]

In her helpful discussion of Bakhtin's concept of dialogical truth in the context of biblical studies, Carol A. Newsom discusses three features of monological truth versus four features of dialogical truth. Newsom highlights that monological truth, the mode that is the default for most of us, is characterized as proposition based, something that moves toward systematization, and single-minded or voiced.[4] A picture of monological truth might be the lecture: a single consciousness delivering abstract systematized propositions. Against that kind of thinking, Bakhtin speaks of dialogical truth.

Newsom helpfully characterizes Bakthin's notion of dialogical truth as something requiring a plurality of minds or voices, personal rather than abstraction, something that does not move toward systematization, and open or unfinalizable.[5] If the lecture is a picture of monological truth, the conversation (or dialogue!) is the picture of dialogical truth, something that requires two or more personalities giving personal perspectives that form the picture of truth.

Others have used this picture of dialogical truth as an essential picture of the task of biblical theology.[6] For example, Brevard S. Childs, in commenting on the task of biblical theology from a Christian perspective, stated that "Biblical Theology attempts to hear the different voices in rela-

---

2. L. Juliana M. Claassens, "Biblical Theology as Dialogue: Continuing the Conversation on Mikhail Bakhtin and Biblical Theology," *JBL* 122 (2003): 129. See Mikhail M. Bakhtin, *Speech Genres and Other Late Essays*, ed. Caryl Emerson and Michael Holquist, trans. Vern W. McGee (Austin: University of Texas Press, 1986), 71–72, 94.

3. See Bakhtin, *Speech Genres*, 106, 162; and Bakhtin, *The Dialogical Imagination: Four Essays*, ed. Michael Holquist (Austin: University of Texas Press, 1981), 284; cf. Claassens, "Biblical Theology as Dialogue," 130.

4. Carol A. Newsom, "Bakhtin, the Bible, and Dialogical Truth," *JR* 76 (1996): 290.

5. Newsom, "Bakhtin, the Bible, and Dialogical Truth," 293–95.

6. See further: Benjamin D. Sommer, "Dialogical Biblical Theology: A Jewish Approach to Reading Scripture Theologically," in *Biblical Theology: Introducing the Conversation*, ed. Leo Perdue, LBT (Nashville: Abingdon, 2009), 1–53; Susan M. Felch, "Dialogism," in *Dictionary for Theological Interpretation of the Bible*, ed. Kevin J. Vanhoozer et al. (Grand Rapids: Baker Academic, 2005), 173–75; Dennis T. Olson, "Biblical Theology as Provisional Monologization: A Dialogue with Childs, Brueggemann and Bakhtin," *BibInt* 6 (1998): 162–80; Claassens, "Biblical Theology as Dialogue."

tion to the divine reality to which they point in such diverse ways."[7] Or one might think of Walter Brueggemann's *Theology of the Old Testament*, whose controlling courtroom metaphor for biblical theology proposes the categories of testimony, dispute, and advocacy as accurately reflecting "the process of theological utterance (and thought) in the Old Testament."[8] This model is inherently dialogical and pictures biblical theology as attending to the various voices within Scripture.[9] This approach may take several different shapes. It may take the form of macrostructural biblical theology such as Brueggemann's that seeks to understand the whole of the Bible as a dialogue, or it may take the form of intertextual readings of discrete portions of Scripture to highlight the inherent dialogue that happens within portions of the biblical text.[10] In this essay I will suggest an example of an instance where the biblical text itself structurally suggests a dialogical reading. It is an instance that is regularly noted as a tension or contradiction within the text. It is my suggestion that attentiveness to a dialogical approach to different perspectives within the text and within the inherently dialogical structure of the text allows for a fuller and more fruitful theological engagement with the text.

The text I will explore is the case of YHWH's repentant and unrepentant nature depicted in 1 Sam 15:10–35. In 1 Sam 15:11 we read that YHWH repented (נחם) that he made Saul king over Israel.[11] Then at the

---

7. Brevard S. Childs, *Biblical Theology of the Old and New Testaments: Theological Reflection on the Christian Bible* (Minneapolis: Fortress, 1992) 85. Childs, in this context at least, is primarily interested in the dialogue that is created in the inclusion of both Old and New Testaments in the Christian canon.

8. Walter Brueggemann, *The Theology of the Old Testament: Testimony, Dispute, Advocacy* (Minneapolis: Fortress, 2005), xvii.

9. In his recent assessment of the future of biblical theology, Walter Brueggemann contends that "dialogic transaction" or "dialogic contestation" is central to the future of biblical theology ("Futures in Old Testament Theology: Dialogical Engagement," *HBT* 37 [2015]: 32–49).

10. See for example, recent intertextual readings of sections of Scripture in Katharine Dell and Will Kynes, eds., *Reading Job Intertextually*, LHBOTS (London: Bloomsbury, 2013); Dell and Kynes, eds., *Reading Ecclesiastes Intertextually*, LHBOTS (London: Bloomsbury, 2014).

11. The use of the term "repentance" here ought not necessarily bring with it the standard context of "repentance from sin," which is probably its most common usage today. For discussion of the terminology of "repentance," especially when used of God, see Terence E. Fretheim, "The Repentance of God: A Key to Evaluating Old Testament God-Talk," *HBT* 10 (1988): 50–52.

end of this pericope we hear again that he repented (נחם) that he made Saul king. In between this *inclusio* of YHWH's repentance is the unequivocal statement by his prophet that "the Enduring One of Israel will not lie or repent [נחם], for he is not a mortal, that he should repent [נחם]" (1 Sam 15:29).[12] This contradiction between the statements in 1 Sam 15:11, 35, and 29 is regularly noted by commentators.[13] The fact that the contradiction in 1 Sam 15 has long been seen does not mean that there is anything near a consensus on how to interpret it, as we will presently see. What I will explore is following on the lead from Brueggemann, who in commenting on 1 Sam 15 argued that "verses 10, 29, and 35 form a marvelous and intriguing place from which to do biblical theology.... The verses pose a theological problem about the character of God, who does not change and yet who changes."[14]

2. Approaches to Answering This Anomaly

Scholars have proposed various means and methods to alleviate the tension between 1 Sam 15:11, 35, and 29, but no discernible consensus has emerged. Some prominent ways of dealing with this tension can be described as harmonizing approaches, source-critical approaches, narrative-critical approaches, and recourse to paradox.

2.1. Harmonizing Approaches

A harmonizing approach can be described as an attempt to alleviate the tension in 1 Sam 15 that leads to the relativization of one of the two claims. Two common harmonizing strategies are employed: one is recourse to the category of anthropomorphism, and the other is recourse to the conditional nature of divine promises.

Some scholars alleviate the tension in 1 Sam 15 by claiming that the statements in verses 11 and 35 should be understood as anthropomorphic or, more accurately, anthropopathic statements and are thus "only an

---

12. Unless otherwise indicated, translations are my own.

13. For example, in his book on theological diversity, John Goldingay uses this as his parade example of a "formal contradiction" in Scripture (*Theological Diversity and the Authority of the Old Testament* [Grand Rapids: Eerdmans, 1987], 16–17).

14. Walter Brueggemann, *First and Second Samuel*, IBC (Louisville: John Knox, 1990), 116.

analogy."[15] In this view, passages that speak of YHWH repenting (e.g., Gen 6:6; 1 Sam 15:11, 35) are to be understood as anthropopathic metaphors, while passages that speak of YHWH not repenting (e.g., Num 23:19; 1 Sam 15:29) are theomorphic statements that actually describe YHWH's character.

In addition to the arbitrary nature of the decision as to which feelings or features are or are not appropriate to YHWH, the anthropomorphic argument fails to take into account the purpose of anthropomorphic language. The metaphoric nature of anthropomorphic statements does not mean that we can reject these statements. Metaphoric statements, as Terence E. Fretheim has argued, do in fact "contain information about God."[16] To appeal to the fact that some statements about YHWH use anthropomorphic language as a way to alleviate tension is to throw the baby out with the bathwater and thus render the metaphor meaningless.[17]

The second harmonizing strategy for dealing with the tension in 1 Sam 15 is to appeal to the conditional nature of some of YHWH's promises and the unconditional nature of others. This view claims that the statement that YHWH does not "repent" (נחם) in 1 Sam 15:29 is unconditional, while the statement that YHWH "repents" (נחם) in 1 Sam 15:11, 35 reflects the fact that Saul's kingship was always conditional upon his obedience (1 Sam 12:14–15). In this view it is sometimes suggested that YHWH's statements and promises are inherently conditional unless he specifically decrees it.[18] However, just what has been decreed in 1 Sam 15:29 that makes that statement unconditional must be argued, and commentators come to different conclusions. On the one hand, some argue that 1 Sam 15:29 is speaking of

---

15. Strictly speaking, anthropomorphism is describing God in human forms, while anthropopathism is describing God in terms of human feelings, which is what is present in the 1 Sam 15 text. See Lester J. Kuyper, "The Suffering and the Repentance of God," *SJT* 22 (1969): 257. The quote is from Timothy R. Ashley, *The Book of Numbers*, NICOT (Grand Rapids: Eerdmans, 1993), 477. For examples of scholars who hold this view, see S. R. Driver, *Notes on the Hebrew Text and the Topography of the Books of Samuel with an Introduction on Hebrew Palaeography and the Ancient Versions*, repr. ed. (Eugene, OR: Wipf & Stock, 2004), 129; see also Carl Friedrich Keil, *Joshua, Judges, Ruth, 1 and 2 Samuel*, vol. 2 of *Commentary on the Old Testament* (Peabody, MA: Hendrickson, 2006), 469.

16. Fretheim, "Repentance of God," 51.

17. See the discussion by Kuyper, "Suffering and the Repentance," 257–58.

18. See Robert B. Chisholm Jr., "Does God 'Change His Mind'?," *BSac* 152 (1995): 387–99.

the rejection of Saul's kingship and that it is Saul's rejection that is unconditional.[19] The strength of this view is the flow of the narrative, which clearly seems to suggest that YHWH has made a final decision regarding Saul's kingship and that this decision is unconditional and final. The weakness of this view is that it does not adequately answer why 1 Sam 15:29 is worded like a general statement.[20] On the other hand, it is possible that 1 Sam 15:29 is speaking of the promise of David's kingship. Thus, it is the promise of David's kingship that is unconditional (see 2 Sam 7:12–17).[21] The strength of this view is that it recognizes the importance of the allusion to Num 23:19 and its Davidic context.[22] The connection to David is certainly the point of this passage. However, the weaknesses of this view are that it still struggles to deal with the timeless and general nature of the statement in 1 Sam 15:29, which we noted above, and within the flow of the narrative neither Samuel nor Saul know anything about David, and it is difficult to see how a reference to David would make sense at this point in the story.[23]

2.2. Source-Critical Approaches

The second major strategy for dealing with the tension in 1 Sam 15 is the appeal to the contradictory verse in 15:29 as a later redaction. Proponents

---

19. E.g., R. P. Gordon, *1 and 2 Samuel: A Commentary* (Exeter: Paternoster, 1986), 146; Chisholm, "Does God 'Change His Mind'?," 392–95; Robert D. Bergen, *1, 2 Samuel*, NAC 7 (Nashville: B&H, 1996), 174.

20. So David Noel Freedman, "When God Repents," in *Divine Commitment and Human Obligation: Selected Writings of David Noel Freedman* (Grand Rapids: Eerdmans, 1997), 422; J. P. Fokkelman, *The Crossing Fates*, vol. 2 of *Narrative Art and Poetry in the Books of Samuel* (Dover, NH: VanGorcum, 1986), 107; R. W. L. Moberly, "God Is Not Human That He Should Repent," in *God in the Fray: A Tribute to Walter Breuggemann*, ed. Tod Linafelt and Timothy K. Beal (Minneapolis: Fortress, 1998), 120. Moberly proposes ובזאת לא ינחם יהוה as something we would expect to see in this view.

21. So Terence E. Fretheim, "Divine Foreknowledge, Divine Constancy, and the Rejection of Saul's Kingship," *CBQ* 47 (1985): 599; Moberly, "God Is Not Human," 120.

22. Fretheim, "Divine Foreknowledge," 598–99; Moberly, "God Is Not Human," 120–21; see also Gerhard von Rad, *Old Testament Theology*, vol. 1, trans. David M. G. Stalker (New York: HarperSanfrancisco, 1965), 325. Von Rad noted that we must read this narrative while looking forward to David.

23. Lyle Eslinger, "A Change of Heart: 1 Samuel 16," in *Ascribe to the Lord: Biblical and Other Studies in Memory of Peter C. Craigie*, ed, Lyle Eslinger and Glen Taylor (Sheffield: Sheffield Academic, 1988), 351.

of this view argue that such a blatant contradiction as exists between 1 Sam 15:11, 35, and 29 is classic sign of a "re-elaborated text."[24]

While this observation may help us understand how the text came to be, it does not adequately wrestle with the tension in the text that we have. To say that the problematic statement in 1 Sam 15:29 is a later redaction is merely to move the interpretive problem from an original author to a redactor. It does not address the question of how the redactor viewed this contradiction. Whether we view verse 29 as part of the original composition of this text or whether we see it as a later redaction still leaves us with a text that affirms two contradictory statements.[25] For the purposes of theological engagement, the recognition of differing and conflicting sources in the biblical text only invites the reader to enter into a dialogue that is already taking place in the text itself.[26]

2.3. Narrative-Critical Approaches

The helpful contribution that a literary analysis adds to the discussion is the recognition that some characters are portrayed as unreliable so that their statements cannot be trusted. If it could be shown that Samuel was making an unreliable statement in 1 Sam 15:29, then it could be rejected. The basic principles for determining whether a character is reliable are to view how the character has been portrayed throughout the narrative

---

24. Fabrizio Foresti, *The Rejection of Saul in the Perspective of the Deuteronomistic School: A Study of 1 Sm 15 and Related Texts*, vol. 5, StThT (Roma: Teresianum, 1984), 25; see also P. Kyle McCarter Jr., *1 Samuel: A New Translation with Introduction, Notes and Commentary*, AB 8 (Garden City, NY: Doubleday, 1980), 269; Artur Weiser, "I Samuel 15," *ZAW* 54 (1936): 4–5. Foresti additionally argues that the apparent duplication of Saul's repentance in 15:24–26 and 15:30–31 is also evidence of a later redaction. V. Philips Long takes up the arguments of Foresti and Weiser (among others) and argues that the repetition of Saul's repentance is in fact a meaningful literary technique, "Interpolation or Characterization: How Are We to Understand Saul's Two Confessions?," *Presb* 19 (1993): 49–53.

25. See the comments of Dale Patrick, who argues that it was the practice of ancient redactors to counterbalance older and unworthy language (15:11 and 35) with newer language (15:29) rather than remove the older language (*The Rendering of God in the Old Testament*, OBT [Philadelphia: Fortress, 1981], 54–55). Thus the reader is forced to encounter and believe both the older and newer formulations.

26. See Benjamin D. Sommer, "The Source Critic and the Religious Interpreter," *Int* 60 (2006): 9–20.

and to judge the statements and actions of the character compared to the truths the reader knows from the reliable narrator (or in biblical texts, the reliable character of God).[27]

So when it comes to the contradiction between 1 Sam 15:11, 35, and 29, whom do we trust? At first blush, the answer appears obvious. We cannot trust Samuel. First and foremost, Samuel's words about the fact that YHWH does not "repent" (נחם, 15:29) clearly contradict the words of the reliable narrator (15:11) and YHWH himself (15:35). Weighing these options, clearly it is Samuel who cannot be trusted.[28] Furthermore, it has often been pointed out that Samuel is something of a questionable character anyway.[29]

However, there are a number of reasons to take a second look at Samuel and suggest that he may, in fact, be reliable in this instance. First, the narrative officially has a high opinion of Samuel and his words, saying that "he [YHWH] did not let any of his [Samuel's] words fall to the ground. And all Israel knew, from Dan to Beer-sheba, that Samuel was a trustworthy prophet of YHWH" (1 Sam 3:19–20).[30]

Second, there does appear to be legitimate commingling of Samuel's words and YHWH's words in this chapter. Richard Middleton asks the perfectly legitimate literary question of whether or not YHWH really commanded Saul to "strike Amalek and put to the ban all that is his. Do not spare him, but kill both man and woman, both child and infant, both

---

27. See Yairah Amit, "'The Glory of Israel Does Not Deceive or Change His Mind': On the Reliability of Narrator and Speakers in Biblical Narrative," *Proof* 12 (1992): 205; Meir Sternberg, *The Poetics of Biblical Narrative: Ideological Literature and the Drama of Reading* (Bloomington: Indiana University Press, 1985), 502; Robert Polzin, *Samuel and the Deuteronomist: A Literary Study of the Deuteronomic History* (New York: Harper & Row, 1989), 140. This does not take into account the possibility of an unreliable narrator or an unreliable God.

28. See Amit, "Glory of Israel," 204; Polzin, *Samuel and the Deuteronomist*, 140.

29. For a negative reading of the character of Samuel, see J. Richard Middleton, "Samuel Agonistes: A Conflicted Prophet's Resistance to God and Contribution to the Failure of Israel's First King," in *Prophets, Prophecy, and Ancient Israelite Historiography*, ed. Mark J. Boda and Lissa M. Wray Beal (Winona Lake, IN: Eisenbrauns, 2013), 69–91. He deals with Samuel's unreliability in 1 Sam 15 at 81–85.

30. Middleton suggests that, even though Samuel is an unreliable character, God has committed to be bound by him and his words (e.g., 1 Sam 3:19–20). So, even if we may distrust him, Middleton argues, we must understand a commingling of divine and human words in the case of Samuel ("Samuel Agonistes," 87–88).

ox and sheep, both camel and donkey" (1 Sam 15:3). Did YHWH actually command this? The narrator does not say. Samuel says he did. Middleton says he did not.[31] Leaving aside the horrific nature of this command, there are a few reasons to suggest that Samuel is in fact reporting the word of YHWH. On the one hand, Samuel's claims for these words are the formal introduction to a prophetic word: "Thus says YHWH of hosts" (כה אמר יהוה צבאות, 1 Sam 15:2). On the other hand, when YHWH's words to Samuel are narrated, we hear YHWH say that Saul "did not keep *my* words" (ואת־דברי לא הקים, 1 Sam 15:11). What are "the words" that Saul did not keep? The most obvious words in the narrative are Samuel's.

Samuel's Command (1 Sam 15:3)	Saul's Actions (1 Sam 15:8–9)
Strike (נחם) Amalek	Saul struck (נחם) Amalek
Put to the ban (חרם), do not have mercy (חמל), and kill (המית) all that is his both man and woman both child and infant both ox and sheep both camel and donkey	He put to the ban (חרם) all the people all that was despised and worthless He had mercy (חמל) and did not put to the ban (חרם) Agag the best of the sheep, cattle, fatlings, lambs, and all that was valuable

In light of the above, it seems most likely that when YHWH says that Saul did not keep his words, this is most obviously in reference to Saul's failure to follow through with the command of Saul to destroy Amalek. Thus in this case YHWH has equated his words (1 Sam 15:11) with Samuel's words (1 Sam 15:3), giving us reason to argue that Samuel is reliable here.[32]

Third, Samuel's claim that YHWH does not repent (נחם) is given in a prophetic oracle that includes the also unconfirmed claim that YHWH has given Saul's kingdom to his neighbor who is better (טוב) than he (1 Sam 15:28). This statement by Samuel is confirmed true when David finally

---

31. Middleton, "Samuel Agonistes," 79–81.

32. See Middleton, "Samuel Agonistes," 87–88, and his view of an unreliable Samuel whose words nevertheless commingle with YHWH's.

takes Saul's kingdom. However, it is hinted at even earlier. The next time we hear the language of "good" (טוב) is when we are introduced to David. He is described as "good of appearance" (טוב ראי, 1 Sam 16:12) and is one who causes "good" (טוב) to come to Saul when he is in a fit (1 Sam 16:16, 23). There is certainly the potential for narrative irony in 1 Samuel when Saul feels "better" (טוב) because of the one who is "better" (טוב) than him.[33] The rest of Samuel's claims in this section appear to be trustworthy, which lends at least some credence to the suggestion that Samuel's claims about YHWH's unrepentant nature are also trustworthy.[34]

Finally, as I will argue below, the structure of 1 Sam 15:10–35 leads the reader to see this as the hinge section of the narrative. It is thus highlighted and shown to be thematically central such that claiming it is Samuel just blowing smoke seems unlikely.

2.4. Paradoxical Approaches

Given the range of ways that scholars have attempted to deal with the tension in 1 Sam 15:10–35, it is not surprising that some scholars have thrown their hands in the air and appealed to some form of divine paradox to explain this tension. For example, in the conclusion to his discussion of this issue Ralph W. Klein writes, "Perhaps the paradox expresses the real truth: he never changes his mind, and yet he does."[35] While in the first instance this approach may feel like a cop-out, there is much to commend it. First, Newsom is probably correct in her study of dialogical biblical theology when she notes that "the truth about human nature, the world, and God *cannot* be uttered by a single voice."[36] Second, in this text we

---

33. See Keith Bodner, *1 Samuel: A Narrative Commentary* (Sheffield: Sheffield Phoenix, 2009), 172–73. This theme is clearer in the LXX which includes an unqualified statement that David is "good" (ἀγαθός) in 16:12. On this variant and this theme, see Benjamin J. M. Johnson, *Reading David and Goliath in Greek and Hebrew: A Literary Approach*, FAT 2/82 (Tübingen: Mohr Siebeck, 2015), 47–48.

34. Stephen B. Chapman writes that "there is no explicit evidence anywhere in 1 Samuel 15 that the narrator considers Samuel's actions selfish or self-motivated. To the contrary, Samuel apparently continues to stand symbolically for the narrator's version of religious orthodoxy" (*Reading 1 Samuel as Christian Scripture: A Theological Commentary* [Grand Rapids: Eerdmans, 2016], 143).

35. Ralph W. Klein, *1 Samuel*, WBC 10 (Waco, TX: Word, 1982), 156. See also Freedman, "When God Repents."

36. Newsom, "Bakhtin, the Bible, and Dialogical Truth," 301, emphasis original.

have a formal contradiction in an assertion and a denial of the same reality, which, according to John Goldingay, "invites us to seek to relate them as well as to contrast them."[37] The point Goldingay makes is to say that the contradiction is intentional and invites us into the tension. It seems he is getting close to a dialogical approach when he says, "Thus both the affirmation and the denial are part of a coherent analogical description of God's involvement in the world, and each would be misleading without the other."[38] The strength of an appeal to paradox in this instance is the attempt to take both claims, about YHWH's repentance and unrepentance, seriously. It is the tension or, perhaps better, the conversation that results in accepting both of these claims that is the most helpful way forward in understanding what 1 Sam 15:10–35 says about YHWH.[39]

3. Caution! Chiastic Claims Ahead

Thus far I have noted the importance of a dialogical approach for theological engagement with the Bible, I have noted the theological tension present in 1 Sam 15:10–35, and I have discussed some of the ways that the tension is dealt with by commentators. In the previous section I noted that the category of paradox is a helpful one for this thorny text. It is my belief that a dialogical approach is the most helpful way to engage with this text. The rest of this essay will seek to show how the chiastic literary structure of 1 Sam 15:10–35 suggests a dialogical approach to this theologically difficult text.

3.1. Dangers of Chiastic Claims

Scholars have long noted the use of chiasms in ancient literature.[40] This is true of Hebrew poetry as well as Hebrew narrative.[41] However, it has also

---

37. Goldingay, *Theological Diversity*, 16.

38. Goldingay, *Theological Diversity*, 17.

39. For a helpful introductory presentation of this kind of approach, see Karl Allen Kuhn, *Having Words with God: The Bible as Conversation* (Minneapolis: Fortress, 2008).

40. The best starting point is John W. Welch, ed., *Chiasmus in Antiquity: Structures, Analyses, Exegesis* (Provo, UT: Research, 1999).

41. On chiasms in Hebrew poetry, see, e.g., Wilfred G. E. Watson, *Classical Hebrew Poetry: A Guide to Its Techniques*, JSOTSup 26 (Sheffield: JSOT Press, 1986), 201–21. On chiasms in Hebrew narrative, see, for example, Jerome T. Walsh, *Style and Structure in Biblical Hebrew Narrative* (Collegeville, MN: Liturgical Press, 2001),

been argued that many chiastic structures are in the eye of the beholder. One of the most infamous examples comes from Mike Butterworth's *Structure and the Book of Zechariah*, where he chose a selection of verses from Isaiah at random and formed a reasonable chiasm![42] In a similar vein, Mark J. Boda critiques what he sees as many errors in identifying a chiasm. He argues that there are often (1) errors in symmetry, which may include lopsided design, irregular arrangement, or atypical patterns; (2) errors in subjectivity, which may include arbitrary omission and inclusion, questionable demarcation, arbitrary labeling, metrical maneuvering, methodological isolation; or (3) errors in probability.[43] For these reasons and others, many scholars are rightfully suspicious of claimed chiastic patterns in biblical literature.[44]

Nevertheless, accepting the above criticisms and cautions, a chiastic literary structure was an available feature of the toolkit of an ancient author, and many, including the authors mentioned above, are willing to keep an eye out for them.

3.2. Functions of Chiastic Structures

However, even if we are persuasive in identifying a chiastic literary pattern, it is not certain what we are to make of that observation. Most often scholars speak of the purpose of the chiasm as something that focuses on the central element of the chiasm.[45] Other views on the function of a chiasm are available. Nathan Klaus, for example, argues that, while chiasms most often focus our attention on the center, occasionally the focus is meant

---

13–34; Elie Assis, "Chiasmus in Biblical Narrative: A Rhetoric of Characterization," *Proof* 22 (2003): 273–304.

42. Mike Butterworth, *Structure and the Book of Zechariah*, JSOTSup 130 (Sheffield: JSOT Press, 1992), 53–57. However, I use the term "reasonable" loosely here. The literary gymnastics Butterworth performs in order to see a chiastic structure is more pronounced than many studies and, I hope, more pronounced than what is attempted in the present study!

43. Mark J. Boda, "Chiasmus in Ubiquity: Symmetrical Mirages in Nehemiah 9," *JSOT* 71 (1996): 56–58.

44. See also Nathan Klaus, *Pivot Patterns in the Former Prophets*, JSOTSup 247 (Sheffield, England: JSOT Press, 1999); and from a New Testament perspective, see David A. DeSilva, "X Marks the Spot? A Critique of the Use of Chiasmus in Macrostructural Analyses of Revelation," *JSNT* 30 (2008): 343–71.

45. E.g., Assis, "Chiasmus in Biblical Narrative," 273.

to be on the outer frame of the structure.[46] Jerome T. Walsh argues that
a chiastic pattern often "invite[s] the reader to see the two sequences as
contrasting in some way, with the central element(s) marking the turning
point."[47] I will pay attention to all of these proposed functions of a chiasm
but will propose another nuance. My thesis is that the present chiastic
structure highlights the parallel elements and puts them into dialogue and
forces the reader to see the parallel elements in dialogical relationship.
However, if the proof of the pudding is in the eating, then perhaps the
proof of the chiasm is in the reading, and to that we now turn.

4. Identifying a Chiastic Literary Structure

4.1. Beginning to See a Parallel Structure

I will argue that 1 Sam 15:10–35 has a relatively developed chiastic literary structure. However, the recognition of a number of the parallel
features of this structure are not new and are, in fact, regularly recognized. The first and perhaps most regularly noted structural feature of
this scene is the fact that it is framed by divine repentance.[48] Not only are
the two phrases of YHWH's repentance in these verses nearly identical,
but they are two of the four uses in the Hebrew Bible of the idiomatic
phrase נחם + כי.[49] It is clear and without dispute that this scene is framed
by divine repentance and that this fact is thematically important for the
narrative. The fact that the scene is clearly framed by statements that
YHWH "repents" (נחם) throws Samuel's statement that YHWH does not
repent (נחם) in 15:29 into sharp relief. We will see how this plays out
structurally below.

A second significant literary parallel is found in Saul's repetitious confessions. On two occasions (15:24–26 and 15:30–31) Saul is said to confess

---

46. Klaus, *Pivot Patterns*, 253–56.

47. Jerome T. Walsh, *Old Testament Narrative: A Guide to Interpretation* (Louisville: Westminster John Knox Press, 2010), 111.

48. See for example, Fokkelmann, *Crossing Fates*, 91–92; Amit, "Glory of Israel,"
201; Freedman, "When God Repents," 419–20; Klein, *1 Samuel*, 151; Polzin, *Samuel
and the Deuteronomist*, 140–41; Fretheim, "Divine Foreknowledge," 595–96.

49. H. Van Dyke Parunak, "A Semantic Survey of *NḤM*," *Bib* 56 (1975): 519. The
other two usages of this idiom are found in Gen 6:6–7, which 1 Sam 15:11 and 35 likely
allude to, and Judg 21:15.

his sins to Samuel. The significance of these parallel confessions have led scholars to suggest that they originated as variant traditions, one in which Samuel refused to return with Saul and one in which he agreed to return with Saul.[50] The verbal connections between these two confessions show how clearly parallel they are:

1 Sam 15: 24–25	1 Sam 15:30–31
Confession: "I have sinned" (חטאתי)	Confession: "I have sinned" (חטאתי)
Request: "and return (שוב) with me"	Request: "and return (שוב) with me"
Reason for Request: "that I may worship YHWH." (ואשתחות ליהוה)	Reason for Request: "that I may worship YHWH your God" (והשתחויתי ליהוה אלהיך)
Samuel's Response: "I will not return with you" (לא אשוב עמך)	Samuel's Response: and Samuel returned after Saul (וישב שמואל אחרי שאול)

Once again, the clear lexical parallelism between these two elements give us firm objective support for asserting a parallel structure here.

Not only are these two scenes clearly parallel, but they frame the scene of the torn robe (15:27–29) and suggest that this scene may be important for understanding these parallel confessions of Saul. We will deal with the significance of this parallelism below; for now it is enough to note the structure that has emerged thus far.

Both clearly parallel elements that we have identified so far point to the scene of the torn robe and Samuel's statement to Saul that YHWH does not repent as being central. They can be outlined as follows:

A.   15:11: YHWH repents (נחם) that (כי) he made Saul king (מלך)
    B.   15:24–26: Saul's first confession (חטאתי), Samuel does not return (שוב)
        X.   15:27–29: Torn robe. YHWH does not repent (נחם)

50. See Foresti, *Rejection of Saul*, 25–28; McCarter, *1 Samuel*, 268; Weiser, "I Samuel 15," 4–5; Hans Wilhelm Hertzberg, *1 and 2 Samuel: A Commentary*, OTL (Philadelphia: Westminster, 1964), 129.

B′. 15:30–31: Saul's second confession (חטאתי), Samuel returns
(שוב)

A′. 15:35: YHWH repents (נחם) that (כי) he made Saul king (מלך)

4.2. Filling out the Literary Structure

The obvious literary parallels noted above cause us to be sensitive to the possibility of other literary parallels. Once we become sensitive to these kinds of parallel elements in this text, an overarching structure begins to emerge.

First we noted the parallelism of YHWH's repentance. Each statement about YHWH's repentance is matched by a statement about Samuel's emotional response to this reality. In 15:11b we are told that "Samuel was angry," and in 15:35aβ we are told that Samuel "mourned" concerning Saul. I suggest that these two instances are parallel and have an interesting relationship. J. P. Fokkelman suggests that one can see that the "one night in which he was to come to terms with Saul's rejection is expanded into a lifelong grief."[51]

Next, there is an elaborate parallelism in the movement of Samuel and Saul. After his initial reaction to the news of Saul's rejection, Samuel rises in the morning and goes "to greet" (לקראת) Saul (15:12a). He is told that Saul has gone and set up a monument for himself, then turned and crossed over and "went down" (ירד) to Gilgal (15:12b). Samuel then "comes" (בוא) to Saul, and the scene is set for their confrontation (15:13a). This pattern of movement—Samuel to Saul to Samuel—is repeated in inverse order and contrasting fashion at the end of the scene in 15:34–35aα. After the confrontation with Agag, Samuel "goes" (הלך) to Ramah (15:34a). This contrasts with his "coming" (בוא) to Saul in 15:13a. We are then told that Saul "goes up" (עלה) to Gibeah (15:34b). This contrasts with his "going down" (ירד) to Gilgal in 15:12b. Finally, we are told that Samuel did not "meet" (לראות) Saul again until the day of his death (15:34aα). This contrasts with Samuel going to "greet" (לקראת) Saul in 15:12a. Not only are the two instances grammatically parallel with the use of ל + infinitive construct, but the concepts are fairly synonymous as well.[52]

---

51. Fokkelman, *Crossing Fates*, 111.

52. In trying to understand the relationship between this statement and the scene where Saul appears "before Samuel" in 19:24, David Toshio Tsumura suggests that לראות ought to be understood as "to meet" here and so does not contradict 19:24 (*The*

Finally, we are left with 15:13b–23 and 15:32–33 unaccounted for in our structure. At first blush this clearly looks like a major gap in the structure that we are highlighting, and perhaps we ought to stop there. However, I suggest that there are good reasons to consider these two sections as being intentionally parallel. First, each of these two sections narrates Samuel's confrontation with two kings, Saul and Agag. That the confrontation with Saul is substantially larger than the confrontation with Agag is only natural, given that the story is about Saul and is only about Agag in respect to Saul.

Second, though it is a textually complex and vague statement, Agag's approach to Samuel saying that "Surely the bitterness of death has turned aside" (15:32) could interestingly be compared to Saul's naive and incorrect statement that he has "carried out the command of YHWH" (15:13).[53]

Third, Samuel's confrontations with these two kings both end in the same way: with the king's denunciation. Furthermore, each king's denunciation is given in a poetic pronouncement that follows the same structure. The poetic parallelism of the denunciations of Saul and Agag fit the following pattern: because [just as] you did X // so [thus] X will be done to you.[54]

Rejection of Saul (15:23)
   Because you have rejected (מאס) the word of YHWH,
   you have been rejected (מאס) from being king.
Rejection of Agag (15:33)
   Just as your sword has bereaved (שׁכל) women,
   thus your mother shall be bereaved (שׁכל) among women.

Commentators have noted that there is an implicit association between Saul and Agag in this chapter. Meir Sternberg has called Agag Saul's "veiled

---

First Book of Samuel, NICOT [Grand Rapids: Eerdmans, 2007], 411). Whatever one thinks about the relationship between 15:35 and 19:24, I think he is right in capturing the sense of לראות as "to meet" which highlights the similarity to לראות in 15:12.

53. See V. Philips Long, *The Reign and Rejection of King Saul: A Case for Literary and Theological Coherence*, SBLDS 118 (Atlanta: Scholars Press, 1989), 165. Polzin also sees significant but slightly different characterization going on in this statement by Agag (*Samuel and the Deuteronomist*, 139). The textual issue revolves around the LXX, which reads εἰ οὕτως πικρὸς ὁ θάνατος, "Is death thus bitter?" On this textual issue, see McCarter, *1 Samuel*, 265.

54. See Fokkelman, *Crossing Fates*, 109.

analogue."[55] Robert Polzin suggests that "the author now captures the heart of the story of Saul in the figure of the captured Agag."[56] Even closer to our point here, Keith Bodner has noted that "Saul is not the only king in this chapter who is on the wrong end of Samuel's poetic thundering."[57]

Given the above observations, we can identify the following chiastic pattern in 1 Sam 15:10–35:

A. 15:10–11a: **YHWH repents** (נחם) that he made Saul king

    B. 15:11b: Samuel is angered (חרה) [about Saul]

        C. 15:12a: Samuel goes *to greet* (לקראות) Saul [in the morning]

            D. 15:12b: Saul *goes down* (ירד) *to Gilgal*

                E. 15:13a: Samuel *comes* (בוא) to Saul

                    F. 15:13b–23: Samuel confronts King Saul with *poetic rejection*

                        G. 15:24–26: Saul's first confession (חטאתי), Samuel does not return (שוב)

                          X. 15:27–29: Torn robe. **YHWH does not repent** (נחם)

                        G'. 15:30–31: Saul's second confession (חטאתי), Samuel returns (וישב)

                      F'. 15:32–33: Samuel confronts King Agag with *poetic denouncement and death*

                E'. 15:34a: Samuel *goes* (הלך) to Ramah

            D'. 15:34b: Saul *goes up* (עלה) *to Gibeah*

        C'. 15:35aα: Samuel is never *to see* (לראות) Saul again [until the day of his death]

    B'. 15:35aβ: Samuel mourns (אבל) about Saul

A'. 15:35b: **YHWH repents** (נחם) that he made Saul king

We will discuss the implications of this parallel structuring in the next section. For now, let us summarize the claim of its presence. Sections A–E and A'–E' are all half-verse length or less.[58] Furthermore, with the exception of A and A', which claim that YHWH repents, each parallel element con-

---

55. Sternberg, *Poetics of Biblical Narrative*, 514.

56. Polzin, *Samuel and the Deuteronomist*, 139.

57. Bodner, *1 Samuel*, 164.

58. The exception is A, which includes the introduction to YHWH's direct speech in 15:10.

trasts at a lexical level. In B Samuel is "angered" (חרה) at Saul's rejection; in B' he "mourns" (אבל) Saul. Though not direct contrasts, the narrative effect of these two emotional states of Samuel is clear, as his "anger" in 15:11b leads him to cry out to YHWH all night, whereas his "mourning" about Saul is a cause of his not seeing him again until the day of his death, an action that seems to imply Samuel being resigned to Saul's state.[59] In C Samuel goes "to greet" (לקראת) Saul "in the morning" (temporal phrase); in C' he does not "see" (לראות) Saul again "until the day of his death" (temporal phrase). In D Saul "goes down" (ירד) to Gilgal; in D' Saul is moving not down but up as he "goes up" (עלה) to Gibeah.[60] In E Samuel "comes" (בוא) to Saul, whereas in E' Samuel is now leaving and "goes" (הלך) to Ramah.[61] It seems we are on relatively strong ground for identifying these parallel elements here.

The remaining parallel elements consist of much larger sections. However, the common elements between them and the narrative significance of these scenes make their parallel nature clear. There is no doubt that the current text includes two parallel statements of Saul's confession before Samuel. We identified above the number of lexical connections between these two texts. Second, the fact that Samuel confronts two kings in this text and each is denounced with almost identically structured poetic statements suggests that we are justified in seeing parallelism here as well. We have now made the case for the presence of a chiastic structure in this chapter. However, if the proof of the pudding is in the eating, we must now highlight how recognizing this structure aids the theological engagement with this text.

5. Implications:
A Characterizing Chiasm and Dialogical Biblical Theology

I suggest that the chiastic structure of this chapter is inherently dialogical. While we noted a number of potential functions of a chiastic structure above, and the present structure is certainly highlighting a number of things, I contend that one of the primary things highlighted in this structure is the dialogue created between the parallel elements. In the final section of this essay it remains to offer a dialogical reading of this chapter informed by the chiastic structure just identified.

---

59. The כי in the first part of 15:35 suggests this causal relationship.
60. On this word pair used in contrasting parallelism, see Pss 104:8; 107:26.
61. For an example of this word pair used in contrasting parallelism, see Ps 126:6.

5.1. Characterizing a Contrast

As Walsh noted, chiastic structures often highlight an inherent contrast, with the center as the turning point.[62] This certainly seems to be one of the functions of this structure. The scene in 15:27–29 seems without question to be playing on the theme of turning. The scene begins, "As Samuel *turned* to go" (ויסב שמואל ללכת, 1 Sam 15:27). With the initial act of turning, the scene emphasizes the unchanging nature of YHWH by stating that "the Enduring One of Israel [נצח ישראל] will not deceive [שקר] or repent [נחם]" (1 Sam 15:29).[63] Perhaps even more interesting is the fact that 4QSam[a] and LXX read "will not turn [שוב/ἀποστρέφω] or repent [נחם/μετανοέω]."[64] Thus there appears to be an interesting dynamic here, as this turning point in YHWH's relationship with his king is marked by emphatic statements that he does not turn, does not repent. He is the Enduring One (perhaps we may suggest Unturning One?). This play on the Unturning One at the turning point in the narrative is further highlighted by the structural pattern identified in the contrasting elements in B–E and B′–E′. Each element is clearly contrasting, and C–E//C′–E′ are all contrasting pictures of movement.

B. 15:11b: Samuel is angered (חרה) [about Saul]

C. 15:12a: Samuel goes *to greet* (לקראת) Saul [in the morning]

D. 15:12b: Saul *goes down* (ירד) to Gilgal

E. 15:13a: Samuel *comes* (בוא) to Saul

B′. 15:35aβ: Samuel mourns (אבל) about Saul

C′. 15:35aα: Samuel is never *to see* (לראות) Saul again [until the day of his death]

D′. 15:34b: Saul *goes up* (עלה) *to* Gibeah

E′. 15:34a: Samuel *goes* (הלך) *to* Ramah

Thus the contrasting parallel elements of this chiastic structure further highlight the narrative irony that the turning point of this chapter hinges

---

62. Walsh, *Old Testament Narrative*, 111.

63. On the emphasis of נצח ישראל as emphasizing YHWH's enduring nature, see David G. Firth, *1 and 2 Samuel: A Kingdom Comes*, PGOT 9 (Sheffield: Sheffield Phoenix, 2013), 170; Bergen, *1, 2 Samuel*, 174 n. 15. Note, however, that the LXX reads here "and Israel will be divided in two" (καὶ διαιρεθήσεται Ισραηλ εἰς δύο). See A. Graeme Auld, *I and II Samuel: A Commentary*, OTL (Louisville: Westminster John Knox, 2011), 174.

64. For discussion of the text, see Auld, *Samuel*, 174.

on emphatic statements about YHWH's unrepentant, unchanging nature and his commitment to Saul's replacement.[65]

5.2. Characterizing Characters

We saw the contrasting nature of the two halves of this literary structure in the contrasting elements surveyed above. In the two immediately juxtaposing sections (F/F′ and G/G′) we see not necessarily contrasting parallels but parallel sections that, when read together in dialogical relationship, highlight the interpretive power of this literary structure.

In the G sections (15:24–26//15:30–31) Saul offers two confessions. We noted the parallels above. We also noted that the response from Samuel is different in each instance. We did not, however, note the significance of these two different confessions and the significance that reading them in relation to each other might make. Although in each instance Saul confesses his sin, his elaboration of each confession is significantly different. In the first confession Saul offers a reason for his sin: he feared the people and listened to their voice (15:24b). In the second confession Saul simply states that he sinned. In the first confession Saul asked for Samuel to *forgive* (נשׂא) his sin (15:25a); in the second Saul asks that Samuel *honor* (כבד) him before the elders and before Israel (15:30a). Forgiveness is nowhere mentioned.[66]

When read together, each scene of Saul's repentance and Samuel's response can be seen to mitigate each other to some degree. Samuel's refusal to go with Saul the first time clarifies our understanding of his eventual acquiescence to this request the second time. Samuel may eventually go with Saul, but YHWH has moved on. Similarly, Samuel's acquiescence to Saul's second request clarifies his refusal of Saul's first request. It is not that he is unwilling to listen to Saul's repentance but that it cannot mitigate YHWH's decision to move on. Reading these two parallel elements dialogically highlights the theological significance of each.

---

65. One thinks of the similar play on perspectives from Mal 3, where the God who does not change (לֹא שָׁנָה, Mal 3:6), calls for his people to turn (שׁוּב) to him so that he might turn (שׁוּב) to them (Mal 3:7b).

66. Long makes many of these observations. Though a number of commentators also note that forgiveness is conspicuously absent from Saul's second confession ("Interpolation or Characterization," 48–53). E.g., Brueggemann, *First and Second Samuel*, 116; Firth, *1 and 2 Samuel*, 176. See Gordon, *1 and 2 Samuel*, 146, who suggests that "Saul's preoccupation is now with saving face."

In the F and F′ scenes we see the rejection of the two kings. It is my contention that this parallel structure helps us to see how the two kings characterize each other. Or, to borrow one of Bakhtin's concepts, we can see that the *character zones* of Saul and Agag overlap.[67] The parallel poetic denunciations of these two kings make them blur and overlap to a certain degree. Thus we are left to wonder just how much of Saul there is in Agag and, perhaps more damagingly for Saul, how much of Agag there is in Saul. We cannot help but read Samuel's assessment of Saul in the light of Samuel's assessment of Agag. So when Samuel tells Saul that "rebellion is like the sin of divination and defiance like iniquity and teraphim," though there is some complexity in how to understand the reference to teraphim, it seems clear that Samuel is comparing Saul's behavior to practices that were expressly forbidden to Israel and indicative of other peoples.[68] Reading Saul's rejection in relation to Agag's denunciation heightens this interpretation of Saul's culpability. Perhaps we are meant to see that the people unfortunately got their wish when they asked for a king just like the nations (1 Sam 8:5). Putting these two elements in dialogue highlights the significance of these two scenes and the similarities of these two kings.

5.3. A Characterizing Contradiction

Finally, we come to the narrative element that led to this investigation in the first place: the parallelism of A and A′ and the contradiction with X. I suggest that recognizing this chiastic literary structure highlights the contradictory statements in 1 Sam 15:11, 29, and 35 that commentators recognize anyway. What the recognition of this structure adds is a frame through which to engage with the contradiction about the character of

---

67. On Bakhtin's concept of *character zones*, see Keith Bodner, *David Observed: A King in the Eyes of His Court*, HBM 5 (Sheffield: Sheffield Phoenix, 2008), 11 n. 4; Barbara Green, *How Are the Mighty Fallen? A Dialogical Study of King Saul in 1 Samuel*, JSOTSup 365 (Sheffield: Sheffield Academic, 2003), 272; Bakhtin, *Dialogical Imagination*, 316, 434.

68. On terephim, see the discussions in McCarter, *1 Samuel*, 263; Tsumura, *First Samuel*, 400; Auld, *Samuel*, 174. Klein notes, "Divination is consistently prohibited in the OT (cf. Deut 18:10 and 2 Kgs 17:17). It is a practice for which the wicked nations are criticized (Num 22:7; Deut 18:14; Josh 13:22; 1 Sam 6:2).... In some passages teraphim seem to be a kind of household god (e.g., Gen 31:34, 35; Judg 17:5; 18:14) but they were apparently also a means of divine inquiry (e.g., Hos 3:4; Ezek 21:26 [EVV 21])" (*1 Samuel*, 153).

YHWH. As Walsh notes in his discussion of chiastic structures, "often, especially when the center comprises only a single element, there will also be a verbal link between the central element and the first and last elements."[69] That is precisely what we have here. By putting these contradictory elements in the frame and center of this chiastic structure the narrative forces us to hold them in dialogical tension.

The recognition of this chiastic literary structure mitigates against reading Samuel's statement about YHWH's unchangeability in 15:29 as either unreliable or contextually specific. The tension between verses 11 and 35 and verse 29 is so central to the structure of the passage and the movement of the narrative that it suggests that it is characterizing something about the nature of YHWH and the dynamic way he works with his people. This is a narrative about YHWH's change of direction in leadership. It is framed by statements about YHWH changing his mind about the leadership in Israel. The turning point in the narrative is a statement about YHWH's unchangeability and stability. There are thus many narrative elements in this structure that highlight that a central aspect to this story is the change of direction of an unchanging God.

What we have in 1 Sam 15 is two truths about YHWH put into dialogical tension. The acceptance of each one is true, as far as it goes, but accepting them together highlights a fuller and more truthful picture of the nature of God. As the frame suggests, YHWH is dynamic. He changes and interacts in response to the actions of his people. As the center suggests, he is unchanging. He is not like human beings who may be fickle and unreliable; he can be relied upon. Each truth helpfully nuances the other. Lest the frame suggest that YHWH is fickle and unreliable, the center reinforces that he is reliable and unchanging. Lest the center suggest that YHWH is rigid and inflexible, the frame suggests that he is dynamic and responsive—and although in this instance YHWH's responsiveness does not work in Saul's favor, the majority of instances of YHWH's repentance in the Hebrew Bible are in the direction of mercy.[70]

I suggest that the statements in the center and frame are universal truths about both the nature of YHWH and his working in the world and

69. Walsh, *Old Testament Narrative*, 229 n. 13.

70. See esp. John T. Willis, "The 'Repentance' of God in the Books of Samuel, Jeremiah, and Jonah," *HBT* 16 (1994): 156–75. He notes that the statements about YHWH's repentance in the direction of mercy are often part of a formula that clearly define the character of God (pp. 168–69).

that this is where a dialogical approach to biblical theology helps us. We are not meant to push toward a synthesis of these two ideas. Rather, we are meant to hold these two truths in dialogue and wrestle with the reality of a God who categorically does not repent or change, and yet he does! The literary structure highlights this dialogical truth and forces us to wrestle with it. Thus what we have in 1 Sam 15 is a characterizing chiastic contradiction, one that highlights a truth that R. W. L. Moberly noted: "Such is the inherently mysterious nature of God and his ways with [humanity] that it is often difficult to make a statement in a theologically reflective way without wishing to qualify it, sometimes by the assertion of an apparently opposite truth."[71] Each truth about God is true as far as it goes. He repents. He does not repent. Each truth is, however, open to misinterpretation. The recognition of the literary structure of 1 Sam 15 suggests a dialogical approach to the theological presentation of God in this text and suggests that the fuller truth about God is in the dialogical relationship between the seemingly contradictory perspectives that it can and must be said that God is unchanging, faithful, trustworthy, and does not repent, yet it can and must also be said that he is dynamic, responsive, and does repent.

Bibliography

Amit, Yairah. "'The Glory of Israel Does Not Deceive or Change His Mind': On the Reliability of Narrator and Speakers in Biblical Narrative." *Proof* 12 (1992): 201–12.

Ashley, Timothy R. *The Book of Numbers*. NICOT. Grand Rapids: Eerdmans, 1993.

Assis, Elie. "Chiasmus in Biblical Narrative: A Rhetoric of Characterization." *Proof* 22 (2003): 273–304.

Auld, A. Graeme. *I and II Samuel: A Commentary*. OTL. Louisville: Westminster John Knox, 2011.

Bakhtin, Mikhail M. *The Dialogical Imagination: Four Essays*. Edited by Michael Holquist. Austin: University of Texas Press, 1981.

---

71. R. W. L. Moberly, *At the Mountain of God: Story and Theology in Exodus 32–34*, JSOTSup 22 (Sheffield: JSOT Press, 1983), 33. On 1 Sam 15, see Freedman, "When God Repents," 423; Klein, *1 Samuel*, 156; Patrick, *Rendering of God*, 54. Childs similarly writes, "The main lines which cross at the heart of the Old Testament's understanding of God are of such diversity and intensity that the risk is acute of flattening the witness through modern systematic categories" (*Biblical Theology*, 354).

———. *Speech Genres and Other Late Essays*. Edited by Caryl Emerson and Michael Holquist. Translated by Vern W. McGee. Austin: University of Texas Press, 1986.

Bergen, Robert D. *1, 2 Samuel*. NAC 7. Nashville: B&H, 1996.

Boda, Mark J. "Chiasmus in Ubiquity: Symmetrical Mirages in Nehemiah 9." *JSOT* 71 (1996): 55–70.

Bodner, Keith. *1 Samuel: A Narrative Commentary*. Sheffield: Sheffield Phoenix, 2009.

———. *David Observed: A King in the Eyes of His Court*. HBM 5. Sheffield: Sheffield Phoenix, 2008.

Brueggemann, Walter. *First and Second Samuel*. IBC. Louisville: John Knox Press, 1990.

———. "Futures in Old Testament Theology: Dialogical Engagement." *HBT* 37 [2015]: 32–49.

———. *The Theology of the Old Testament: Testimony, Dispute, Advocacy*. Minneapolis: Fortress, 2005.

Butterworth, Mike. *Structure and the Book of Zechariah*. JSOTSup 130. Sheffield: JSOT Press, 1992.

Chapman, Stephen B. *Reading 1 Samuel as Christian Scripture: A Theological Commentary*. Grand Rapids: Eerdmans, 2016.

Childs, Brevard S. *Biblical Theology of the Old and New Testaments: Theological Reflection on the Christian Bible*. Minneapolis: Fortress, 1992.

Chisholm, Robert B., Jr. "Does God 'Change His Mind'?" *BSac* 152 (1995): 387–99.

Claassens, L. Juliana M. "Biblical Theology as Dialogue: Continuing the Conversation on Mikhail Bakhtin and Biblical Theology." *JBL* 122 (2003): 127–44.

Dell, Katharine, and Will Kynes, eds. *Reading Ecclesiastes Intertextually*. LHBOTS. London: Bloomsbury, 2014.

———, eds. *Reading Job Intertextually*. LHBOTS. London: Bloomsbury, 2013.

DeSilva, David A. "X Marks the Spot? A Critique of the Use of Chiasmus in Macro-structural Analyses of Revelation." *JSNT* 30 (2008): 343–71.

Driver, S. R. *Notes on the Hebrew Text and the Topography of the Books of Samuel with an Introduction on Hebrew Palaeography and the Ancient Versions*. Repr. ed. Eugene, OR: Wipf & Stock, 2004.

Eslinger, Lyle. "A Change of Heart: 1 Samuel 16." Pages 341–61 in *Ascribe to the Lord: Biblical and Other Studies in Memory of Peter C. Craigie*.

Edited by Lyle Eslinger and Glen Taylor. Sheffield: Sheffield Academic, 1988.

Felch, Susan M. "Dialogism." Pages 173–75 in *Dictionary for Theological Interpretation of the Bible*. Edited by Kevin J. Vanhoozer, Craig G. Bartholomew, Daniel J. Treier, and N. T. Wright. Grand Rapids: Baker Academic, 2005.

Firth, David G. *1 and 2 Samuel: A Kingdom Comes*. PGOT 9. Sheffield: Sheffield Phoenix, 2013.

Fokkelman, J. P. *The Crossing Fates*. Vol. 2 of *Narrative Art and Poetry in the Books of Samuel*. Dover, NH: VanGorcum, 1986.

Foresti, Fabrizio. *The Rejection of Saul in the Perspective of the Deuteronomistic School: A Study of 1 Sm 15 and Related Texts*. Vol. 5. StThT. Roma: Teresianum, 1984.

Fox, Michael V. *Proverbs 10–31: A New Translation with Introduction and Commentary*. AB 18B. New Haven: Yale University Press, 2009.

Freedman, David Noel. "When God Repents." Pages 409–46 in *Divine Commitment and Human Obligation: Selected Writings of David Noel Freedman*. Grand Rapids: Eerdmans, 1997.

Freedman, David Noel. "When God Repents." Pages 409–46 in *Divine Commitment and Human Obligation: Selected Writings of David Noel Freedman*. Grand Rapids: Eerdmans, 1997.

Fretheim, Terence E. "Divine Foreknowledge, Divine Constancy, and the Rejection of Saul's Kingship." *CBQ* 47 (1985): 595–602.

———. "The Repentance of God: A Key to Evaluating Old Testament God-Talk." *HBT* 10 (1988): 50–52.

Goldingay, John. *Theological Diversity and the Authority of the Old Testament*. Grand Rapids: Eerdmans, 1987.

Gordon, R. P. *1 and 2 Samuel: A Commentary*. Exeter: Paternoster, 1986.

Green, Barbara. *How Are the Mighty Fallen? A Dialogical Study of King Saul in 1 Samuel*. JSOTSup 365. Sheffield: Sheffield Academic, 2003.

Hertzberg, Hans Wilhelm. *1 and 2 Samuel: A Commentary*. OTL. Philadelphia: Westminster, 1964.

Johnson, Benjamin J. M. *Reading David and Goliath in Greek and Hebrew: A Literary Approach*. FAT 2/82. Tübingen: Mohr Siebeck, 2015.

Keil, Carl Friedrich. *Joshua, Judges, 1 and 2 Samuel*. Vol. 2 of *Commentary on the Old Testament*. Peabody, MA: Hendrickson, 2006.

Klaus, Nathan. *Pivot Patterns in the Former Prophets*. JSOTSup 247. Sheffield, England: JSOT Press, 1999.

Klein, Ralph W. *1 Samuel*. WBC 10. Waco, TX: Word, 1982.

Kuhn, Karl Allen. *Having Words with God: The Bible as Conversation*. Minneapolis: Fortress, 2008.

Kuyper, Lester J. "The Suffering and the Repentance of God." *SJT* 22 (1969): 257–77.

Long, V. Philips. "Interpolation or Characterization: How Are We to Understand Saul's Two Confessions?" *Presb* 19 (1993): 49–53.

———. *The Reign and Rejection of King Saul: A Case for Literary and Theological Coherence*. SBLDS 118. Atlanta: Scholars Press, 1989.

McCarter, P. Kyle, Jr. *1 Samuel: A New Translation with Introduction, Notes and Commentary*. AB 8. Garden City, NY: Doubleday, 1980.

Middleton, J. Richard. "Samuel Agonistes: A Conflicted Prophet's Resistance to God and Contribution to the Failure of Israel's First King." Pages 69–91 in *Prophets, Prophecy, and Ancient Israelite Historiography*. Edited by Mark J. Boda and Lissa M. Wray Beal. Winona Lake, IN: Eisenbrauns, 2013.

Moberly, R. W. L. *At the Mountain of God: Story and Theology in Exodus 32–34*. JSOTSup 22. Sheffield: JSOT Press, 1983.

———. "God Is Not Human That He Should Repent." Pages 112–23 in *God in the Fray: A Tribute to Walter Breuggemann*. Edited by Tod Linafelt and Timothy K. Beal. Minneapolis: Fortress, 1998.

Murphy, Roland E. *Proverbs*. WBC 22. Nashville: Nelson, 1998.

Newsom, Carol A. "Bakhtin, the Bible, and Dialogical Truth." *JR* 76 (1996): 290.

Olson, Dennis T. "Biblical Theology as Provisional Monologization: A Dialogue with Childs, Brueggemann and Bakhtin." *BibInt* 6 (1998): 162–80.

Parunak, H. van Dyke. "A Semantic Survey of *NḤM*." *Bib* 56 (1975): 519.

Patrick, Dale. *The Rendering of God in the Old Testament*. OBT. Philadelphia: Fortress, 1981.

Polzin, Robert. *Samuel and the Deuteronomist: A Literary Study of the Deuteronomic History*. New York: Harper & Row, 1989.

Rad, Gerhard von. *Old Testament Theology*. Vol. 1. Translated by David M. G. Stalker. New York: HarperSanfrancisco, 1965.

Sommer, Benjamin D. "Dialogical Biblical Theology: A Jewish Approach to Reading Scripture Theologically." Pages 1–53 in *Biblical Theology: Introducing the Conversation*. Edited by Leo Perdue. LBT. Nashville: Abingdon, 2009.

———. "The Source Critic and the Religious Interpreter." *Int* 60 (2006): 9–20.

Sternberg, Meir. *The Poetics of Biblical Narrative: Ideological Literature and the Drama of Reading*. Bloomington: Indiana University Press, 1985.

Tsumura, David Toshio. *The First Book of Samuel*. NICOT. Grand Rapids: Eerdmans, 2007.

Walsh, Jerome T. *Old Testament Narrative: A Guide to Interpretation*. Louisville: Westminster John Knox Press, 2010.

———. *Style and Structure in Biblical Hebrew Narrative*. Collegeville, MN: Liturgical Press, 2001.

Watson, Wilfred G. E. *Classical Hebrew Poetry: A Guide to Its Techniques*. JSOTSup 26. Sheffield: JSOT Press, 1986.

Weiser, Artur. "I Samuel 15." *ZAW* 54 (1936): 1–28.

Welch, John W., ed. *Chiasmus in Antiquity: Structures, Analyses, Exegesis*. Provo, UT: Research, 1999.

Willis, John T. "The 'Repentance' of God in the Books of Samuel, Jeremiah, and Jonah." *HBT* 16 (1994): 156–75.

Ashamed before the Presence of God: Theological Contexts of Shame in the Book of Ezekiel

Soo J. Kim

"When YHWH turned again the captivity of Zion, we were like them that dream." As the psalmist sings, returning home from exile is usually experienced with great joy as a sign of God's mercy. If this is a response from the returnees, God also expresses his compassion and forgiveness toward the exiles through the prophecies of restoration. But how does the book of Ezekiel depict the same event? Is the restoration a happy homecoming?

Baruch Schwartz argues that the book of Ezekiel offers a uniquely dim view of restoration. According to him, YHWH's turning point regarding the restoration came as the result of two realizations: his damaged reputation after the fall of Judah and no inclination for repentance from Israel even after that disaster. Thus Schwartz asserts that the ultimate goal of Israel's restoration is to restore God's honor among nations, but YHWH decides to retain Israel ashamed before him.[1] Schwartz's analysis is profound and

---

A shorter version of this paper was presented in the joint session, Ezekiel 40–48 and Its Relationship to Pentateuchal-Legal Texts and Concepts, in the Theological Perspectives on the Book of Ezekiel section, at the 2013 Society of Biblical Literature Annual Meeting in Baltimore.

1. Baruch J. Schwartz, "Ezekiel's Dim View of Israel's Restoration," in *The Book of Ezekiel: Theological and Anthropological Perspectives*, ed. Margaret S. Odell and John T. Strong, SBLSymS 9 (Atlanta: Society of Biblical Literature, 2000), 43–68; Schwartz, "The Ultimate Aim of Israel's Restoration in Ezekiel," in *Birkat Shalom: Studies in the Bible, Ancient Near Eastern Literature, and Postbiblical Judaism Presented to Shalom M. Paul on the Occasion of His Seventieth Birthday*, ed. Chaim Cohen, Victor Avigdor Hurowitz, and Jeffrey H. Tigay, 2 vols. (Winona Lake, IN: Eisenbrauns, 2008), 1:305–20.

comprehensive, but it makes me ponder the following questions. Does this pessimistic view really represent an end of the exilic community story and the goal of writing the book of Ezekiel? Thinking from God's perspective, what could be the first step to bring the exiles home if the people identify themselves as victims and continually refuse to confess their guilt? If shame is the goal of the restoration, as Schwartz argued, what is the ultimate goal of that shame? What are Ezekiel's theological conceptions of exile, and how are they reflected in the concept of restoration?

This essay seeks answers for those theological questions on shame and restoration in the book of Ezekiel through a syntactical, structural, semantic study of Ezek. 43:10–11. These two verses deserve our attention because they most explicitly show the appropriate reaction that serves as a precondition for restoring Israel's relationship with YHWH who returns to dwell in the temple.

1. Review and Direction

A study of the rhetorical and theological concepts of restoration presented in Ezekiel is not a new topic.[2] Nonetheless, the difficulty of synthesizing the logical sequence of restoration in the book of Ezekiel or its theological conceptualization indeed lies in the gap between the two contrasting

---

2. The works in the general discussion: Peter R. Ackroyd, *Exile and Restoration: A Study of Hebrew Thought of the Sixth Century BC* (London: SCM, 1968); Dalit Rom-Shiloni, "Deuteronomic Concepts of Exile Interpreted in Jeremiah and Ezekiel," in Cohen, Hurowitz, and Tigay, *Birkat Shalom*, 69–81; John J. Ahn, *Exile as Forced Migrations: A Sociological, Literary, and Theological Approach on the Displacement and Resettlement of the Southern Kingdom of Judah*, BZAW 417 (Berlin: de Gruyter, 2010); Rainer Albertz, *A History of Israelite Religion in the Old Testament Period*, 2 vols. (London: SCM, 1994).

The works focusing on the book of Ezekiel: Jon D. Levenson, *Theology of the Program of Restoration of Ezekiel 40–48*, HSM 10 (Atlanta: Scholars Press, 1976); M. E. Andrew, *Responsibility and Restoration: The Course of the Book of Ezekiel* (Dunedin: University of Otago Press, 1985); Katheryn Pfisterer Darr, "The Wall around Paradise: Ezekielian Ideas About the Future," *VT* 37 (1987): 271–79; Tova Ganzel, "The Description of the Restoration of Israel in Ezekiel," *VT* 60 (2010): 197–211; Jacob Milgrom and Daniel I. Block, *Ezekiel's Hope: A Commentary on Ezekiel 38–48* (Eugene, OR: Cascade, 2012); John T. Strong, "Grounding Ezekiel's Heavenly Ascent: A Defense of Ezek 40–48 as a Program for Restoration," *SJOT* 26 (2012): 192–211; Marvin A. Sweeney, *Reading Ezekiel: A Literary and Theological Commentary* (Macon, GA: Smyth & Helwys, 2013).

presentations: repeated divine commands to repent in the earlier chapters in a realistic prophetic form and the sudden appearance of restoration in the later nine chapters in a visionary form. While there was no response of repentance from the exiles, only complaints from the human side and rebukes from the deity up to Ezek 37, chapters 40–48 project a vision of the already-restored world. It is well known that the vision encouraged readers to appreciate the reversed experience between reality and fantasy so that the exiles already stood before the newly completed temple precinct in the land of Israel. Accordingly, exhortations to return to the land or oracles against Babylon as part of the process of return seldom appear in these nine vision chapters,[3] and, as a result, scholars have paid little attention to Ezek 43:10–11 as the verses relate to the process of restoration.[4] Nonetheless, the significance of this passage lies in the fact that it allows us to see at a glance the process and condition of restoration. We should acknowledge that Ezek 40–48 has both descriptive and prescriptive presentations. If a new temple and a new city description, initiated and completed by YHWH, is the former, the latter is offered in the divine commands to humans as the potential beneficiaries who shall live in that new structure. Ezekiel 43:10–11 is one of the starting moments of that prescriptive presentation.

This essay pays particular attention, using rhetorical criticism, to the sequences of the restoration and the theological concepts underlying the presentations.[5] Here James W. Watts's and Michael V. Fox's critiques, especially regarding the concept of aural reception, are worth mentioning. Emphasizing the use of the written text for oral presentation, Watts encourages us to recognize elements of persuasion in the speech as a key

---

3. This phenomenon can be explained in many ways including historical reflections on the Babylonian exile and return in the Persian era, but selective imitation of the first exodus pattern in the author's mind might be a possible answer, too.

4. John T. Strong sees the return of God's glory itself as a starting point of the restoration procedure since it is the sign of his victory over battles against gods ("God's *Kābôd*: The Presence of Yahweh in the Book of Ezekiel," in Odell and Strong, *The Book of Ezekiel*, 83). Baruch Schwartz's "Ultimate Aim of Israel's Restoration" might be the exception of this tendency. He deals with 43:10–11 as one of his prooftexts of "shame" as the goal of restoration.

5. In understanding rhetoric as the art of persuasion, this essay attempts to clarify how the same passages can produce different presentations and effects to the different audiences throughout generations. Thus, it will be overlapped with audience-oriented criticism.

to understanding the text. Fox also emphasizes the importance of the interaction between the speaker and the audience.[6] Based on this background, I pursue the speaker's rhetorical intentions and their effects on the word "shame" (כלם) in Ezekiel's restoration vision in order to appreciate the abundant and dynamic theological concepts it contains.

2. Ezekiel 43:10–11 (in 43:1–27)

2.1. Speaker and Audience

Before moving to an analysis of the text's rhetorical intention and effects, let us clarify the term *audience*. Too many overlapping kinds of audience in both literary and rhetorical analyses have created interpretive confusion.[7]

In light of the gap between the retrospective in composition (diachronic dimensions of the passages) and the projective in presentation (synchronic dimensions), I distinguish the terms *implied audience* and *literary audience* for this discussion. This distinction is essential especially in an analysis of ancient texts that have a long history of composition and reception, with the result that the text before us has different layers of audiences.[8] Those who are directly addressed by the speaker on the literary level are the literary audience (thus also a character), while the author's ideal and targeted audience is the implied audience.[9] Due to the difficulty

---

6. James W. Watts, "Rhetorical Strategy in the Composition of the Pentateuch," *JSOT* 68 (1995): 4; Watts, "Public Readings and Pentateuchal Law," *VT* 45 (1995): 540–57; Michael V. Fox, "The Rhetoric of Ezekiel's Vision of the Valley of the Bones," *HUCA* 51 (1980): 2–4.

7. For the general overview of *audience* in literary and rhetorical analyses, see Chaïm Perelman and L. Olbrechts-Tyteca, *The New Rhetoric: A Treatise on Argumentation* (Notre Dame, IN: Notre Dame Press, 1969), 30. For the various kinds of audience study, see Wayne Booth, *The Rhetoric of Fiction*, 2nd ed. (Chicago: University of Chicago Press, 1983), 137–38, 151–52, 421–31; Wolfgang Iser, *The Implied Reader: Patterns of Communication in Prose Fiction from Bunyan to Beckett* (Baltimore: Johns Hopkins University Press, 1978), 274–94; Paul Strohm, "Chaucer's Audience(s): Fictional, Implied, Intended, Actual," *The Chaucer Review* 18 (1983): 137–45.

8. Robert Polzin also points out that Deuteronomy has more than one audience: those who were on the plains of Moab and "those of the narrator/author of Deuteronomy" (*Moses and the Deuteronomist: A Literary Study of the Deuteronomic History 1, Deuteronomy, Joshua, Judges* [New York: Seabury, 1980], 72, 92).

9. For a different application on the audiences/readers of the book of Ezekiel, see Thomas Renz, *The Rhetorical Function of the Book of Ezekiel*, VTSup 76 (Leiden: Brill,

of determining the precise compositional dates and a lack of evidence for their performance records, the text's real audiences are hard to determine. In other words, it is possible that neither the literary audience nor the implied audience is the actual audience.[10]

This recognition enhances not only our understanding of the rhetorical intention of the text but also our appreciation of the rhetorical effects on the audience/reader. As we shall see in detail, the transformation in the book of Ezekiel is designed through the generational transition. In most prophecies, the earlier generation—identified as the dried bones in Ezek 37—appears as the character to whom Ezekiel should deliver the divine messages. Unfortunately, however, this literary audience/character is not the people whom YHWH considers to bring back to the land because God's covenantal sincerity, at least in the book of Ezekiel, seems to be fulfilled after passing over this first generation of exile.

Nevertheless, more explicitly speaking from the reader's perspective, this time distinction alone—the first and second, or earlier and later generation—is not a sufficient tool to discuss restoration in the book of Ezekiel because both kinds of audience are often presented as virtual if not fictional. The book of Ezekiel indeed pushes all characters, including YHWH, Ben Adam, and the captives, into the air, by presenting the prophet Ezekiel's mysterious encounter with his deity in the exiled land as first-person diary-like writing. Regardless of its genre, whether a realistic prophetic commission report or a fantastic vision report, the book chooses its strategy to be free from the pressure of the fulfillment in due time. This indeterminacy in time is intentional; likewise, the specific date entries in each unit are a smart strategy to provide the historical weight to the text as well as the justification for the generational transition. Thus,

---

1999), 19–20. He distinguishes the "implied reader" as the reader presupposed at the beginning of the communication from "the ideal reader" as the intended result of the communicative act.

10. This phenomenon already appears in Deuteronomy's typical addressee "All Israel" (כל ישראל) as the fictional ancestors of later generations. Timothy A. Lenchak identifies "all Israel" as an ideal lay community of Deuteronomy (*"Choose Life!": A Rhetorical-Critical Investigation of Deuteronomy 28,69–30,20*, AnBib 129 [Rome: Pontifical Biblical Institute, 1993], 85). My explanation of the relationship between literary audience and implied audience can be compared to Harry P. Nasuti's clarification of "you" in the biblical law speech. He argues that the literary "you" may reach beyond the narrative characters ("Identity, Identification, and Imitation: The Narrative Hermeneutics of Biblical Law," *Journal of Law and Religion* 4 [1986]: 10).

whoever situates himself or herself in the returnee's position becomes the implied audience/reader as Edwin Black's second persona or even Philip Wander's third persona.[11] By separating from the literary audience or even excluding themselves from the harsh rebukes, these kinds of readers can identify themselves as beneficiaries of YHWH's restoration plan rather than the target of his wrath.

On the contrary, the literary audience is identified as whoever remains in the exiled land as the fictional counterpart of the implied audience. The uniqueness of the book of Ezekiel lies in the fact that the division does not depend on one's obedient personality or choice to repent but on YHWH's solemn decision of the proper time. In other words, the book of Ezekiel employs temporality to create this generational gap and even seems to manipulate that all the adult exiles are to perish as the old persona while their children will be reborn as the new human race.[12] With this scenario, the implied audience would learn from the speaker's severe rebuke of the literary audience. For example, frequent appearances of the concept of shame in the book of Ezekiel produce the aura of the basic recommended attitude for listening/reading.

Now, let us examine the speaker and audience of our passage Ezek 43:10–11 in the context of chapter 43. The main speaker in the vision report up to Ezek 42 was idenfied as Bronze Man, but now, after the glory of YHWH has returned, a new speaker is introduced: "someone speaking [masc. sg. *piel* participle מדבר] out of the house" (43:6). We can conjecture him as YHWH based on his characterization as the one who has the throne in the temple (43:7). Thus, YHWH is the speaker although the passage keeps blurring the boundary of the two speakers, Bronze Man and YHWH.

---

11. According to Edwin Black, the second persona is the implied auditor, while Philip Wander proposes the third persona who is excluded from a certain discourse. See Edwin Black, "The Second Persona," in *Landmark Essays on Rhetorical Criticism*, ed. Thomas W. Benson, Landmark Essays 5 (Davis, CA: Hermagoras Press, 1993), 161–72; Philip Wander, "The Third Persona: An Ideological Turn in Rhetorical Theory," *Central States Speech Journal* 35 (1984): 209.

12. It is true that the book of Ezekiel does not explicitly distinguish between earlier and later generations within the exilic community; nonetheless, historical presentations of the biblical accounts regarding the exilic period (ca. sixty years from 597 BCE, King Jehoiachin's captivity, to 536 BCE, King Cyrus's decree) suggest that the contemporary of Ezekiel must be hardly identical with the returnees in the book of Ezra-Nehemiah.

Following is a description of the dynamic relationship among the four characters: YHWH, Bronze Man, Ben Adam,[13] and the virtual audience. First, there is no dialogue between YHWH and Bronze Man, between Bronze Man and Ben Adam (only one-way discourse from Bronze Man to Ben Adam), between YHWH and Ben Adam (only one-way discourse from YHWH to Ben Adam), and, of course, between Ben Adam and his audience.

Second, regarding the relationship between Ben Adam and the audience, Ben Adam the receiver of the divine commands is supposed to deliver the vision to his audience later because Ezek 40–48 is a vision for Ezekiel alone.[14] At the same time, however, we observe the speaker's flexible accessibility from his listener Ben Adam to the implied audience (captive) Israelites whenever YHWH directly rebukes the virtual audience by using the second-person pronoun "you" in the midst of his speech to Ben Adam. In other words, the text often shows its presupposition that audience members are already participating as eavesdroppers of the words of YHWH/Bronze Man; that is, the author technically allows his audience/reader to use the physical body of Ben Adam for their virtual vision tour.

Third, both Ben Adam and Bronze Man act as agents: Ben Adam for the virtual audience and Bronze Man for invisible YHWH. These agents are quite restricted so as not to show their personas but embed the invisible entities in their tasks. As an agent of the audience, Ben Adam experienced God's vision for the future of Israel in the temple tour vision. Despite his passive role, therefore, this first-person report grants him a crucial role as the only witness and authoritative person for the later generation.[15] This is

---

13. "Ben Adam" is the transliterated appellation of character Ezekiel בֶּן אָדָם. YHWH always uses this term when he calls him. While NRSV's "mortal" emphasizes Ezekiel's limited nature as human, my term Ben Adam focuses more on his representativeness of humans as the only contact person to the deity in this liminal period.

14. Steven L. Cook, *Ezekiel 38–48: A New Translation with Introduction and Commentary*, AYB 22B (New Haven: Yale University Press, 2018), 191.

15. Hanna Liss argues that the purpose of the introduction of the utopian world is to change the audience's perception of their own world. See Hanna Liss, " 'Describe the Temple to the House of Israel': Preliminary Remarks on the Temple Vision in the Book of Ezekiel and the Question of Fictionality in Priestly Literatures," in *Utopia and Dystopia in Prophetic Literature*, ed. Ehud Ben Zvi, Publications of the Finnish Exegetical Society 92 (Göttingen: Vandenhoeck & Ruprecht, 2006), 122–43; T. J. Betts, *Ezekiel the Priest: A Custodian of Tôrâ*, StBibLit 74 (New York: Lang, 2005). Cf. James W. Watts, "Reader Identification and Alienation in the Legal Rhetoric of the Pentateuch," *BibInt* 7 (1999): 101–12.

Ben Adam's priestly role, since his embodiment is not limited to serve as the representative of human beings before God. He should also perform as the representative of YHWH before the people (cf. 4:3), although the verification of the actual performance is beyond the horizon of the book of Ezekiel.

Meanwhile, YHWH's literary audience of Ezek 43 at the surface level is Bronze Man or Ben Adam, but his targeted implied audience is the exiles, both earlier and later generations. As a result, shifts of the audience from Ben Adam to children of Israel or some specific audience, including kings, priests, and the Levites, frequently occurred as necessary.

Although most prophets and some of Ezekiel's figures in the book are classified as divine messengers, Ezekiel's role in the final vision (Ezek 40–48) is not limited to being the messenger but also the spectator and scribe. In his "Vision of the Valley" analysis, Fox pays attention to Ezekiel's role as spectator and argues that this spectator's position is employed from a strategic plan to give the impression of objectivity to the vision.[16] He also explains the situation of the next generation in exile as those who neither knew about the homeland nor had experienced the trauma of the exile.[17]

Emphasizing Ezekiel's scribal role in the vision, Renz points out that the vision report as a script expects readers to internalize and experience the messages from Ezekiel, as though the prophet "ate" the scroll (2:9–3:3).[18] Leaving a written document can mean the author's preparation for his absence shortly.[19] If the year of the vision in 40:1 refers to Ezekiel's twentieth year of ministry, then, as Sweeney proposes, that year for Ezekiel is time to retire from his supposed priestly duty.[20] Encountering hopeless daily life in Babylon and disappearing from history, Ezekiel may be desperate to see his deity who would command him to deliver the torah, God's new plan for the exiles.[21] In this context, Ezekiel resembles or imitates Moses in the plain of Moab, who, when he was about to disappear from

---

16. Fox, "Rhetoric of Ezekiel's Vision," 8.

17. Fox, "Rhetoric of Ezekiel's Vision," 11–12.

18. Renz, *Rhetorical Function*, 18.

19. I would like to add my observation of the two figures in their psychological characterizations to Levitt Kohn's comparison of the two figures. See Risa Levitt Kohn, *A New Heart and a New Soul: Ezekiel, the Exile, and the Torah*, JSOTSup 358 (London: Sheffield Academic, 2002), 107–10.

20. Marvin A. Sweeney, *Tanak: A Theological and Critical Introduction to the Jewish Bible* (Minneapolis: Fortress, 2012), 338.

21. Andrew Mein, "Ezekiel as a Priest in Exile," in *The Elusive Prophet: The Prophet*

history, delivered the next generation more warnings and cautions than blessings. If Moses's gloomy tendency comes from the lessons of the failed history through the wilderness period and solitary emotions in separation from the audience, Ezekiel's stricter application of the earlier traditions, verbose warnings, and interruptive rebukes even in the restored vision report might also come from the similar psychological pressure. As Moses was commanded to write the words of God, Ezekiel was ordered to write and tell the words of God.

Unfortunately for Ezekiel, however, a crucial difference exists between Moses's and his situation. For the Deuteronomy audience, as the literary setting of the location suggests, the day of entering the Promised Land is imminent; right after the leadership will shift, and the literary audience will experience another miracle: the crossing of the Jordan River. In the case of Ezekiel, however, both the speaker and his literary audience are still in Babylon; in reality, they have not taken a single step toward the Promised Land. With this uncertainty, unlike the Deuteronomy farewell discourse, which emphasizes the active initiative of the audience, the book of Ezekiel relies on the descriptive characteristic of the genre "vision" in meeting with his audience/readers.

2.2. Shame in the Syntactical Context

As a part of a divine speech (43:7–27) in the vision report, the literary subgenre of 43:10–11 is a casuistic law form of act/consequence: when X happens, if one does A, then B will happen. The conditional clause in the casuistic law form must have been familiar to those ancients and would already have elicited a perlocutionary response from them. Its rhetorical genre is exhortation, which uses the vision form to evoke more effectively an emotional response from the audience. By translating 43:11b as "live by its design and intent," Stephen Cook also interprets this passage as the rhetorical exhortation.[22]

If the rhetorical genre characteristic of our passage contains exhortation, in what situation is the exhortation planned? In the vision setting, the exilic community is imagined in the land already, as though Ezekiel were brought to the land by YHWH's supernatural power. In this final

---

as a Historical Person, Literary Character, and Anonymous Artist, ed. Johannes C. de Moor, OtSt 45 (Leiden: Brill, 2001), 199–213.

22. Cook, *Ezekiel 38–48*, 192.

vision, there is no conditional/temporal clause starting with a conjunction כי, to express "when/if you (or they) enter/return the Land of Israel," which frequently appears in the Pentateuch discourses. Thus, feeling ashamed or showing their shame is neither a crucial condition for return home nor the ultimate goal of the restoration.

The exhortation using the protasis and apodosis also appears in Deut 30:1–10, which shows the two possible scenarios and a permanent threat with the heaven and earth as witnesses if the hearers do not follow the speaker's recommended option. Interestingly, Ezek 43:10–11 does not present another possible choice of "if you do not do A," probably because exile, the worst punishment, has already occurred for the literary audience,[23] as well as possibly because the restoration agenda is already set up in YHWH's mind no matter how the audience responds. The passage assumes (or even encourages) their choice of showing themselves to be "ashamed" and continues in that direction. With the lack of threat, we may conjecture that shame is a strong recommendation as a preliminary attitude toward God before being reconnected to him.

Jacqueline E. Lapsley offers a slightly different interpretation: shame as an absolute condition to shift from general to advanced knowledge of God.[24] While agreeing with her syntactical conclusion, I consider its performative dimension, too. What if the exiles show no shame or no response at all? If the story goes that way, according to Lapsley's interpretation the audience will have no more chance due to their one-time decision, and the rest of the instructions will not be delivered. However, my analysis suggests that Ben Adam's performance will repeat and repeat until his audience responds to the command to be shamed so that, ultimately, the commission in 43:10–11 is fulfilled.[25] As Kalinda Stevenson and Bennett Simon argue, respectively,[26] this shame is a key to entering the new life

---

23. See Brian Neil Peterson, *Ezekiel in Context: Ezekiel's Message Understood in Its Historical Setting of Covenant Curses and Ancient Near Eastern Mythological Motifs*, PTMS 182 (Eugene, OR: Pickwick, 2012).

24. Jacqueline E. Lapsley, *Can These Bones Live? The Problem of the Moral Self in the Book of Ezekiel*, BZAW 301 (Berlin: de Gruyter, 2000), 177–79.

25. Liss briefly mentions the performative characteristic of 43:11, too ("Describe the Temple," 142).

26. Both Kalinda Stevenson and Bennett Simon read 43:10 as a rhetorical strategy to connect the geometrical measurement to the morality or holiness against the chaotic past. See Kalinda Rose Stevenson, *The Vision of Transformation: The Territorial Rhetoric of Ezekiel 40–48*, SBLDS 154 (Atlanta: Scholars Press 1996), 26, 163; Ben-

in the land; it is for them a vehicle for the practice of all instructions for a holy life. Thus, I prefer to translate ואם in 43:11a as "and when" rather than "and if."

Below is the syntactical analysis of 43:10–11, indicating the imperatives and their volitional clauses via different indentions.

> [10]As for you, Ben Adam,
> Describe (הגד) to the house of Israel the House
>> so that they may be ashamed (ויכלמו) of their iniquities;
>> so that they shall measure (ומדדו) proportion accurately.
>
> [11] And *when they are ashamed* (ואם-נכלמו) of all that they have done (עשו),
>> the fashion (צורה) of the house, its arrangement, its exits and its entrances, its whole design (צורה) and all its statutes; its whole design (צורה) and all its instructions—(D.O.)
> make known (הודע) to them
> and write (וכתב) it down in their sight,
>> so that they may observe (וישמרו) its whole form (צורה) and all its statutes
>> so that they practice (ועשו).

2.3. Shame in the Structural Context

In structuring this unit, scholars have been often driven by diachronic or thematic concerns and attempted to treat 43:11 and 43:12 as belonging to two different units.[27] However, both formal and content signs in the present text clearly show that those subunits (43:7–9, 10–11, and 12–27) should be regarded as one larger unit of the divine speech.

Focusing on *inclusio* between 40:3–4 and 43:10–11 as the same command to deliver what Ben Adam saw and heard, Daniel Block also separates verses 11 and 12. According to Block, the description of the return of the glory should be the conclusion of building or dedication of the temple, and

nett Simon, "Ezekiel's Geometric Vision of the Restored Temple: From the Rod of His Wrath to the Reed of His Measuring," *HTR* 102 (2009): 414, 430–31.

27. For diachronic approaches, see Georg Fohrer, *Ezechiel*, 2nd ed., Handbuch zum Alten Testament (Tübingen: Mohr Siebeck, 1955), 237–45; Steven S. Tuell, *Law of the Temple in Ezekiel 40–48*, HSM 49 (Atlanta: Scholars Press, 1992), 38–44. For a thematic approach, see Walter Zimmerli, *Ezekiel 2: A Commentary on the Book of the Prophet Ezekiel Chapters 25–48*, Hermeneia (Minneapolis: Fortress, 1983), 412.

the New Torah section should cover 43:12–46:24.[28] Despite his attractive divisions into New Temple (40:1–43:11), New Torah (43:12–46:24), New Land (47:1–48:29), and New City (48:30–35), Block's structural analysis seems to rely too much on themes. Clearer formal signs, including a character's verbs of movement and the speech formula, encourage interpreters to pay attention to the syntactical structure. Meanwhile, Ronald Hals analyzes 43:12 as the conclusion of 43:1–12,[29] but verse 12 obviously shows the second phase of the commands. Thus, although YHWH's command can be completed without pause between verses 11 and 12, it would be better to appreciate the text as the script that requires the performer to pause for a while and wait for a response from the audience. Only when the condition of 43:10–11 is fulfilled positively can verse 12 and following be performed. As I suggested above, the performer leads the expression of shame for the audience.

After the completion of the first temple tour focusing on its overall structures (Ezek 40–42), the vision report reaches the new phase by divine epiphany in 43:2. The first divine speech goes up to 43:27bγ, the end of chapter 43. The phrase "the wall of separation between the sacred and the common" in 42:20 now functions as an ending marker of the measurement of the temple structure scene, which 43:10 receives as the content to perform before the audience. Interestingly, the first issue chosen by YHWH is the instruction regarding the altar, which the text skips to show during the first temple tour in Ezek 40–42. I read this focalization as the authorial allusion for the counter passage, Ezek 8:4–6. In the Jerusalem temple vision (Ezek 8–11), YHWH picked this idolatrous altar gate as the first station and led Ben Adam to encounter a perilous scene: the idols and the glory of YHWH together in one space. Now, therefore, it is significant that, unlike the structures measured by Bronze Man and shown to Ben Adam in Ezek 40–42, the special instruction for the altar is given to Ben Adam directly from YHWH's mouth.

In between the ending of the first tour to see the overall structure of the temple (42:20) and the instruction of the torah of the temple (43:12–27), the reporter describes three significant things: the return of YHWH's glory (43:2–5); an accusation against the Israelites/kings regarding the incorrect use of the temple structure and emendation (43:7–9); and a

---

28. Daniel I. Block, *Ezekiel 25–48*, NICOT (Grand Rapids: Eerdmans, 1997), 576.

29. Ronald Hals, *Ezekiel*, FOTL 19 (Grand Rapids: Eerdmans, 1989), 304–5.

commission to Ben Adam to deliver the torah (43:10–11). All three connect the previous unit with the following unit. The conclusion of the first temple tour would/should evoke shame in the exiles by reminding them of the abuse of the temple structures. Moreover, emphasizing the temple as the place of his throne (43:7), YHWH claims his kingship over human kings. Regardless of our understanding of the phrase ובפגרי מלכיהם במותם ("by the carcasses of their kings in their high places"),[30] for YHWH this returning time is the appropriate time to announce the reason for his abandonment of the temple and redress for the future prevention of wrong practice. As illustrated in Ezek 8–11, the abominable practice at the sanctuary is the most intolerable trespass against God. This shame evocation is more concretely and explicitly addressed again in 43:11 in teaching about the shape of the temple, its exits and entrance, and its cultic ordinances, all of which imply their past encroachment of the boundary of the holy hierarchy. The book of Ezekiel understands this encroachment as the cause of the universal chaos.

Below is the structural analysis of 43:10–11 within Ezek 40–43.

1. Preliminary temple tour for the overall temple structure (40:1–42)
2. The appearance of the glory of God and the divine speech at the east gate (43:1–27)
   2.1. Appearance of the glory of God at the temple through the east gate (43:1–5)
   Shame is expected when performed.
   2.2. Setting of the divine speech (43:6)
   2.3. Divine speech per se (43:7–27)
      2.3.1. Rebuke and emendation on the past wrongdoings (43:7–9)
      Shame is expected when performed.
      2.3.2. Commission to tell the structure (43:10a)
      Shame is explicitly expected when performed: wait for the "shame" response from the audience; if the result is negative, make more efforts for a positive result.

---

30. Among various views are intramural royal graves (John William Wevers, *Ezekiel* [Osprey, FL: Nelson, 1969], 312; Matthew J. Suriano, *The Politics of Dead Kings*, FAT 48 [Tübingen: Mohr Siebeck, 2010], 102); as a cult of the dead (Block, *Ezekiel 25–48*, 583–86); and as a child sacrifice (Brian B. Schmidt, *Israel's Beneficent Dead: Ancestor Cult and Necromancy in Ancient Israelite Religion and Tradition*, FAT 11 [Tübingen: Mohr Siebeck, 1994], 251).

2.3.3. When they show shame, tell the Torah of the Temple
(43:10b–11)
(Proper practice will be expected based on the shame)
    2.3.4. Torah of the temple per se (43:12–27)
        2.3.4.1. General introduction (43:12)
        2.3.4.2. Instruction for the structure of the altar (43:13–17)
        2.3.4.3. Instruction for the dedication of the altar (43:18–27)

2.4. Shame in the Semantic Context

Now, how shall we understand our thematic emotion shame in the book of Ezekiel? Its unique usage in Ezekiel lies in the presentations of two kinds of shame: disgrace and discretion.[31] Disgrace-shame happens when people are humiliated in front of an enemy; they feel discretion-shame from divine exhortation or rebuke. Focusing on the latter phenomenon, Schwartz argues that shame is the ultimate goal of restoration; consequently, the book of Ezekiel's restoration agenda is not so cheerful.[32] While Schwartz focuses on the literary and theological dimensions of this shame, other Ezekiel scholars, including Jacqueline Lapsley, Thomas Renz, and Johanna Stiebert, pay attention to the rhetorical aspects of shame in the book and come to more positive conclusions.[33]

---

31. Jacqueline E. Lapsley, "Shame and Self-Knowledge: The Positive Role of Shame in Ezekiel's View of the Moral Self," in Odell and Strong, *Book of Ezekiel*, 143–74. Here she uses Carl D. Schneider's terms "disgrace-shame" and "discretion-shame." See Carl D. Schneider, *Shame, Exposure, and Privacy* (Boston: Beacon, 1977). For more recent works by psychologists and theologians, see Thomas J. Scheff, "Shame in Self and Society," *Symbolic Interaction* 26 (2003): 239–62; Fraser Watts, *Psychology, Religion, and Spirituality: Concepts and Applications* (Cambridge: Cambridge University Press, 2017), especially chapter 5, "Religious Experience"; and Daniel Y. Wu, *Honor, Shame, and Guilt: Social-Scientific Approaches to the Book of Ezekiel*, BBRSup 14 (Winona Lake, IN: Eisenbrauns, 2016).

32. Schwartz, "Ezekiel's Dim View" and "Ultimate Aim."

33. Contrary to Schwartz's idea that restoration is part of punishment to provoke Israel's feeling ashamed, Lapsley defines "feeling ashamed is part of divine restoration and mercy" (*Can These Bones Live*, 173; "Shame and Self-Knowledge," 143–74; see also Renz, *Rhetorical Function*, 19–21, 101–30, 144–47; Johanna Stiebert, *The Construction of Shame in the Hebrew Bible: The Prophetic Contribution*, JSOTSup 346 [Sheffield: Sheffield Academic, 2002], 3, 47, 129–73). Pointing out the parallels between 43:10–12 and 40:5, Milgrom and Block also argue that the purpose of mentioning the temple design in Ezek 43 is to evoke shame (*Ezekiel's Hope*, 113–15).

Despite its frequent appearance throughout the book, in the final vision the word "shame" in any Hebrew term appears only here (43:10–11), in the term כלם. This tells us two things: in the overall restoration vision, shame is not a main interest of the author; at the same time, the use of the word in Ezek 43 sends an inescapable signal to readers. In fact, the demand for the emotion shame fits well with the return of the glory of God even before the exhortation starts in 43:10. According to Martin A. Klopfenstein, among בש, כלם, and חרפה, all of which refer to feeling shame or disgrace, the word group כלם is the full antonym of כבד.[34] When the people notice their king's return, they should be humbled before the presence of God the King. Moreover, the rebuke of the passage implies that YHWH's glory was mostly stolen by kings or political authorities due to their encroachment upon the sacred boundary.

To understand the theological conception of shame in the book of Ezekiel, Stiebert's definition is helpful: "shame, then, is an emotion focused on the vulnerability and conspicuousness of one's self-image (subjective, internalized) concerning a perceived ideal (objective, external)."[35] Cairns offers a similar semantic meaning of shame as self-judgment, not only as a group but even on the individual solitary level.[36] In other words, feeling shame means that one now recognizes oneself in comparison to external standards. Back to Stiebert's term, if that "perceived ideal" refers to other nations, shame might be the objective shame ("disgrace-shame" in Stiebert and Carl D. Schneider's terms; "being shamed" in Schwartz's terms). Israel, its land, and ultimately its deity YHWH with regard to his defamed reputation have experienced this objective shame due to the fall of Judah and Jerusalem temple. But if this perceived ideal is attributed to Israel's deity YHWH, feeling shame becomes a synonym of sincere recognition of YHWH as one's only true God and oneself as mortal ("discretion-shame" for Stiebert and Schneider; "feeling ashamed" for Schwartz).[37] This kind of shame must be the same emotion of self-

---

34. Martin A. Klopfenstein, *Scham und Schande nach dem Alten Testament: Eine begriffsgeschichtlich Untersuchung zu den hebräscen Wurzeln* בוש, כלם *und* חפר, ATANT 62 (Zürich: Theologischer Verlag, 1972), 208.

35. Stiebert, *Construction of Shame*, 3, 47, 129–73.

36. Douglas L. Cairns, *Aidôs: The Psychology and Ethics of Honour and Shame in Ancient Greek Literature* (Oxford: Clarendon, 1993), 16.

37. With this knowledge, the semantic names of the generic term Ben Adam (בן אדם) can be understood as mortal, descendant of a man from the dust (not God), as

humiliation in Lev 26:41: יכנע לבבם הערל "if their uncircumcised heart becomes humbled." According to Lev 26:40–45, this self-humbling is one of the key factors to let God restore the people from exile. In a discussion of "divine initiative and human response," Paul Joyce interprets the new heart and new spirit in its moral dimension as obedience to God.[38] Lapsley also connects shame with self-morality.[39] In that vein, I suggest that shame can be analogous to a pacemaker that operates a given new heart. Without the new heart, one cannot feel ashamed (the discretion-shame); without being controlled by the pacemaker, shame, however, one cannot keep the new heart working properly. These two faculties thus work together to observe the torah, especially the torah of the temple in the restoration vision.

With this semantic dimension of the word shame, both ancient and modern readers come to know that the boundary encroachment in YHWH's accusation (43:7–9) results from not thoroughly recognizing YHWH as God and causes the people to go into exile. Thus, the way of returning to God and home should be found most of all by setting the appropriate hierarchy between God and humans as well as among humans. The theme of Israel's recognition of their deity as the true God is promoted in the book of Ezekiel both by through dreadful judgment and undeserved deliverance.[40] In sum, the book of Ezekiel leads audience/readers to a dramatic shift from shame before the world to shame before the presence of God. This action-reaction analogy from a lever principle is possible when God visited and initiated his new creation to the exiles. Interestingly this interaction of two kinds of shame also appears in Ezra's confessional prayer in Ezra 9:6 (בשתי ונכלמתי, before God) and 9:7 (בשת פנים, before the nations).

---

well as the priestly figure as a representation of human beings. Stierbert uses Carl D. Schneider's term in her book. See Carl D. Schneider, "A Mature Sense of Shame," in *Many Faces of Shame*, ed. Donald M. Nathanson (London: Guilford, 1987), 194–213. For Schwartz's reference, see "Ezekiel's Dim View," 66–67.

38. Paul Joyce, *Divine Initiative and Human Response in Ezekiel*, JSOTSup 51 (Sheffield: Sheffield Academic, 1989), 111.

39. Lapsley, *Can These Bones Live*, 138–40, 170–72.

40. A. A. Diestel, *"Ich bin Jahwe": Der Aufstieg der Ich-bin-Jahwe-Aussage zum Schlüsselwort des alttestamentlichen Monotheismus*, WMANT 110 (Neukirchen-Vluyn: Neukirchener Verlag, 2006); John Frederick Evans, "An Inner-Biblical Interpretation and Intertextual Reading of Ezekiel's Recognition Formulae with the Book of Exodus" (PhD diss., University of Stellenbosch, 2006).

3. Shame in Theological Contexts

So far we have learned that being ashamed before God is the required procedure for a new life in the land, so the performer of the text never stops encouraging the audience to show that virtue.

Now we ask again why it is so important. I started this essay with the statement that, if the book of Ezekiel is a book of transformation, that transformation is planned through a generational transition. The matter of being ashamed makes a decisive difference in the destinies of the parent generation and their children. Thus, this section has three agendas: to identify characteristics of earlier and later generations through the image of the human scapegoat; to unpack the literary contexts of the proximate chapters of the final vision, Ezek 37–39; and to synthesize the overall theological perspectives of the book of Ezekiel within the framework of shame.

3.1. The Day of Atonement and the Human Scapegoat

In his study of the book of Ezekiel, Sweeney briefly mentions Yom Kippur as the *Sitz im Literatur* of the vision ("In the beginning of the year, in the tenth day of the month," 40:1) and the possible "scapegoat" imagery of the exiles, first referred to in Lev 16.[41] However, this insight needs further consideration, since the apparent gap between the animal scapegoats and the human exiles seems huge.[42] Detailed instructions on the scape-

---

41. Marvin A. Sweeney, *The Prophetic Literature*, Interpreting Biblical Texts (Nashville: Abingdon, 2005), 135, 142; Sweeney, *Form and Intertextuality in Prophetic and Apocalyptic Literature* (Eugene, OR: Wipf & Stock, 2005), 145, 153; Sweeney, *Reading Ezekiel*, 195. Block also sees a Nisan New Year as Rosh Hashanah based on the cultic ritual reference in 45:18–25 (*Ezekiel 25–48*, 513). For the Jubilee Year argument, see Jan Van Goudoever, "Ezekiel Sees in Exile a New Temple-City at the Beginning of a Jobel Year," in *Ezekiel and His Book: Textual and Literary Criticism and Their Interrelation*, ed. Johan Lust, BETL 74 (Leuven: Leuven University Press/Peeters, 1986), 344–49. Hanna Liss argues the date of 40:1 as Day of Atonement with the connection to Year of Jubilee ("Describe the Temple," 130). For the general discussion of the cult and character relationship, see Roy Gane, *Cult and Character: Purification Offerings, Day of Atonement, and Theodicy* (Winona Lake, IN: Eisenbrauns, 2005).

42. Scapegoat imagery has become a more popular topic in the field of psychology. Most psychological analyses easily adopt the characteristics of actual scapegoat and apply to human beings such as the character Joseph. See Sylvia Brinton Perera, *The Scapegoat Complex: Toward a Mythology of Shadow and Guilt*, Studies in Jung-

goat ritual in Leviticus give readers a practical impression rather than a symbolic understanding, which causes us to hesitate to connect the two entities directly.

Therefore, it is helpful to ponder first the meaning of Yom Kippur in the final vision of the book of Ezekiel. YHWH the God of Israel who had departed the Jerusalem temple and lived among the exiles for a while, finally returned to the rebuilt holy of holies with his glory on Yom Kippur. On that day, the deity began to speak about the torah of the temple to Ben Adam, who had desperately longed for the temple and the presence of YHWH but was sent to the profane land, the inaccessible land of doom. This is a summary of the vision. If we consider the significance of Yom Kippur and its renewal characteristic through purgation, this event natu-rally embraces something beyond God's consolation and mercy. It is God's proclamation of the new start par excellence.

One of the quintessential rituals of Yom Kippur according to Lev 16 is to send away the chosen scapegoat. This randomly chosen scapegoat from between two dedicated goats has four important traits: (1) to "bear the sins (נשא עון) of the whole community as reparation;[43] (2) to be "sent away" (שלח) alive into the wilderness ("cut-off" land, ארץ גזר); (3) to be abandoned to "rot away" there (pine away, מקק); and (4) never to return (שוב). When we recall the unique vocabulary of Ezekiel, we easily find similarities between the scapegoat and the captives' situation: "sent away" to the wilderness (cut-off land) and "rot away" (pine away). But two other traits, to bear people's sins and never to return, need more clarification.

If Lev 16 regulates the ritual at the tent of meeting and the future temple in the Promised Land with the appropriate sacrificial goat and scapegoat, the desperation of the exilic community in the book of Ezekiel can be understood as a confession or complaint from the mouth of the

---

ian Psychology by Jungian Analysts 23 (Toronto: Inner City Books, 1986), 26–32, 88; Roger De Verteuil, "The Scapegoat Archetype," *Journal of Religion and Health* 5 (1966): 209–25.

43. Although it needs more detailed explanation, for now I merely mention the reference. The concept of concreteness, inheritance, and contagiousness of sins is intrinsic in the Hebrew Bible. See Rolf Knierim, *Die Hauptbegriffe für Sünde im Alten Testament* (Gütersloh: Mohn, 1965); Klous Koch, "עָוֹן 'āwōn," *TDOT* 10:546–60; and Baruch J. Schwartz, "The Bearing of Sin in the Priestly Literature," in *Pomegranates and Golden Bells: Studies in Biblical, Jewish, and Near Eastern Ritual, Law, and Litera-ture in Honor of Jacob Milgrom*, ed. David P. Wright, David Noel Freedman, and Avi Hurvitz (Winona Lake, IN: Eisenbrauns, 1995), 3–21.

human scapegoat community. They identify themselves as (1) those who (unfairly) bear sins of Israel inherited from the ancestors; (2) were sent away from the presence of YHWH; (3) have wandered and finally rotted away in the dry cut-off land; and, of course, have (4) no hope of returning or surviving.

3.2. Making the Human Scapegoat Return

Application of the scapegoat imagery to certain biblical characters was not the invention of modern interpreters. The book of Jubilees (34:10–19) connects various symbols of the Joseph story in Genesis to Yom Kippur and understands Joseph as a symbolic figure of the scapegoat who was sent away alive to the cut-off land, bearing his brothers' sins, and never returned home to the Promised Land.[44] Gershon Hepner even argues that the Genesis stories are created out of the pentateuchal laws to produce narrative settings, one such example being the Joseph story for Yom Kippur and scapegoat ritual.[45] What I would like to draw attention to is God's presence with Joseph in Egypt. Even though the two concepts—expulsion from the presence of God in his wrath and God's dwelling with him—are not compatible, the author of Jubilees and his readers connect the two figures using God's dynamic moveable image. In Ezekiel, too, God visited Ezekiel, who stayed in the unclean land and even made God himself there his temporal sanctuary, מקדש מעט (11:16).

The description of the wilderness as the place where the scapegoat is sent also gives us reason to see the exiles as the human scapegoat. In Lev 16, the goat goes not just to the wilderness (מדבר) but specifically to a cut-off land (גזר ארץ) that is inaccessible. That land is a place of doom, as expressed in exilic literature such as Ezek 37:11 ("we were cut off," נגזרנו) and Lam 3:54 ("I am cut off," נגזרתי).[46]

---

44. Another explicit image of the human scapegoat is presented in the suffering Servant Song in Isa 53. For its origin and reception history, see Bernd Janowski and Peter Stuhlmacher, eds., *The Suffering Servant: Isaiah 53 in Jewish and Christian Sources* (Grand Rapids: Eerdmans, 2004), especially Bernd Janowski, "He Bore Our Sins: Isaiah 53 and the Drama of Taking Another's Place," 48–74.

45. Despite his interesting intertextual readings, Hepner's assumption above needs more textual evidence and examination. See Gershon Hepner, *Legal Friction: Law, Narrative, and Identity Politics in Biblical Israel*, StBibLit 78 (New York: Lang, 2010), 539.

46. Calum Carmichael, "The Origin of the Scapegoat Ritual," *VT* 50 (2000): 167–82, especially 169–70.

The imagery of Jerusalem as a wandering figure in the wilderness is one of the main characteristics presented in the midst of diatribe in Ezek 16. Jerusalem was found in the wilderness; no one knows how she was born and who abandoned her in the wilderness. Her origin is briefly described as the affiliation of the Canaanite nations in terms of Jerusalem's origin. Of course, the discovery of the infant Israel first refers to her infant status during her forty years of the wilderness journey after the exodus, but the point is that she is described as a "cast" (*hophal* second fem. sg. *wayyiqtol*, ותשלכי) child in an unclean condition both physically and ritually. Because of this, no one pitied her; she was in the dry and cut-off land. YHWH picked her up, raised her, and made her his bride. Before reaching Ezek 33, the time of Jerusalem's fall, Lady Jerusalem continued to be alive. Although her status has been dramatically changed from a poor baby to a beloved daughter, from a beautiful lady queen to an unfaithful wife to the abandoned whore, she is the same "person" (more precisely the same persona). In Ezek 37 we finally see that some children of that lady had been killed a long time ago, and their bones had already dried out in the desolate wilderness. Some of her children nonetheless remained without parents in the wilderness, again like her childhood in Ezek 16. Who shall take care of her children and how so?

Now let us move back to the earlier topic: two remaining traits of the scapegoat. We take up the fourth one first. The notion of never returning to the sanctuary immediately prompts questions of restoration, reformation, or even re-creation. To begin with the question of how to make the children return, according to Lev 16 the scapegoat was never to return. The fact that the exodus generation could never (re)enter the Promised Land, even if they as a human scapegoat could leave the cut-off land, clearly hinders our effort to combine the image of the scapegoat who can never return and the exiles who finally returned to the land. Hepner cannot find a solution to this contradiction and brings another image of expulsion, ostracism, to apply it to Jacob's case. He argues that the ostracism that Jacob experienced allows the person to return while the human scapegoat Joseph cannot be allowed to return.[47]

I suggest a different solution: a shift of generations. Although Hepner focuses on the fact that Joseph did not return to the Promised Land, I focus on the fact that Joseph's two sons became the children of Israel through

---

47. Hepner, *Legal Friction*, 537–45.

their grandfather Jacob's adoption of them. If their father Joseph was the human scapegoat and was destined to die in the cut-off land, the same destiny for his children as cast-offs might also be expected.

However, our Genesis story solves this problem brilliantly.[48] Jacob adopted Joseph's two sons and made it possible for them to become the members of twelve tribes and to live in the land. Likewise, YHWH in the book of Ezekiel will adopt the children of the earlier exilic generation to make them his children. The means of nullifying the destiny of the human scapegoat is adoption by the higher authoritative party, especially divine adoption! It is not surprising that we often see God's adoption formula in Ezekiel ("I will become [ל + היה] your God, and you will become [ל + היה] my people/children"; see 11:20; 36:28; 37:23, 27). Of course, it is not a formula unique to the book of Ezekiel, but the rhetorical effect is significant, especially when God proclaims that message to the hopeless exiles.

If there were a shift of destiny from Joseph to his two sons, to what extent can we apply this principle to the exiles? Do we have other examples of a generational shift in the Bible? How about the children who were born in the wilderness in the Pentateuch texts? The literary audience of the Leviticus passage is the first generation of the exodus. Although the characters did not know their destiny, from the author's retrospective view, they ultimately will wander and die in the wilderness. However, their history will continue in their children who will enter the Promised Land. This is the destiny and the role of the first generation in the Pentateuch, which is similar to the rhetorical situation of the book of Ezekiel.

In the Deuteronomy passage, the literary audience is *the* second generation, right before entering the Promised Land. Their responsibility is essential; depending on their obedience or disobedience, the blessings or curses will follow in the future, which demands an active response by the audience. In Ezek 40–48, the literary audience must be the mixed generations of the exiles, as I argued their flexible identification earlier.[49] Despite

---

48. Here I do not attempt to consult intertextual parallels among the Joseph story in Genesis, the scapegoat ritual in Lev 16, and the conception of the exile in the book of Ezekiel in terms of authorial intention. I am not even sure that this picture was in the mind of the author of the book of Ezekiel. It is my application of the human scapegoat image to the exiles with the help of the account the book of Jubilees.

49. The date entry of the final vision is "the fourteenth year after the fall of Jerusalem" as the relatively early stage of Babylonian exile. For the discussion about the multiple generations in the exilic era, see Ahn, *Exile as Forced Migrations*, chs. 3–6.

YHWH's rebuke for their own iniquities, the earlier exilic generation identifies themselves as victims of their ancestors' sin. If we consider the ultimate generational shift, the complaint of the earlier generation might be legitimate: they have no hope for returning; they will rot away, seeing each other in their sins. However, as Joseph's sons could enter and live in the Promised Land, their children, the generation born in the wilderness-like Babylon, can enter the land, too. Even if the earlier generation bears their own and their ancestors' sins and thus suffer now, God will miraculously work to bring their children home. Therefore, the restoration program in Ezek 40–48 is hardly for the literary audience themselves to apply but rather for the implied audience, that is, whoever identifies as the later generation.

Who will teach and deliver this vision to the next generation in the indefinitely open period? Obviously, the literary audience through the priest/prophet Ezekiel.[50] One of the efforts for this education, I believe, was illustrated in Ezek 18's sour grape dispute. To date this dispute has been most frequently interpreted as a prophetic speech to correct the exilic audience's biased view that they suffer on account of their ancestors' sins. However, another interpretation is completely plausible and fits well in our discussion. By delivering this new message to the earlier exilic generation (literary audience) who complained of their innocent suffering, the prophet first argues that they are the wicked children of wicked fathers. At the same time, however, to the future implied audience, which coexists within the group of the literary audience at that time, the prophet urges that they can become good children of the wicked fathers whose parents will soon perish in the cut-off land. In other words, the prophet wants to make room for the later generation to be freed from the burden of bearing their ancestors' sins. Moreover, through the application of the complaints in Ezek 18 to the future implied audience, this discourse not only cuts off the destiny of the earlier generation from their ancestors as traditionally

---

Renz distinguishes the first generation and second generation in the Babylonian exile, comparing them with the two generations in the wilderness in Exodus (*Rhetorical Function*, 1, 83–84). Sweeney also points out that any scenario of deliverance should wait until the end of the current round of punishment. See Marvin A. Sweeney, "Ezekiel's Conceptualization of the Exile in Intertextual Perspective," *Hebrew Bible and Ancient Israel* 1 (2012): 171.

50. Lapsley, *Can These Bones Live*, 176.

understood but also encourages the next generation to have hope by cutting off their parents' behaviors.

3.3. Literary Location of Gog's Invasion Episode: Free from Disgrace-Shame

The literary location of the Gog of Magog episode in Ezek 38–39 can also be understood in this context. It is presented before the final temple vision report although, in the logical or chronological order of the projected time, the invasion of Gog will occur later than the fulfillment time of the final temple vision in Ezek 40–48.[51] In other words, the invasion could happen before God brings the exiles to the land, but the present text clearly mentions that it will happen after the exiles return to the land of Israel (38:8).[52] One of the possible purposes of this setting is to let readers understand the sequence of restoration: God's fame is honored again before the world; the land of Israel is completely purified by fire; then the glory of YHWH comes back to the land. Through these events the returnees (the later generation of the exile) experience YHWH's almighty power so that they thoroughly recognize him as their only God.

Meanwhile, Levitt Kohn argues that portrait of Ezekiel as a new Moses comes from a confluence of Priestly and Deuteronomic traditions.[53] As a Priestly part, I suggest the invasion of Gog of Magog in Ezek 38–39 as the extensive unfolding drama of Lev 26:33b–35: the Sabbatical desolation of the land as the final preparation for the return of God's glory. Of course, the two literary corpora have differences, too. First, the land in Leviticus enjoys its desolation in the status of "empty" land when the exiles were bound in the foreign land; Ezek 38–39 depicts the purgation of the land by war and the burial of the corpses of enemies with the presence of returnees. Thus, the fulfillment has been differently presented, but the general picture and conceptions are similar.

---

51. William Tooman, *Gog of Magog*, FAT 2/52 (Tübingen: Mohr Siebeck, 2011), 75.

52. Tooman, *Gog of Magog*, 150–60. Tooman argues that this is an authorial intention to interpret the restoration as a new exodus. On the contrary, paying attention to the phrase מימים רבים in verse 8, Zimmerli and Block argue that the target audience of the oracle is not identical with the Ezekiel's audience, since the invasion will happen in the inconsiderable future. See Zimmerli, *Ezekiel 2*, 307; Block, *Ezekiel 25–48*, 443; Block, "Gog and the Pouring Out of the Spirit: Reflections on Ezekiel xxxix 21–9," *VT* 37 (1987): 257–70.

53. Levitt Kohn, *New Heart,* 109–10.

If Ezek 38–39 functions as the waiting period of purging all the unclean things of the land,[54] the agenda of the book of Ezekiel has many common aspects with Leviticus, especially the Holiness Code.[55] If the latter part of Ezek 36 and 37 deal with the purification of the people by transforming their heart and spirit, Ezek 38 and 39 focus on the land purification. The method of the land purification may sound somewhat surprising in this context, since it uses the invasion of the foreign kings including Gog from Magog. However, we need to think about the essential characteristic of this battle: we hear no casualty report among the Israelites; only invaders are killed, even before they attempt to attack (38:20–22), but Israelites clean their corpses and weapons for a full seven-year period (39:9–16).

Accordingly, we can rgard this battle as designed for the purification of the land and confirmation that YHWH is on Israel's side. It occurs on an international and universal scale, but the focal point is that the land of Israel will first experience its uprooted turmoil (not a partial desolation) by the invasion of the nations and severe natural disasters. Granted, this is chaos, implying that the desolated or waste status of the land during the exilic period is not enough for its purification. Note that prophecies of the fall of Jerusalem in earlier chapters of Ezekiel focus on the description of how people will suffer and be killed. Now another focalization is made for the land concern, especially its intentional desecration for the complete re-creation. Just as the Israelites need to be cast away, experience death-like suffering in the wilderness, and be transformed in order to come back home as new people of God, the land must experience total disaster first both by war and natural disaster. Here, through the illustration of the restoration agenda regarding the land and people, we see Ezekiel's typical theological preference as stricter applications of his earlier traditions again.

---

54. Sweeney, *Reading Ezekiel*, 186–87; Margaret Odell, "The City of Hamonah in Ezekiel 39:11–16: The Tumultuous City of Jerusalem," *CBQ* 56 (1994): 479–89.

55. Regarding H and Ezekiel, Michael Lyons discusses Ezekiel's creative application of H based on Ezekiel's inversion of word order, creation of new word pairs, and splitting and recombining of sayings. Lyons's analysis on the Ezekiel's contextualization, including laws becoming instructions, is especially insightful for our discussion. See Michael Lyons, *From Law to Prophecy: Ezekiel's Use of the Holiness Code*, LHBOTS 507 (New York: T&T Clark, 2009). Recently, in his commentary, *Ezekiel 38–48*, Stephen Cook also argues the Holiness Code or the Holiness school as the source of the book of Ezekiel.

3.4. Standing on the Fathers' Failures

After acknowledging how the later generation can come back to the land although their fathers perished like the human scapegoat, finally, we ask why YHWH needs to bring them back to the Promised Land. This question is related to the rhetorical intention of the accusations and the rhetorical effect on the commands for being ashamed. The simplest answer is that it is because Israel is forever YHWH's children; no matter what happens, this is the most crucial bond. In this context, biblical authors claim that God's abandonment of Israel and the loss of the nation and temple are to be understood not as total and eternal abandonment but as temporary suffering (cf. Ps 89:46–47; Isa 64:7) due to God's hidden face.[56] It should be surprising for all audiences that the last word of YHWH (39:29) before the final vision started was, "but now I will not hide my face from them [ולא־אסתיר עוד פני מהם] because I poured my spirit upon the house of Israel."

Rebecca Idestrom examines various echoes of the book of Exodus in the book of Ezekiel.[57] For future study, I also suggest applying this intertextual reading to the history presented in the Former Prophets. In disclosing the restoration agenda, the author of the book of Ezekiel indeed not only considers the first exodus but also expresses concerns about theological accounts from Exodus to expulsion throughout Israel's history. If we keep the pictures of the pentateuchal literature and the Former Prophets together while reading the book of Ezekiel, we can see how Ezekiel the theologian and historian traces Israel's failures throughout its history and attempts to transform all perceived ruined spots into the newly created world. Whenever Ezekiel's eyes stay on the moments of failure in contemplating history, he painstakingly changes the conventions of the earlier traditions with his projected view.[58] This transformation or somewhat new creation project in Ezek 36–48 has three crucial characteristics: a shift from human efforts to the divine initiative; an elimination of all possible

---

56. See Richard Elliott Friedman, *The Hidden Face of God* (New York: Harper Collins, 1996); Samuel E. Balentine, *The Hidden God: The Hiding of the Face of God in the Old Testament*, Oxford Theological Monographs (Oxford: Oxford University Press, 1983).

57. Rebecca G. S. Idestrom, "Echoes of the Book of Exodus in Ezekiel," *JSOT* 33 (2009): 489–510.

58. See Michael Fishbane, *Biblical Interpretation of Ancient Israel* (Oxford: Clarendon, 1985), 410–12.

pitfalls to prevent another failure; the use of the emotion shame to make the new heart work properly.

In other words, Ezekiel's concern can be understood by reminding the wilderness generation after exodus. Did God choose the second generation based on their virtues? Does their repentance of their ancestors' iniquities function as a ticket for the Promised Land? No! The book of Numbers claims that it was God's decision when his judgment time on the first generation passed. Unfortunately, the history in the Former Prophets shows that the second generation and their offspring who lived in the land also failed to obey God. What should Ezekiel, the exiled priest/prophet learn from this? Once YHWH decided to adopt this later exilic generation as his children, how was he to discipline this undisciplined and inexperienced generation? Can we find the secure feeling of restoration from Ezekiel's agenda? Unless radical changes took place, chronic failure would haunt again and again even after the exiles returned home by miraculous divine power. This is the serious recognition of reality in the book of Ezekiel. By the same token, what do we see in the final vision of Ezek 40–48? In order to retain security in the land, the new community needs many innovative rules, including a new heart and its pacemaker, shame; the temple and the city should be separated; the temple structure and its access should be more strictly applied; kingship should be subdued under the control of the priesthood; Levites should bear their iniquities not to rebel against the Zadokite priests, and so on.

As we have observed, Ezekiel's restoration agenda is not just reformation or purification; it is a complete new start, a new creation. The old and new worlds, despite apparent similarities, are barely connected with the collective memory of history to produce the necessary discretion shame. Ezekiel 43:10–11 describes the literary audience from the perspective of continuity: those who are asked to show the shame have the capacity of memory to recall their (or their ancestors') past wrongdoings. If the physical conditions and essential content of memory indicate continuity, a new heart and new spirit with the shameful emotion point to discontinuity, the children as an entirely different human race. One's attitude from complaint to contrition is only possible when one can reevaluate the past with a transformed memory. By this logic, we conjecture that Ezek 43:10–11 expects its audience to undergo a dramatic transition of discontinuity within the context of continuity.

From the author's perspective, it would not be an exaggeration to say that the history of ancient Israel in the Hebrew Bible is the repetition of the ancestors' failure, again and again if the parent generation in the book of Ezekiel is none but the descendants of the second generation in the wilderness, who had experienced the massive and painful deaths of their parents there. In front of this tragic circle, the book of Ezekiel solemnly puts the strong and perpetual feeling, shame, as the gate of the new world. This is the only way to escape from the evil cycle that the fathers failed and pined away as dried bones. Ezekiel might learn from that failure that human initiatives have limitations and partial emendation of the wrong behaviors cannot guarantee returning home, living in security, and keeping the relationship with God.

In sum, even if shame seems the ultimate goal of restoration on the literary level, I should say that the ultimate goal of the shame according to the book of Ezekiel is to reach an in-depth knowledge of God and self so that the people keep their eternal relationship forever. Ashamed before the presence of God is the essential virtue of the newly transformed human race.

Bibliography

Ackroyd, Peter R. *Exile and Restoration: A Study of Hebrew Thought of the Sixth Century BC*. London: SCM, 1968.

Ahn, John J. *Exile as Forced Migrations: A Sociological, Literary, and Theological Approach on the Displacement and Resettlement of the Southern Kingdom of Judah*. BZAW 417. Berlin: de Gruyter, 2010.

Albertz, Rainer. *A History of Israelite Religion in the Old Testament Period*. 2 vols. London: SCM, 1994.

Andrew, M. E. *Responsibility and Restoration: The Course of the Book of Ezekiel*. Dunedin: University of Otago Press, 1985.

Balentine, Samuel E. *The Hidden God: The Hiding of the Face of God in the Old Testament*. Oxford Theological Monographs. Oxford: Oxford University Press, 1983.

Betts, T. J. *Ezekiel the Priest: A Custodian of Tôrâ*. StBibLit 74. New York: Lang, 2005.

Black, Edwin. "The Second Persona." Pages 161–72 in *Landmark Essays on Rhetorical Criticism*. Edited by Thomas W. Benson. Landmark Essays 5. Davis, CA: Hermagoras Press, 1993.

Block, Daniel I. *Ezekiel 25–48*. NICOT. Grand Rapids: Eerdmans, 1997.

———. "Gog and the Pouring Out of the Spirit: Reflections on Ezekiel xxxix 21–9." *VT* 37 (1987): 257–70.

Booth, Wayne. *The Rhetoric of Fiction*. 2nd ed. Chicago: University of Chicago Press, 1983.

Cairns, Douglas L. *Aidôs: The Psychology and Ethics of Honour and Shame in Ancient Greek Literature*. Oxford: Clarendon, 1993.

Carmichael, Calum. "The Origin of the Scapegoat Ritual." *VT* 50 (2000): 167–82.

Cook, Steven L. *Ezekiel 38–48: A New Translation with Introduction and Commentary*. AYB 22B. New Haven: Yale University Press, 2018.

Darr, Katheryn Pfisterer. "The Wall around Paradise: Ezekielian Ideas About the Future." *VT* 37 (1987): 271–79.

De Verteuil, Roger. "The Scapegoat Archetype." *Journal of Religion and Health* 5 (1966): 209–25.

Diestel, A. A. *"Ich bin Jahwe": Der Aufstieg der Ich-bin-Jahwe-Aussage zum Schlüsselwort des alttestamentlichen Monotheismus*. WMANT 110. Neukirchen-Vluyn: Neukirchener Verlag, 2006.

Evans, John Frederick. "An Inner-Biblical Interpretation and Intertextual Reading of Ezekiel's Recognition Formulae with the Book of Exodus." PhD diss., University of Stellenbosch, 2006.

Fishbane, Michael. *Biblical Interpretation of Ancient Israel*. Oxford: Clarendon, 1985.

Fohrer, Georg. *Ezechiel*. 2nd ed. Handbuch zum Alten Testament. Tübingen: Mohr Siebeck, 1955.

Fox, Michael V. "The Rhetoric of Ezekiel's Vision of the Valley of the Bones." *HUCA* 51 (1980): 1–15.

Friedman, Richard Elliott. *The Hidden Face of God*. New York: Harper Collins, 1996.

Gane, Roy. *Cult and Character: Purification Offerings, Day of Atonement, and Theodicy*. Winona Lake, IN: Eisenbrauns, 2005.

Ganzel, Tova. "The Description of the Restoration of Israel in Ezekiel." *VT* 60 (2010): 197–211.

Hals, Ronald. *Ezekiel*. FOTL 19. Grand Rapids: Eerdmans, 1989.

Hepner, Gershon. *Legal Friction: Law, Narrative, and Identity Politics in Biblical Israel*. StBibLit 78. New York: Lang, 2010.

Idestrom, Rebecca G. S. "Echoes of the Book of Exodus in Ezekiel." *JSOT* 33 (2009): 489–510.

Iser, Wolfgang. *The Implied Reader: Patterns of Communication in Prose Fiction from Bunyan to Beckett*. Baltimore: Johns Hopkins University Press, 1978.

Janowski, Bernd. "He Bore Our Sins: Isaiah 53 and the Drama of Taking Another's Place." Pages 48–74 in *The Suffering Servant: Isaiah 53 in Jewish and Christian Sources*. Edited by Bernd Janowski and Peter Stuhlmacher. Grand Rapids: Eerdmans, 2004.

Joyce, Paul. *Divine Initiative and Human Response in Ezekiel*. JSOTSup 51. Sheffield: Sheffield Academic, 1989.

Klopfenstein, Martin A. *Scham und Schande nach dem Alten Testament: Eine begriffsgeschichtlich Untersuchung zu den hebräscen Wurzeln בוש, כלם und חפר*. ATANT 62. Zürich: Theologischer Verlag, 1972.

Knierim, Rolf. *Die Hauptbegriffe für Sünde im Alten Testament*. Gütersloh: Mohn, 1965.

Lapsley, Jacqueline E. *Can These Bones Live? The Problem of the Moral Self in the Book of Ezekiel*. BZAW 301. Berlin: de Gruyter, 2000.

———. "Shame and Self-Knowledge: The Positive Role of Shame in Ezekiel's View of the Moral Self." Pages 143–74 in *The Book of Ezekiel: Theological and Anthropological Perspectives*. Edited by Margaret S. Odell and John T. Strong. SBLSymS 9. Atlanta: Society of Biblical Literature, 2000.

Lenchak, Timothy A. *"Choose Life!": A Rhetorical-Critical Investigation of Deuteronomy 28,69–30,20*. AnBib 129. Rome: Pontifical Biblical Institute, 1993.

Levenson, Jon D. *Theology of the Program of Restoration of Ezekiel 40–48*. HSM 10. Atlanta: Scholars Press, 1976.

Levitt Kohn, Risa. *A New Heart and a New Soul: Ezekiel, the Exile, and the Torah*. JSOTSup 358. London: Sheffield Academic, 2002.

Liss, Hanna. " 'Describe the Temple to the House of Israel': Preliminary Remarks on the Temple Vision in the Book of Ezekiel and the Question of Fictionality in Priestly Literatures." Pages 122–43 in *Utopia and Dystopia in Prophetic Literature*. Edited by Ehud Ben Zvi. Publications of the Finnish Exegetical Society 92. Göttingen: Vandenhoeck & Ruprecht, 2006.

Lyons, Michael. *From Law to Prophecy: Ezekiel's Use of the Holiness Code*. LHBOTS 507. New York: T&T Clark, 2009.

Mein, Andrew. "Ezekiel as a Priest in Exile." Pages 199–213 in *The Elusive Prophet: The Prophet as a Historical Person, Literary Character, and Anonymous Artist*. Edited by Johannes C. de Moor. OtSt 45. Leiden: Brill, 2001.

Milgrom, Jacob, and Daniel I. Block. *Ezekiel's Hope: A Commentary on Ezekiel 38–48*. Eugene, OR: Cascade, 2012.

Nasuti, Harry P. "Identity, Identification, and Imitation: The Narrative Hermeneutics of Biblical Law." *Journal of Law and Religion* 4 (1986): 9–23.

Odell, Margaret. "The City of Hamonah in Ezekiel 39:11–16: The Tumultuous City of Jerusalem." *CBQ* 56 (1994): 479–89.

Perelman, Chaïm, and L. Olbrechts-Tyteca. *The New Rhetoric: A Treatise on Argumentation.* Notre Dame, IN: Notre Dame Press, 1969.

Perera, Sylvia Brinton. *The Scapegoat Complex: Toward a Mythology of Shadow and Guilt.* Studies in Jungian Psychology by Jungian Analysts 23. Toronto: Inner City Books, 1986.

Peterson, Brian Neil. *Ezekiel in Context: Ezekiel's Message Understood in Its Historical Setting of Covenant Curses and Ancient Near Eastern Mythological Motifs.* PTMS 182. Eugene, OR: Pickwick, 2012.

Polzin, Robert. *Moses and the Deuteronomist: A Literary Study of the Deuteronomic History 1, Deuteronomy, Joshua, Judges.* New York: Seabury, 1980.

Renz, Thomas. *The Rhetorical Function of the Book of Ezekiel.* VTSup 76. Leiden: Brill, 1999.

Rom-Shiloni, Dalit. "Deuteronomic Concepts of Exile Interpreted in Jeremiah and Ezekiel," Pages 69–81 in vol. 1 of *Birkat Shalom: Studies in the Bible, Ancient Near Eastern Literature, and Postbiblical Judaism Presented to Shalom M. Paul on the Occasion of His Seventieth Birthday.* Edited by Chaim Cohen, Victor Avigdor Hurowitz, and Jeffrey H. Tigay. 2 vols. Winona Lake, IN: Eisenbrauns, 2008.

Scheff, Thomas J. "Shame in Self and Society." *Symbolic Interaction* 26 (2003): 239–62.

Schmidt, Brian B. *Israel's Beneficent Dead: Ancestor Cult and Necromancy in Ancient Israelite Religion and Tradition.* FAT 11. Tübingen: Mohr Siebeck, 1994.

Schneider, Carl D. "A Mature Sense of Shame." Pages 194–213 in *Many Faces of Shame.* Edited by Donald M. Nathanson. London: Guilford, 1987.

———. *Shame, Exposure, and Privacy.* Boston: Beacon, 1977.

Schwartz, Baruch J. "The Bearing of Sin in the Priestly Literature." Pages 3–21 in *Pomegranates and Golden Bells: Studies in Biblical, Jewish, and Near Eastern Ritual, Law, and Literature in Honor of Jacob Milgrom.* Edited by David P. Wright, David Noel Freedman, and Avi Hurvitz. Winona Lake, IN: Eisenbrauns, 1995.

———. "Ezekiel's Dim View of Israel's Restoration." Pages 43–68 in *The Book of Ezekiel: Theological and Anthropological Perspectives*. Edited by Margaret S. Odell and John T. Strong. SBLSymS 9. Atlanta: Society of Biblical Literature, 2000.

———. "The Ultimate Aim of Israel's Restoration in Ezekiel." Pages 305–20 in vol. 1 of *Birkat Shalom: Studies in the Bible, Ancient Near Eastern Literature, and Postbiblical Judaism Presented to Shalom M. Paul on the Occasion of His Seventieth Birthday*. Edited by Chaim Cohen, Victor Avigdor Hurowitz, and Jeffrey H. Tigay. 2 vols. Winona Lake, IN: Eisenbrauns, 2008.

Simon, Bennett. "Ezekiel's Geometric Vision of the Restored Temple: From the Rod of His Wrath to the Reed of His Measuring." *HTR* 102 (2009): 411–38.

Stevenson, Kalinda Rose. *The Vision of Transformation: The Territorial Rhetoric of Ezekiel* 40–48. SBLDS 154. Atlanta: Scholars Press 1996.

Stiebert, Johanna. *The Construction of Shame in the Hebrew Bible: The Prophetic Contribution*. JSOTSup 346. Sheffield: Sheffield Academic, 2002.

Strohm, Paul. "Chaucer's Audience(s): Fictional, Implied, Intended, Actual." *The Chaucer Review* 18 (1983): 137–45

Strong, John T. "God's *Kābôd*: The Presence of Yahweh in the Book of Ezekiel." Pages 69–95 in *The Book of Ezekiel: Theological and Anthropological Perspectives*. Edited by Margaret S. Odell and John T. Strong. SBLSymS 9. Atlanta: Society of Biblical Literature, 2000.

———. "Grounding Ezekiel's Heavenly Ascent: A Defense of Ezek 40–48 as a Program for Restoration." *SJOT* 26 (2012): 192–211.

Suriano, Matthew J. *The Politics of Dead Kings*. FAT 48. Tübingen: Mohr Siebeck, 2010.

Sweeney, Marvin A. "Ezekiel's Conceptualization of the Exile in Intertextual Perspective." *Hebrew Bible and Ancient Israel* 1 (2012): 154–72.

———. *Form and Intertextuality in Prophetic and Apocalyptic Literature*. Eugene, OR: Wipf & Stock, 2005.

———. *The Prophetic Literature*. Interpreting Biblical Texts. Nashville: Abingdon, 2005.

———. *Reading Ezekiel: A Literary and Theological Commentary*. Macon, GA: Smyth & Helwys, 2013.

———. *Tanak: A Theological and Critical Introduction to the Jewish Bible*. Minneapolis: Fortress, 2012.

Tooman, William. *Gog of Magog*. FAT 2/52. Tübingen: Mohr Siebeck, 2011.

Tuell, Steven S. *Law of the Temple in Ezekiel 40–48*. HSM 49. Atlanta: Scholars Press, 1992.

Van Goudoever, Jan. "Ezekiel Sees in Exile a New Temple-City at the Beginning of a Jobel Year." Pages 344–49 in *Ezekiel and His Book: Textual and Literary Criticism and Their Interrelation*. Edited by Johan Lust. BETL 74. Leuven: Leuven University Press/Peeters, 1986.

Wander, Philip. "The Third Persona: An Ideological Turn in Rhetorical Theory." *Central States Speech Journal* 35 (1984): 197–216.

Watts, Fraser. *Psychology, Religion, and Spirituality: Concepts and Applications*. Cambridge: Cambridge University Press, 2017.

Watts, James W. "Public Readings and Pentateuchal Law." *VT* 45 (1995): 540–57.

———. "Reader Identification and Alienation in the Legal Rhetoric of the Pentateuch." *BibInt* 7 (1999): 101–12.

———. "Rhetorical Strategy in the Composition of the Pentateuch." *JSOT* 68 (1995): 3–21.

Wevers, John William. *Ezekiel*. Osprey, FL: Nelson, 1969.

Wu, Daniel Y. *Honor, Shame, and Guilt: Social-Scientific Approaches to the Book of Ezekiel*. BBRSup 14. Winona Lake, IN: Eisenbrauns, 2016.

Zimmerli, Walter. *Ezekiel 2: A Commentary on the Book of the Prophet Ezekiel Chapters 25–48*. Hermeneia. Minneapolis: Fortress, 1983.

Contributors

Georg Fischer, SJ, is a member of the Society of Jesus and studies in Munich, Innsbruck, and Rome (Pontifical Biblical Institute). Since 1995, he has been chair of Old Testament Biblical Studies and Oriental Languages at the Theological Faculty of the University of Innsbruck, Austria. His main research areas are torah, Jeremiah, and biblical theology. He is the author of about twenty books and many articles.

David Frankel is Senior Lecturer of Bible at the Schechter Institute of Jewish Studies in Jerusalem. His publications include *The Murmuring Stories of the Priestly School: A Retrieval of Ancient Sacerdotal Lore* (Brill, 2002), *The Land of Canaan and the Destiny of Israel: Theologies of Territory in the Hebrew Bible* (Eisenbrauns, 2011), and numerous articles.

Benjamin J. M. Johnson (Ph.D., University of Durham) is Tutor in Biblical Interpretation at Wycliffe Hall, Oxford. He is the author of *Reading David and Goliath in Greek and Hebrew: A Literary Approach* (Mohr Siebeck, 2015).

Soo J. Kim is Academic Dean and Professor of Old Testament at America Evangelical University, Los Angeles, California. She is a specialist in biblical theology, and she is currently preparing a monograph on visionary experience in the book of Ezekiel. She currently serves as cochair of the SBL Theology of the Hebrew Scriptures Section (2017–2022).

Wonil Kim is Associate Professor of Religious Studies at La Sierra University in Riverside, California. He is a specialist in Old Testament theology and previously served as cochair of the Society of Biblical Literature Theology of the Hebrew Scriptures Section (1999–2005).

Jacqueline E. Lapsley is Associate Professor of Old Testament and Director of the Center for Theology, Women, and Gender at Princeton Theological Seminary. She is interested in literary theory, ethics (especially creation ethics), theological anthropology, and gender theory as tools for reading the Old Testament theologically. Her current research and writing focuses on the relationship between human dignity and creational dignity.

Julia M. O'Brien is Paul H. and Grace L. Stern Professor of Hebrew Bible/ Old Testament at Lancaster Theological Seminary in Lancaster, Pennsylvania. Specializing in prophetic literature and gender studies, she is the author of commentaries on *Micah* (Liturgical Press, 2015), *Nahum through Malachi* (Abingdon, 2004), and *Nahum* (Sheffield, 2002) and monographs entitled *Challenging Prophetic Literature* (Westminster John Knox, 2008) and *Priest and Levite in Malachi* (Scholars Press, 1990). She also is the editor of the *Oxford Encyclopedia of Bible and Gender Studies* (Oxford University Press, 2014) and *The Aesthetics of Violence in the Prophets* (with Chris Franke, T&T Clark, 2010). She is formerly cochair of the Society of Biblical Literature Theology of the Hebrew Scriptures Section (2011– 2016).

Dalit Rom-Shiloni is Associate Professor at the Department of Biblical Studies at Tel Aviv University, Israel. She works on Hebrew Bible theology of the sixth century BCE and is currently completing a monograph on *Theodical Discourse: Justification, Doubt, and Protest in the Face of Destruction*. She is also interested in the internal ideological conflict over identity within Judean communities of the Neo-Babylonian and the early Persian periods.

Marvin A. Sweeney is Professor of Hebrew Bible at the Claremont School of Theology. He is a specialist in Jewish biblical theology and in prophetic literature who has published widely in the fields of Hebrew Bible and the history of Judaism and Jewish thought. Among his fifteen volumes in the field are *Tanak: A Theological and Critical Introduction to the Jewish Bible* (Fortress, 2012); *Reading the Hebrew Bible after the Shoah: Engagement with Holocaust Theology* (Fortress, 2008); *The Prophetic Literature* (IBT, Abingdon, 2005); *and Introduction to the Pentateuch: The Foundation of Israel's Identity* (CBS, Abingdon, forthcoming). He is cochair of the Society of Biblical Literature Theology of the Hebrew Scriptures Section (2013–).

Andrea L. Weiss is Associate Professor of Bible at Hebrew Union College-Jewish Institute of Religion in New York and Campaign Coordinator for "American Values Religious Voices: 100 Days, 100 Letters." She was associate editor of *The Torah: A Women's Commentary* (URJ, 2008) and author of *Figurative Language in Biblical Prose Narrative: Metaphor in the Book of Samuel* (Brill, 2006).

Biblical References Index

Modern Authors Index

CPSIA information can be obtained
at www.ICGtesting.com
Printed in the USA
FFHW022104040619
52833803-58377FF